BASKETBALL
SKILLS & DRILLS

THIRD EDITION

JERRY V. KRAUSE
DON MEYER
JERRY MEYER

Human Kinetics

Library of Congress Cataloging-in-Publication Data

Krause, Jerry, 1936-
  Basketball skills & drills / Jerry V. Krause, Don Meyer, Jerry Meyer. -- 3rd ed.
    p. cm.
  Includes bibliographical references and index.
  ISBN-13: 978-0-7360-6707-2 (soft cover)
  ISBN-10: 0-7360-6707-8 (soft cover)
  1. Basketball--Coaching. I. Meyer, Don. II. Meyer, Jerry. III. Title. IV. Title: Basketball skills and drills.
  GV885.3.K68 2008
  796.323077--dc22

                          2007012745

ISBN-10: 0-7360-6707-8
ISBN-13: 978-0-7360-6707-2

Acquisitions Editor: Jason Muzinic; **Developmental Editor:** Leigh Keylock; **Assistant Editor:** Christine Horger; **Copyeditor:** Susan Campanini; **Proofreader:** Jim Burns; **Indexer:** Betty Frizzéll; **Permission Manager:** Carly Breeding; **Graphic Designer:** Robert Reuther; **Graphic Artist:** Sandra Meier; **Cover Designer:** Keith Blomberg; **Photographer (cover):** Neil Bernstein; **Photographer (interior):** photo on page 183 © Marin Media; photos on pages 1, 23, 39, 71, 113, 133, 155, 211, and 233 © Human Kinetics; all other photos by Doug Dreyer; **Photo Asset Manager:** Laura Fitch; **Visual Production Assistant:** Joyce Brumfield; **Photo Office Assistant:** Jason Allen; **Art Manager:** Kelly Hendren; **Associate Art Manager:** Alan L. Wilborn; **Illustrators:** Tom Roberts and Alan L. Wilborn; **Printer:** United Graphics

We thank Northern State University in Aberdeen, South Dakota, for assistance in providing the location for the photo shoot for this book.

Human Kinetics books are available at special discounts for bulk purchase. Special editions or book excerpts can also be created to specification. For details, contact the Special Sales Manager at Human Kinetics.

Printed in the United States of America   20 19 18

The paper in this book is certified under a sustainable forestry program.

Human Kinetics
Website: www.HumanKinetics.com

United States: Human Kinetics
P.O. Box 5076
Champaign, IL 61825-5076
800-747-4457
e-mail: info@hkusa.com

Canada: Human Kinetics
475 Devonshire Road, Unit 100
Windsor, ON N8Y 2L5
800-465-7301 (in Canada only)
e-mail: info@hkcanada.com

Europe: Human Kinetics
107 Bradford Road
Stanningley
Leeds LS28 6AT, United Kingdom
+44 (0)113 255 5665
e-mail: hk@hkeurope.com

For information about Human Kinetics' coverage in other areas of the world,
please visit our website: www.HumanKinetics.com

BASKETBALL

SKILLS & DRILLS

THIRD EDITION

Contents

DVD Contents

Basic Body Control
Mass Quick Moves Drill
Line Drill: Quick Starts, Steps, Turns, and Stops
Line Drill: Starts, Stops, and Turns

Advanced Body Control
V-Cut Drill
On-the-Ball Screens
Off-the-Ball Screens

Ballhandling
Passing and Catching Principles
Line Drill: Starts, Stops, and Turns
Two-Player Passing and Catching Drill
Moving Pairs Passing
Mass Dribbling
Ballhandling Basics

Shooting
Line Drill: Shooting Addition
Layup Progression Shooting
Field-Goal Progression
Soft Touch or Killer Shooting
Pairs or In-and-Out Shooting
Free-Throw Progression

**Outside Offensive Moves:
Playing the Perimeter**
Outside Moves Using a Spin Pass
Closeout
Partner Penetrate and Pitch Drill
Timed Layups

Inside Offensive Moves: Playing the Post
Post Warm-Up Drill
Spin Pass Post Moves
Big Spacing and Post Feeding Drill

Individual Defense
Stance and Steps Progression
Progression for Stance and Steps Addition
Line Drill: Individual Defense
On-the-Ball and Off-the-Ball Drill
Closeout Drills
Defensive Charge

Rebounding
Rebounding Rules
Line Drill: 2-and-2, Capture and
    Chin Rebound Addition
Line Drill: Offensive Rebound Addition
Rebound and Outlet Drill
Garbage Drill
NBA (No Babies Allowed) or Survival
    Rebounding
Cutthroat Rebounding

Team Offense
Skeleton Offense Drill
Blitz Fast-Break Drill

Team Defense
Full-Court Drills
Half-Court (Shell Drill)

Total running time ...... 2 hours, 17 minutes

Preface

Better Basketball Basics (Leisure Press) was the original foundation book for Basketball Skills and Drills that focused only on fundamental skills of the game. This 1983 publication, which featured 550 sequential pictures, became extremely popular with coaches and sold out its two printings. In 1991, the concepts of this book were refined and developed into the first edition of Basketball Skills & Drills (Human Kinetics). The 1991 book quickly became a bestselling teaching and learning reference for basketball. Almost 100,000 players and coaches agree that this book is the simplest, most comprehensive treatment of basketball basics, the fundamental skills of the sport. The addition of Don Meyer and Jerry Meyer as coauthors on the second edition brought new contributions with expertise in successful playing and coaching from two more generations of linked experts who built their careers around successful execution of basketball fundamentals.

> "I seek to leave the world a little better place than I found it."
>
> James Naismith, Inventor of Basketball

Basketball Skills & Drills, Third Edition (actually the fourth edition and sixth printing) is a significant improvement on previous editions. The CD-ROM two-pack that accompanied the last edition has been replaced with a new DVD to add a new format video and visual component for those who prefer this mode for demonstrations and drills. We hope this latest "skills and drills" package will be a legacy for future basketball players and coaches and that it will indeed make the basketball world better.

This edition brings to bear over 100 years of overlapping, related basketball experience (all age and skill levels and both genders) that is concentrated on the basics. Thus, Basketball Skills & Drills can function as the definitive source of fundamentals for coaches, players, and parents. It is designed to be the primary basketball reference focused on elementary, middle, or secondary school and youth basketball levels. It also can be used as a textbook for classes in basketball coaching theory where the focus is on fundamentals. Improvements include the following:

* updated and expanded primary concepts for each skill,
* additions to the teaching methods, alternate ways to teach and learn skills in order to teach all players better,
* references to players and coaches who also emphasize fundamental skills,
* addition and modification of court diagrams and clear, accurate illustrations,
* a more comprehensive teaching and learning package; concepts, critical cues, and other new teaching tips,

- expansion of the sequential, progressive drills for each chapter,
- troubleshooting sections where common problems and remedies can be found, and
- skills assessments, both observational (in the troubleshooting sections) and quantitative measures for status and improvement.

The basic skills are the foundation for success at all levels of basketball. For example, Michael Jordan, Tim Duncan, and Dwayne Wade, three of the greatest players ever, combined the proper and quick execution of exceptional fundamental skills with great natural abilities. These superior skills were developed through years of dedication to continuous improvement. Hall of Fame player and coach John Wooden stated that all players must learn to execute the fundamental skills properly and quickly in order to be successful. *Basketball Skills & Drills* can help all coaches and players reach that goal.

Introduction

Players and coaches need to develop lifetime habits of learning, because life is about learning. They need to commit themselves to constant learning, to move forward and to make progress in basketball and in life, to prevent the repetition of past mistakes, to benefit from the experience of others, and to improve performance (including basketball performance) over time. Learning is one of the most valuable ways to spend time.

Both players and coaches need to appreciate the value of learning. It can be a natural, enjoyable, productive, and satisfying activity when approached with a positive attitude. When they are open to learning and growth, they will learn. They need to make a connection between what they want to achieve and what they need to learn in order to achieve their goals.

The knowledge of how to learn effectively helps both players and coaches make the most of the instruction that this book offers. The essential concepts are the following:

> *"I'm a teacher and coach. Teaching is what I love most, the heart of my coaching style. The best thing about my profession is that I can teach."*
>
> Mike Krzyzewski, Hall of Fame Coach, 2008 USA Olympic Coach, Duke University

- Admit mistakes or ignorance. Acknowledge that you don't know something and even be willing to look foolish while you learn and make mistakes. Develop a *mistake mentality* by asking questions and taking risks.

- Begin learning with questions. Let what you know about basketball skills be a starting point each day. Start with a challenge, a problem, or a question that propels you to learn more. Have the humility to use your limited knowledge as a starting point for further learning.

- Bring your knowledge to life. Learn why you are doing a skill and that skill will have more meaning.

- Take responsibility for your own learning and for the learning of those around you. This combined synergy allows individual and team learning to occur at a much faster rate.

- Learn from experience. Turn information into knowledge by applying it and working with it. Use drills to develop skills that can be used to play the game better. Play the game to discover weaknesses that can be improved through drills focused on specific skills.

- Learn from other people, especially those who are successful. Coaches can study the lives of Hall of Fame coaches to learn "the best ideas from the best people." Players can also learn from each other and from more skilled, older players. Seeing from someone else's perspective is a great way to learn.

- Learn by teaching. Players should be encouraged to teach and learn from each other (buddy coaching) and to teach younger, less experienced players. One of the best ways to teach others is by doing your best. Others are more interested in what you do than in what you say.

- Never stop learning. When you integrate learning into all that you do, you benefit immensely. Every moment, every time that you make learning a priority, you bring something positive into your life—a learning experience.

Basketball Skills and Drills

CRITICAL CUE:
Movement skills are learned over time—patience is essential.

Basketball Skills & Drills is about learning the fundamental skills of basketball that coaches teach and players learn. The acquisition of basic skills is highly dependent on optimizing the teaching and learning process for a successful end product—athletes who have learned basketball skills at the highest level.

Any athlete brings to the game inherited genetic movement traits called abilities. These fundamental movement components—such as reaction time, predominant type of muscle fibers, and depth perception—are the building blocks for movement potential. The focus of teaching and learning, however, needs to be on the skills developed from those abilities. Many coaches and basketball experts assert that players focus on "style over substance" and prefer to use inherited abilities (the quick fix) rather than develop skills (the slow process). It is easier to dunk the ball than to execute a challenging pass and catch for a team basket. The focus in this book is on the controllable and gradual process required to teach and learn basic basketball skills, a process that depends on the substance of the skilled athlete rather than that of the stylistic athlete who relies on movement abilities. Coaches and players need to focus on teaching and learning the basic skills of basketball and on the process more than the product (a single performance). They need to build on each player's ability base for developing basketball skills.

CRITICAL CUE:
Basketball skills: learned movements built on inherited abilities.

CRITICAL CUE:
Focus on skills, not drills.

Coaches and players often use drills as necessary tools to enhance skill learning. However, they are only tools, not the end result. Thus, the focus should always be on the desired skills, not on the drills. The drills in this book have been carefully selected to assist players and coaches in improving fundamental basketball skills.

Coaches and players can modify and develop their own drills to learn basketball skills as game moves at game speed. Naismith Hall of Fame coach Henry "Hank" Iba said it this way, "Practice the game in the manner in which it is to be played." Legendary football coach Joe Paterno said, "A coach must replicate what is the game."

Levels of Learning

Movement learning experts have found that basketball skills are learned in three stages:

1. Cognitive stage: The player forms a mental picture of the skill, usually by using a demonstration or explanation from the teacher or coach.

2. Practice stage: This occurs when the player imitates the demonstration, the imitations are corrected and reinforced, and the skills are repeated.

3. Automatic stage: Players can perform skills without thinking. The movements have become habits and can be performed as game moves at game speed.

CRITICAL CUE: Drills should be aimed at game moves at game speed.

Basic skill learning in stages can also involve the senses:

1. The *look* of a skill: A player knows what a proper skill looks like and uses the dominant visual sense to learn the skill. Partner or buddy coaching allows a player to develop this stage—watching (and seeing) teammates perform the skill and then reinforcing what they are doing correctly as well as correcting their mistakes. To maximize team learning of basic skills, coaches should convince all players to take responsibility for the basic skill learning of all of their teammates. A team is only as strong as its weakest link, and its strength is also dependent on each player teaching all of the other players (e.g., the use of echo calls, as discussed later).

2. The *sound* of a skill: How a movement sounds is another element of learning in this model. After players know the look of a proper skill, their focus can shift to sound, such as the sound of a dribble on the floor or the sound of proper passing (ping) and catching (click).

3. The *feel* of a skill: The player's feeling is the highest sensory development of skills, for example, when shooting a free throw in practice with the eyes closed or dribbling a basketball while keeping the eyes focused on the net or the rim.

Visualization is a mental tool that can be applied in all three sensory areas. Learning takes place in a relaxed state when a player mentally practices the skill by picturing perfect performances. This is best done when players focus on mentally re-viewing their own successful performance—how it looks, sounds, and feels. Thus, players need to become aware of the look, sound, and feel of a skill.

Communication

One of the paramount components of teaching and learning is communication. The ability to disseminate palatable information to players is a valuable tool, one that players and coaches have to sharpen each day. It's not what coaches teach, but what players learn, that is important. Not all players learn the same way or at the same speed; what is effective for one may not be effective for all. For coaches, the challenge is to know how to teach players in a way that allows them to learn best. Communication, like learning itself, requires patience, open mindedness, and a common goal (usually knowledge gained). When those elements are present, coaches, players, and teams have the greatest opportunity to grow and succeed.

An example of an effective communication tool is echo calls—when players repeat a critical teaching or learning cue or a coach communication to ensure that all players learn it. Players who teach and communicate with each other learn more efficiently. This kind of audible communication also encourages an environment where team interaction takes place. Players on the floor can never communicate too much.

In his bestselling coaching book *Successful Coaching*, Rainer Martens identifies six areas of development for communication skills:

1. Credibility
2. Positive approach
3. Information over emotion
4. Consistency
5. Listening skills
6. Nonverbal communication

Credibility with players is based on respect. Each player should be allowed the opportunity to build confidence and self-respect during the basketball experience. To develop self-respect while earning the respect of others should be the rule for both players and coaches.

Communication between players and coaches should generally be positive in nature, emphasizing praise and rewards more than punishment and criticism. Telling players *what to do* rather than *what not to do* is a preferred technique of the positive approach. For example, when teaching shooting, coaches might tell players to shoot up, rather than telling them that the shot is too low. Coaches should look for what players are doing right instead of focusing on what they are doing wrong, which is a problem common to most coaching styles.

Messages to players should be filled with factual information as opposed to emotional outbursts. Players need to know what to do correctly; they do not need to be yelled at for making mistakes. Positive emotion or praise tends to be more helpful, especially when players can gather needed information from it in order to learn skills or to correct mistakes. Coaches can use negative emotion and punishment sparingly and only when the negative approach is the best alternative. The feedback sandwich described later is an excellent way to provide necessary information. Information is used best by players when it is specific. A statement such as "Your head is centered" might be better than "Great balance!" in terms of information. Reducing judgment and increasing information are good guidelines for coaches.

Consistency of communication is also important for coaches. Players are looking for consistent messages and feedback from more mature adults. Consistency provides a zone of comfort for communication with players, whether the communication is verbal or nonverbal. What coaches say should match what they do whenever possible. Athletes are quick to sense hypocrisy. They expect coaches to be honest and real. As Martens states, "Be as good as your word."

One of the most challenging areas of communication development is listening. Good listeners maintain eye contact, constantly search for meaning, have respect for the communicator, and become active listeners. Coaches should focus on two-way communication in which players can interact and voice their concerns and questions. Players' acceptance of a mistake mentality is helpful for enhancing listening and reducing fear, doubt, and worry that can accompany communication. Nonverbal communication in the form of positive body language is also important when listening. Body gestures, appropriate touching behavior, and voice quality are all useful skills to improve communication and listening.

The primary measure of communication is what players learn, not what coaches know. Thus, it is imperative for coaches to improve their communication, for themselves and for their players, in order to enhance learning.

Feedback

The learning process happens faster when appropriate feedback on skills is given according to these guidelines:

- Feedback can best be provided by an experienced coach, but players need to learn how to provide their own feedback whenever possible. For example, a player can observe the starting point and landing spot of the feet before and after a jump shot.

- Players must be told what is correct (reinforcement) and incorrect (information on mistakes). Mistakes should be known, acknowledged, and understood by the players; then a specific plan is needed to correct those mistakes.

- The correction of player errors should be consistent. For players, the best learning approach to mistakes is to recognize them (with the coach's help), to acknowledge and admit them (to other players), and to learn from them and then forget them.

- Specific information is better than general feedback: "Great full follow-through" is better than "Nice shot."

- Provide feedback as soon after performance as possible, the sooner the better. An exception might be postgame feedback when emotions of both coaches and players may be too involved.

- Use feedback sandwiches. Dennis Docheff, teaching expert, recommends a three-part feedback message: reinforcement (find something being done correctly), information (correct the skill or behavior that needs improvement), and praise (provide encouragement at the end). An example might be something like this: "Jim, on your last shot, great follow-through at the elbow, but you need to get lower and have your feet wider for better balance . . . that's the way to keep working at game speed." Champion college coach Mike Dunlap uses this format for coaching feedback:
    1. Praise (find a positive)
    2. Talk and tell (prompt and correct and tell them the next step)
    3. Leave them (to learn)

> **CRITICAL CUE:**
> Feedback increases the learning rate.

General Tips on Teaching and Learning

1. Coaching is teaching:
    - Know why you teach a skill; knowing helps the teacher as well as the learner.
    - Focus on the skill first (not on the drill or strategy).
    - Focus on how well you do something rather than what you do (execution over repetition and quality over quantity).
    - When teaching or coaching, preview first (tell what you are going to teach), view (teach it), and then review (tell what you taught).
    - Help players remove their learning blocks of fear, doubt, and worry.

2. Demonstrate and explain the following properly:
    - Make sure that all players can see and hear you.
    - Do it correctly, to show the big mental picture.

- Repeat demonstrations—two angles, two repetitions, or more.
- Use precise and concise explanations.
- Use only critical cues (don't talk too much).
- Practice immediately—players learn by doing and may forget the demonstration and explanation unless they are applied quickly.
- Emphasize practice to make behavior permanent (good or bad habits).

3. Use teaching progressions:
   - Slow to fast—do it right and then do it quickly (the final goal is game moves at game speed).
   - Simple to complex.
   - Teach in sequence and reverse it (start to finish reversed).

4. Players and coaches need to remain open to learning (green and growing, not ripe and rotten):
   - Adopt (the whole skill) as a beginner or adapt (one idea) when experienced.
   - Improve every day of the year (can't maintain, must progress).
   - Look for the lesson; there is always a lesson to learn (search for it).
   - Learn from others—good and bad experiences have lessons.
   - Communicate and encourage teammates (generally, coaches criticize and players praise and encourage each other).
   - Control what you can (all people have total control of their attitudes, actions, and responses) and let go of the rest.

5. Know how each player learns best:
   - Visual (see the skill), read about it or see a demonstration.
   - Auditory (hear the skill), get more explanation or listen for sounds.
   - Kinetic (feel the skill), walk through the skill.

6. Coaches should use:
   - Word pictures (e.g., footfire for moving the feet).
   - Analogies and metaphors (e.g., quick start like a sprinter).
   - Critical cues (e.g., full follow-through).

7. Teach fundamental skills and more:
   - Conditioning.
   - Toughness and effort.
   - Life and character lessons.
   - Communication (early, loud, and often).
   - How to compete.
   - Competitive greatness (see John Wooden's Pyramid of Success in figure 1).

8. Become a full-package coach—able to teach players and assist in their learning and development physically (condition and skill), mentally (psychologically), and socially (as a team player).

9. Evaluate all that you do as players and coaches. One quick and effective evaluation tool, called the one-minute assessment, can be used to gather feedback and information about what players are doing on and off the court. The assessment can be used by coaches to evaluate a practice session, team strategy (offense or defense), or a team rule. It consists of three parts: one

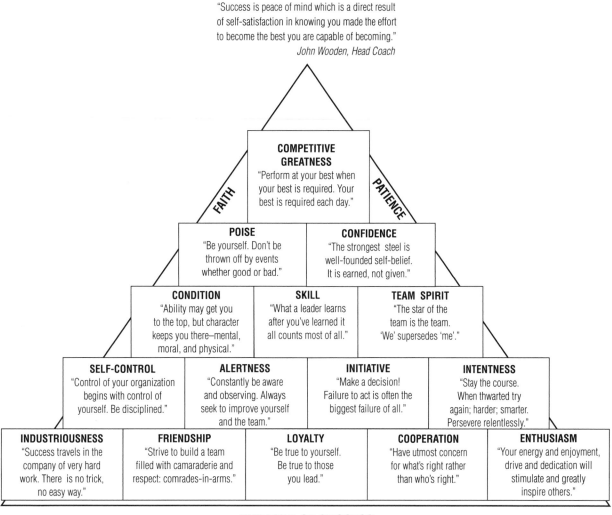

PYRAMID OF SUCCESS

FIGURE 1 **John Wooden's Pyramid of Success.**
From WOODEN ON LEADERSHIP (McGraw-Hill) and www.CoachWooden.com.

quality, action, or performance that is praiseworthy (and why); one element that could be improved (and how); and relevant insights or comments.

10. Coaches and players both need to know themselves, to develop their own unique talents, and to serve others.

The instruction and information in this book is considerable. The potential for learning basketball skills depends on first having the skills to teach and learn effectively. Coaches and players can use these guidelines to help gain the most from the basketball skills and drills in this book.

Key to Diagrams

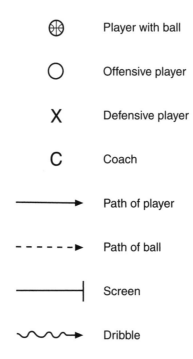

⊕   Player with ball

○   Offensive player

X   Defensive player

C   Coach

⟶   Path of player

----▶   Path of ball

⊢   Screen

〰▶   Dribble

Basic Body Control

"Footwork and balance are necessary every moment of a game while ballhandling is needed less than 10 percent of the game."

Pete Newell, Naismith Hall of Fame Coach

One of the foremost tasks of a coach is to teach players how to move and control their bodies. Fundamental movements, sometimes called basketball basics, are essential tools for all players.

Coaches need to teach players to move effectively (getting the job done) and efficiently (moving the best way). They teach players to conserve time and space and to move with a purpose, reducing wasted motion. In essence, basketball is a game of balance and quickness—all movements should focus on these purposes. Players should strive to "tighten" their game, to increase balance and quickness.

The overall consideration for coaches and players should be on the development of individual balance and quickness. Balance depends almost solely on footwork, starting in the feet but ending with the head. Because of its size (almost 10 pounds [4.5 kilograms]) and body position, the head is a key to balance; it should be centered over the base of support. The head moves in the desired direction to become unbalanced, thus committing the player to quick movement in that direction. Similarly, quickness is related to both the head and the feet, but in the opposite order. Quickness is first a state of mind (think quick and then be quick), starting in the head and ending in the feet (it depends on footwork). Both balance and quickness depend on proper footwork and are closely related to head position and state of mind.

CRITICAL CUE:
Move correctly first,
then move quickly.

Basketball is also a game of quickness (hand and foot) and speed (overall body motion) that are used at the proper time. Coaching should continually emphasize the principle of doing things right, then quickly—making the right move quickly at the right time—while developing and maintaining individual, physical, emotional, and team balance and correct offensive and defensive position.

The six fundamental positions and movements of basketball are stance, starts, steps, turns, stops, and jumps. Because quickness is so important, these basic positions are all designated with the word *quick*.

Quick Stance

Players need to develop the habit of a good basic basketball position to ready them for quick movements. Quick stance requires adequate levels of muscle strength and endurance in the core area (abdominal muscles in front, lower-back muscles behind). Teaching quick stance on offense and defense is a challenging task, and patience is essential with younger players who may not have the strength and muscle endurance to stay in this position very long. The most important part of a quick stance is achieving and maintaining bent-knee and bent-elbow positions. All joints should be flexed and ready. The game is played low to the floor. The lower players get, the higher they can jump; the more explosive their moves to the basket are, the quicker they are on defense, and so the better they can protect the ball. "Play low and stay low" is a critical concept for all players.

CRITICAL CUE: Play
and stay low to the
floor. Get in and stay
in a quick stance.

Teach players the feeling of quick stance—being ready for anything, feeling quick. Maintaining this basic position is hard work; players must become comfortable in an awkward, unnatural, monkey-like position. Players should sit into the stance—get low—and stay in the stance. Consistent and early emphasis on quick stance teaches athletes to assume it automatically. Quickness is a combination of thinking quick, feeling quick, and becoming quick by improving skills. A good test for quick stance is for a player to imagine sitting in a chair with the head positioned behind the knees, as shown in figure 1.1.

Foot Position

The best foot placement in most situations is the slightly staggered stance with the toes pointing slightly outward, not straight ahead. The feet should be about shoulder-width apart, with the instep of the front foot along the same horizontal line as the big toe of the other foot (see figure 1.2). Players should use this position when they need to move in any direction. To get into this foot position, players should put the feet together, move the preferred foot forward until the big toe of the back foot is next to the instep of the forward foot, and then step sideways with the preferred foot until it is about shoulder-width for balance and quickness.

The parallel stance shown in figure 1.3 is best used for side-to-side movement as well as for catching the ball and stopping, stopping after dribbling, and responding defensively when a defender moves laterally. In time, players use both stances interchangeably.

FIGURE 1.1 **Quick-stance test—sit into the stance (side view).**

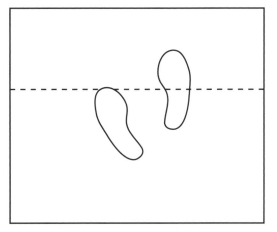

FIGURE 1.2 **The staggered stance (top view). An instep-and-toe relationship, with the feet shoulder-width apart and the back foot toed slightly outward. The figure shows offensive quick stance (right-handed player).**

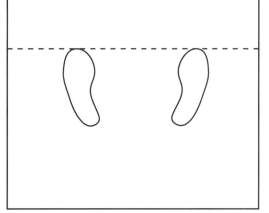

FIGURE 1.3 **The parallel stance (top view). Toe-to-toe relationship, with the feet shoulder-width apart and the toes pointed slightly outward.**

> **CRITICAL CUE:**
> Stagger the stance with the toes pointed slightly outward for the quick stance.

Weight Distribution

Body weight should be evenly distributed from side to side, from front to back, and between the feet. The heels should be down, with most of the weight (60 percent) on the balls of the feet, although pressure should be felt on the toes and heels. The toes should be curled and the heels kept down.

Players may incorrectly place all of their weight on the balls of the feet with the heels off the floor, but this position is slower because the heel has to be brought down before forceful movement can occur. A good way to teach the feeling of proper position is to ask players to take an *eagle claw* position, with the heels down and the toes curled.

> **CRITICAL CUE:**
> Weight distribution for the quick stance—eagle claw stance, weight on the whole foot.

When players are on defense, they should add footfire to their basic quick-stance position. Footfire means keeping the feet active and in constant motion without leaving the floor surface, a technique that helps keep the leg muscles stretched and ready for action and makes the defender quicker. Players can imagine that they are standing on a bed of hot coals, without their feet leaving the floor. For offensive or defensive quick stance, the weight has to be on the whole foot.

Head and Trunk Position

For proper balance, players should keep the head centered over the support base—at the apex of a triangle, with the legs as two equal sides and a line between the feet as the base when viewed from the front (figure 1.4). They should also center the head from front to back, taking an erect trunk position, with the shoulders back and the trunk slightly forward of vertical. The back is straight and the chest is out. The head is behind the knees. Players should sit into this stance.

FIGURE 1.4 **Offensive quick stance (triple-threat position):** *(a)* Front view—the head, the key to balance, carried up and alert—the apex of the triangle. *(b)* Side view—sit into the stance, the back straight, the chest out, and the head up; pit and protect the ball.

Arms and Legs

Teach players to keep their joints (ankles, knees, hips, shoulders, elbows, and wrists) bent and ready. Coach John Wooden suggests that all joints be bent for quickness. Players on offense can tighten their game by bending joints and keeping the ball close to the body (pit and protect the ball in the shooting pocket). The shooting hand is behind the ball, and the offensive player is in triple-threat position, ready to shoot, pass, or drive quickly. Defensive players also can tighten their game (movements) by bending joints, keeping the arms short (bent elbows) and near the body, and adding footfire to their footwork. See figure 1.5. Players should keep the hands and arms bent and close to the body for balance and quickness. The whole sole of each foot should be touching the floor. Remind the players to stay low—the angle at the knee joint in back of the legs should be 90 to 120 degrees in order to maintain the low center of gravity needed for quickness and balance.

FIGURE 1.5 **Defensive quick stance with joints bent:** *(a)* front view, *(b)* side view.

COACHING POINTS FOR QUICK STANCE

- ☐ Be ready for action: feet ready, hands ready.
- ☐ Keep all body joints bent.
- ☐ Play and stay low; sit into the game.
- ☐ Get and stay in a quick stance.
- ☐ Keep the head up, the chest out, and the back straight.
- ☐ Keep body weight on the whole foot, with the heels down (eagle claw position).

Quick Starts, Steps, Turns, and Stops

Starting, stepping, turning (pivoting), and stopping are the fundamental motions used in moving effectively and efficiently in and out of quick stance for offensive and defensive moves. Teach players to execute the skill correctly, quickly, and at the right time every time. Players need to go slowly and get a feel for executing the skill properly, get a rhythm, and then speed up progressively until they make a mistake. They then learn from the mistakes and go toward game moves at game speed.

CRITICAL CUE: Do it correctly and then do it quickly.

A player's overall speed (moving the body from point A to B) is important in basketball, but not as critical as quickness (hand and foot speed). Coaches should strive to improve the quickness of each player. Thinking quick and being quick should be the player's constant focus.

Quick Starts

Starting is the first skill players must learn that uses quick stance. To start quickly, players shift body weight (and the head) in the desired direction of movement. For example, to move to the left, body weight is shifted over the left foot by leaning to the left. Because the head is key to balance, it always leads the weight shift (figure 1.6).

FIGURE 1.6 Moving laterally left: body weight toward the desired direction of movement (over the left foot).

To be quick at the right time, players must remember that all motion change begins on the floor. This means taking short, choppy steps whenever a change of motion or quick start is needed. Teach players to keep their feet in contact with the floor as much as possible and to use the floor to their advantage by staying close to it.

Front (Lead) Foot First. From basic position, players should shift weight in the direction of movement and start by taking the first step with the nearest foot. For example, to move to the right, take the first step with the right foot. To move forward, take the first step with the front foot (push from the back foot and step with the lead foot). This technique is most often used in basketball when focus and attention to the ball are necessary. Sometimes, it is quicker to step across with the trail (back) foot and run or sprint in the desired direction of movement, particularly when a defensive player is beaten by the opponent and must run to recover.

Defensive Quick Start. On defense, players should use a sliding motion. They should keep their feet at shoulder width and use short, quick shuffle steps. This technique is called the *push step*, or step (lead foot) and slide (rear foot). The lead foot moves in the desired direction from the force of the trail foot at the same time as a short, quick push step (lead foot first) is taken (figure 1.6). The force for the push step comes from a power push from the trail foot, which moves the body and transfers the weight to the lead foot, quickly followed by a pulling slide step taken with the trail foot to regain basic position, without bringing the feet together. Players should keep their feet wide at all times: *Step and slide, low and wide, you can't get too low, you can't get too wide.* The lead step and the pull and slide steps are short (12 to 24 inches [30 to 60 centimeters]), and the stance is kept low and wide.

Players should learn to execute defensive starts and slides in side-to-side, forward, backward, and diagonal directions (figure 1.7), with the head level. Head bouncing shows that a player is rising out of the stance instead of using a push step or step sliding and not staying in a stance. Such bouncing, known as the *bunny hop*, brings the feet together in the air, loses the advantage of the floor, and is a waste of time and space, reducing quickness of motion. The head must be kept level. Players can imagine a steel plate above the head during all push-step motion.

Offensive Quick Start. On offense, players with a live ball (i.e., who still can dribble) can do a quick start from triple-threat position using the lead foot first. On live-ball moves, offensive players should establish a permanent pivot foot (PPF) (left foot for right-handed players and vice versa for lefties) and a permanent stepping foot for dribble-driving past a defender and for when the ball is held. Using the PPF, a player

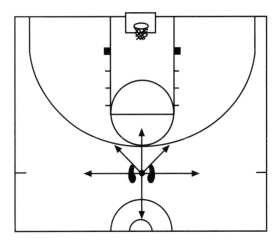

FIGURE 1.7 **Defensive directions for starts and steps.**

can do a quick start with the stepping foot (front foot first). These live-ball moves are called direct drives (to the strong or preferred side) and crossover drives (to the nonpreferred side). Figures 1.8 and 1.9 illustrate both moves.

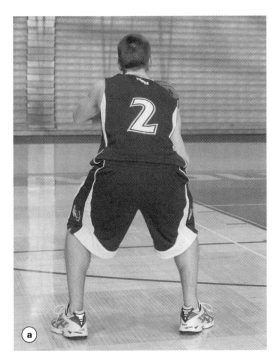

FIGURE 1.8 **Live-ball move—direct drive:** *(a)* **offensive quick stance (triple-threat position),** *(b)* **first step—long and low.**

Quick Steps

Quick steps are the basic motion changes that allow players to use speed and quickness to complete plays and execute offensive and defensive strategies. They consist of changes in speed or pace and in direction at an angle (usually 90 and 180 degrees to the original motion direction). Quick steps are usually slow-to-quick moves that use quickness at the right time.

FIGURE 1.9 **Live-ball move—crossover drive:** *(a)* triple-threat position, *(b)* circle tight with ball, *(c)* long and low crossover step.

COACHING POINTS FOR LIVE-BALL MOVES

- Start from offensive quick stance or triple-threat position.
- Direct drive: long and low on the first step past the defender, using the front foot and straight-line movement. The driver must *win the battle*, getting the head and shoulders past the defender on the first step, and then *win the war* on the second step (with hip contact on the defender to prevent recovery of the defensive position).
- Crossover drive: circle tight from pit to pit (armpit to armpit in front of the body) while changing hands behind the ball, without a foot fake. Step long and low, with the stepping foot in a straight line, and move past the opposite side of the defender to drive past the defender, all in the first step.

COACHING POINTS FOR QUICK STARTS

- Be ready to start by getting in and maintaining a quick stance.
- Learn that using the floor works to your advantage; keep the feet on the floor when starting.
- Shift body weight in the desired direction and lead with the head moving first.
- Stay down and pump the arms when starting (the arms lead the action).
- Use the principle of front (lead) foot first.
- On direct or crossover drives with the ball, use a long and low first step in a straight line toward the basket. Reduce lateral motion.
- For defensive slides, use the push-step technique. Slide, don't hop, and keep the feet wide. *Step and slide, low and wide*: push (from trail foot), step (with lead foot), and slide (with trail foot to quick stance).
- Start and move in straight lines.

Change of Pace and Change of Direction. Change-of-pace steps, including running or sliding at different speeds, are important skills of body control designed to apply the concept of quickness at the right time. For example, an offensive player may be running or dribbling at a moderate speed and then use a burst of speed to get past the defender. Likewise, a defender could be sliding along and then accelerate quickly to get a legal position in the path of an offensive player to disrupt movement or take the charge.

Change-of-direction steps are also designed to apply quickness at the right time. When players run down the floor on offense and need to change to defense, they can use a stride stop, change direction 180 degrees (180-degree cut), and sprint quickly back in the opposite direction. V-cuts, used on either offense or defense, are change-of-direction steps at sharp 90-degree angles that are made by going into the cut slowly, making a sharp-angled change-of-direction move, and accelerating quickly out of the cut. V-cuts are also called L-cuts, 7-cuts, or fake-and-break moves, depending on how they are used.

Live-Ball Moves. A player with the ball who hasn't dribbled can execute quick steps called live-ball moves: direct drive (to the preferred or dominant side) and crossover drive (to the nonpreferred or nondominant side) (see chapter 5 for a full description). From a quick stance, live-ball moves are designed to allow the offensive player with the ball to move quickly past the defender on the dribble drive. This is a straight-line move to the basket to penetrate the defensive perimeter with the use of a long, low, quick first step. By rule, the offensive player with the ball needs to get the head and shoulders past the defender's trunk in order to gain an advantage legally on the quick first step. Then the offensive player attempts to get near-hip contact with the defender in order to maintain the position advantage while moving past the defender to penetrate the defense on the dribble drive and to force another defender to help, thus creating an advantageous 2-on-1 situation for the offense.

Quick Turns and Pivots

Turning, or pivoting, is motion that rotates the body in a circular fashion around the ball of one foot while the player maintains the basic position or quick stance (figure 1.10). Sixty percent of body weight should be on the pivot foot as the heel of the turning foot is lifted slightly to pivot on the ball of the foot. Players on offense should use a PPF and a permanent stepping foot, especially when they have the ball.

As the basic skill for beginning all motion changes, the pivot, or turn, is one of the most important player tools for quickness and balance. It is also one of the least used and most poorly learned skills in basketball.

Pivoting can be done with either foot as the stationary center of rotation, but a PPF is recommended with the ball. When body rotation is toward the front—a pivoting motion that moves the trunk forward around the pivot—the pivot is called a front turn (see figure 1.11). Likewise, a rear turn is used to pivot a player's backside to the rear (figure 1.12).

Players on offense must learn to make pivots with and without the ball. When players with the ball are closely guarded but

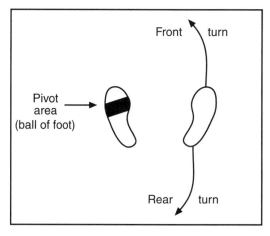

FIGURE 1.10 **Pivoting or turning: a rotation of the body around the ball of the turning foot.**

FIGURE 1.11 **Right-foot pivot—front turn:** *(a)* starting position and *(b)* ending position.

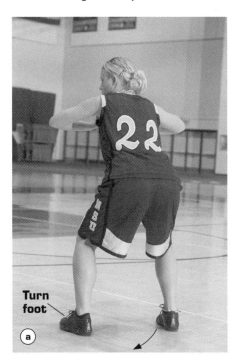

FIGURE 1.12 **Left-foot pivot—rear turn:** *(a)* starting position and *(b)* ending position.

CRITICAL CUE: For quick turns, keep the head level, lead with the elbow (rear turn), and punch into the turn or lead with the elbow (front turn).

want to face the basket, rear turns on the nondominant foot (as the PPF) are usually used to clear space, although some coaches prefer front turns. On defense, players use the pivot as the first move when changing from one position to another and when rebounding, as shown in figure 1.13. This is sometimes called a *swing step*.

Quick Stops

To be quick with balance and control, players must be able to use quick stance, start properly and quickly, move quickly (by stepping, running, turning, or sliding), and

COACHING POINTS FOR QUICK TURNS

- Stay down in basic stance and keep the head level and low for quickness.
- Lead with the elbow of the stepping foot (rear turn) or punch into the turn (front turn).
- Keep the feet shoulder-width apart for balance.
- Maintain balance, and keep the head up.
- Pivot quickly but properly in a quick turn.
- Use the pivot to turn up to half a turn (180 degrees); repeat pivots if more turning is necessary.
- Use a rear turn to face the basket when closely guarded (to clear space).
- With the ball, use a front or rear turn to face the basket. Catch the ball and face the basket with a front or rear turn while receiving the ball and before dribbling (pass first, dribble last).

FIGURE 1.13 **Defensive rebounding:** *(a)* front turn, *(b)* rear turn, and *(c)* block-out contact.

stop quickly in a balanced position. The two recommended basic basketball stops are the one-count quick stop and the two-count stride stop.

Quick Stop. The preferred stop for most situations, the quick stop, is executed at the end of a running or sliding motion. It should not be called a *jump stop* (jumping results in slower stops and too much air time). When running, a player does a quick stop by hopping slightly from one foot, skimming the floor surface, landing in a parallel or slightly staggered stance (basic or quick stance position; figure 1.14), and sticking the landing with *soft feet*. Feet hit the floor at the same time in a one-count motion: Hop from and skim the floor with one foot and land on two feet.

The quick stop conserves time and space and can be used on defense or offense (with or without the ball); it is a complement to the quick turn, one of the primary

FIGURE 1.14 **Quick stop:** *(a)* hop from one foot (left or right) and *(b)* land on two feet.

tools of body control and movement. Basketball rules allow players with the ball to use either foot for pivoting after a quick stop. This gives them a wide variety of motion possibilities with control and balance and prevents them from traveling with the ball if the incorrect foot is chosen as the turning foot. The quick stop is important for getting players into a quick stance for shooting, passing, or dribbling when receiving a pass. The critical cue on the quick-stop landing is to stick it (similar to a gymnastics dismount) with soft feet, which means landing on the whole foot while stopping firmly but softly in a balanced position.

Stride Stop. The stride stop, shown in figure 1.15, is a two-count stop executed by landing on the rear foot (first count) with the front foot hitting immediately afterward (second count). Its primary use is to reverse direction when players are running forward (and in other situations for advanced players). For all other motion situations, players should use the quick stop. With the stride stop, players should keep body weight back and sit on the rear foot.

COACHING POINTS FOR QUICK STOPS AND STRIDE STOPS

- Use the quick stop unless changing direction (180 degrees) when running; then use the stride stop.
- On a quick stop, stick the landing with soft feet (land on the whole foot).
- On a quick stop, hop from one foot and land in quick stance on two feet at once (one count). Stay close to the floor.
- On a stride stop, stay low and sit on the back foot. The rear foot (which hits first) must be the pivot foot when players turn with the ball after using a stride stop.
- In most cases, use the quick-stop technique even though some coaches prefer the stride stop in shooting, in which it is called the plant (back foot) and pivot (into the shot) with the stepping foot, or the step-plant move.

FIGURE 1.15 **Stride stop:** *(a)* changing direction; *(b)* when shooting (plant and pivot or step-plant move).

Quick Jumps

Jumping is an especially important skill in a sport with an elevated goal. Coaches often consider jumping a natural ability that cannot be taught and that players do or do not have. Nothing could be further from the truth.

The basic principles for improving jumping skill include being in quick stance and ready to jump in order to jump quickly in any situation. Players also can jump higher if they increase the muscle strength in their legs. Coaches should help players improve leg strength with resistance training as well as work on jumping skill.

How players land after a jump determines how quick and how high the next immediate jump will be. The best landing position is in a quick stance with balance and a wide base. Then players are ready to jump again with balance and quickness. Body position and control are best taught when players have first learned to jump using both feet and both arms.

The sections that follow explain how to execute two-foot jumps, quick jumps, and one-foot jumps and when to use each type of jump in game situations.

Two-Foot Power Jumps

A two-foot takeoff for jumping is slower but more stable than jumping from one foot on the move. It is best used in high-traffic situations (such as battling for a rebound) or on power layups with close defenders. It is a slow but strong move from a balanced position. The jumping position for power jumps is shown in figure 1.16*a*, with the arms ready to be swung forcefully forward and up.

The takeoff feet should be planted firmly before the jump (players should visualize stamping their feet through the floor) to provide maximum contraction of the leg muscles (i.e., quick stop and jump).

CRITICAL CUE:
Power jump—
two hands, two feet,
use arm momentum
or swing for
maximum height.

FIGURE 1.16 **Power jump for 2-and-2 rebounding:** *(a)* preparation; *(b)* two hands, two feet (tall and small); and *(c)* landing big and wide.

Whenever possible, players should use the forward momentum of a running jump with forceful contact on the takeoff and swing the arms forcefully upward to add to the body's momentum when time and space permit.

Successful rebounding almost always requires the use of two-foot power jumps. The best rebounders do so from two feet with two hands—2-and-2 rebounding—for which the critical cue is combined with another critical cue to teach proper technique—*going up tall and small* (i.e., two hands fully extended toward the ball) and *coming down big and wide* (doing a quick stop on two feet). See figure 1.16, *b* and *c*.

Quick Jumps

Quick jumps are the best compromise between conserving time and space and maintaining body position and control. A quick jump should be used wherever there is congestion, contact, or a contested jump around the basketball. Repeated, successive jumps in rebounding are usually quick jumps. Before a quick jump, the hands are held head high, with the upper arms nearly horizontal and the forearms vertical. Two-foot jumps using two hands (2-and-2 jumps), without momentum, that start from a quick stance are shown in figures 1.17 and 1.18).

> **CRITICAL CUE:**
> Circle tight with the arms for quick jumps.

The critical cue for successive quick jumps is a circle tight move to add arm momentum to the quick jump. From the ready position (figure 1.17*a*), the hands are circled slightly down, inside, and up (figure 1.17*b*) to the tall and small jumping position.

FIGURE 1.17 Quick jumps: *(a)* the hands up, *(b)* inside circle move with the hands for momentum.

FIGURE 1.18 Quick-jump rebounding: *(a)* block out with hands up, *(b)* 2-and-2 rebounding, and *(c)* capture and protect the ball.

One-Foot Jumps

Jumping from one foot is beneficial when movement and maximum height are required. Players should know how to do one-foot takeoffs so they can attack the basket on layups and jump high toward the basket or backboard (high jump, not long jump). One-foot jumps involve opposition, stamping hard on the jumping foot and raising the opposite foot or knee, and a high jump, stamping the jumping foot and using the opposite leg drive to produce a vertical rather than a horizontal or long jump. The shooting hand and knee are connected as though on a string; both of them come up together.

COACHING POINTS FOR JUMPS

- Be ready to jump: get in quick stance, jump, and land in quick stance.
- For power jumps and quick jumps, jump from two feet with two hands (2-and-2 jumps) most of the time, especially when rebounding.
- Whenever possible, use quick jumps with a circle hand move that is tight for repeated jumping efforts.
- For power, balance, and control, use a two-foot takeoff (2-and-2 rebounding), and for speed and height, use a one-foot takeoff (layups).
- Whenever there is time, use the momentum transfer from running forward and from the arms swinging upward.
- When shooting a jump shot, use quick stops and quick jumps.
- For maximum height and quickness, use a one-foot opposition jump.

TROUBLESHOOTING

Most problems in learning and teaching basic body-control moves occur with balance and quickness, unbalanced moves executed too quickly. In the beginning, players should slowly imitate the demonstration and get the feel of the move (get a rhythm). Finally, they can increase quickness until they make mistakes. Players should note and acknowledge mistakes, correct them, learn from them, and then forget them (i.e., develop a *mistake mentality*).

Basic Body-Control Drills

These drills can be used to develop and maintain the basic athletic stance for basketball, the quick stance, and to teach players to move and stop quickly during basketball play. The idea is to move with balance and quickness while maintaining control. The goal of game moves at game speed is always preceded by proper skill development.

QUICK-STANCE CHECK

Purpose: To develop the skills of recognizing various basic stances, getting in a basic stance quickly, and maintaining that stance.

Equipment: Half-court floor space (minimum).

Procedure: Players spread out on the basketball court facing the coach, assume a basic stance variation as directed (offensive or defensive quick stance and ready), and maintain the stance while it is checked by a coach (or partner). Players need to think quickly and respond to the ready command as they get into a quick stance, to know the look of a quick stance, and to know how to get into and stay in a quick stance.

Coaching Points

- Sit into the stance with the head behind the knees.
- Keep body weight on the whole foot with the toes pointed slightly outward.
- Keep the butt down, the chest out, and the back straight.
- Use defensive quick stance: add footfire.
- Use offensive quick stance: pit and protect the ball (or the imaginary ball).

QUICK-STANCE MIRROR

Purpose: To self-evaluate variations in stance by recognizing the look of a correct stance.

Equipment: Player and a full-length mirror.

Procedure: Each player checks all stance variations in front of a mirror, holding each basic stance at least 5 seconds (front and side view). A partner system may be used if a mirror is not available.

Coaching Points

- Coaches and players match what they think they are doing with what they are actually doing.
- Sit into the stance with the head behind the knees.
- Keep body weight on the whole foot with the toes pointed slightly outward.
- Keep the butt down, the chest out, and the back straight.
- Use defensive quick stance: add footfire.
- Use offensive quick stance: pit and protect the ball (or the imaginary ball).

MASS QUICK MOVES DRILL

Purpose: To develop the skills of recognizing various basic stances, getting in a basic stance quickly, and maintaining that stance.

Equipment: Half-court floor space (minimum).

Procedure: Players spread out on the basketball court facing the coach, assume a basic stance variation as directed (offensive or defensive quick stance and ready), and maintain the stance while it is checked by a coach (or partner). Players need to think quickly and respond to the ready command as they get into a quick stance. The coach should evaluate each player's ability to get into a quick stance as well as the quick-stance critical cues (weight on whole foot, all leg and arm joints bent, head up and centered over base, back straight, and chest out). Check the look of the stance and test balance by pushing on a player's shoulder area (forward, back, right, left).

Players can be moved on command to carry out the basic quick moves:

1. **Live-ball direct and crossover moves** (ready, direct drive with long and low step, move, crossover drive with long and low step, move) as shown in figures 1.8 and 1.9 on pages 7 and 8.

Coaching Points for Live-Ball Direct and Crossover Moves

- Start from triple-threat position.

- Focus on quickness and balance, with economy of motion.

- Step long and low past the imaginary defender.

- Use a straight line attack (to the basket) and make contact with the imaginary defender.

- Use the commands: *direct drive, long and low, go; crossover drive, circle tight (ball), long and low, go.*

2. **Quick jumps** (three consecutive jumps) and power jumps. (The commands are *quick-jump position, jump; power-jumping position, jump.*) See figures 1.16 to 1.18 on pages 14 and 15.

Coaching Points for Quick Jumps

- Circle tight with the hands for quick jumps (keep the arms up and the elbows at right angles).

- Jump quickly with a pop, and land ready to repeat.

- Coil and gather with the arms low; the arm explosion triggers the leg explosion for power jumps.

- Command: *quick-jump position, jump.*

For power jumps, add an imaginary ball and 2-and-2 rebounding. Go up tall and small and come down big and wide.

3. **Quick stops:** step right (with right foot) and into quick stop (command is *move*), and step left (with left foot) into a quick stop (command is *move*). See figure 1.14 on page 12.

Coaching Points for Quick Stops

- Stick the landing with soft feet.

- Land on a one count (both feet at the same time).

- Land in a balanced quick stance.

- Commands: *right-foot step, move; left-foot step, move.*

Repeat half turns and increase the pace of turns until mistakes are made.

4. **Quick turns** (ready, front turn, move and ready, rear turn, move). See figures 1.11 and 1.12 on page 10.

Coaching Points for Quick Turns

- Front turn—lead with a punch.

- Rear turn—lead with an elbow.
- Stay low and keep the head level.
- Commands: *front turn, move*; *rear turn, move.*

LINE DRILL: QUICK STARTS, STEPS, TURNS, AND STOPS

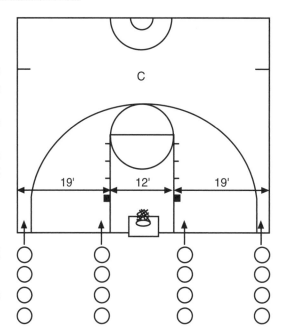

FIGURE 1.19 **Line drill: starts, steps, turns, and stops.**

Purpose: To develop skill in starting, turning, and stopping.

Equipment: Full court.

Procedure: All players are divided into four groups behind the baseline at one end of the court with the coach in the middle (figure 1.19). Coaches call out the options that players are to perform. Coaches teach offensive spacing and timing concepts using the 12-by-19-foot (3.7-by-5.8-meter) free-throw lanes as a reference. Coaches start the first group together; next players start when player ahead is 15 to 18 feet (4.6 to 5.5 meters) up the court (optimal spacing). The lines are already 15 to 18 feet apart.

Options

- All players use a quick-start technique from a quick stance. When players step on the court, they should be ready and in a quick stance.
- Stutter steps: Start from the baseline and go to the opposite end line, keeping the hands up and making the shoes squeak. Use the floor to your advantage; use short, choppy steps.
- Change-of-pace moves: Alternate two or three slow and fast moves after a quick start. Be quick and use a varied number of steps (avoid the same patterns).
- Quick stops: At the free-throw line, half-court line, and opposite free-throw line.
- Quick turns: Full front and rear turns (two half turns) after quick stops.
- Split-vision jog: Four players start simultaneously and jog at half speed, focusing on the far basket while using peripheral vision to stay in a straight line from side to side.
- Stride stops and 180-degree change of direction.
- Progressive stride stops: Progressive forward and backward moves are made from the baseline to the free-throw line (stride stop, reverse), back to the baseline (reverse), from the baseline to the half-court line (reverse), back to the free-throw line, and then to the opposite free-throw line, back to the half-court line, and then to the opposite baseline (figure 1.20).
- Spacing jog (a more advanced skill that also can be used with change-of-pace moves): The first four players start on command and move at their own pace, staying even with the leader (usually from the left line). The next person in line starts when the player ahead is 15 to 18 feet (4.6 to 5.5 meters) away (proper spacing between offensive players) and maintains that distance. This spacing jog is especially challenging in combination with change-of-pace moves. The four players stay in a line from left to right and are spaced 15 to 18 feet apart from side to side and behind the group ahead of them.

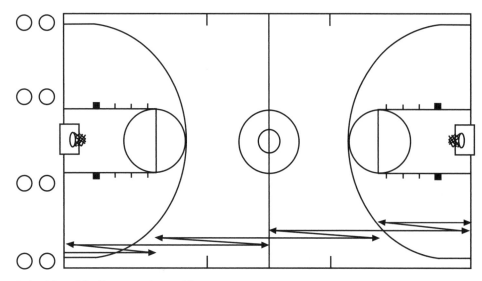

FIGURE 1.20 **Progressive stride stops.**

Coaches may hold players in any quick-stop position to check position and correct mistakes. Players may simulate dribbling a ball or sprinting without the ball (on offense). If defensive quick stops are used, the feet should be active at all times.

The coach can advance to a whistle-stop drill: Four players start and, on each short whistle, stride stop (or quick stop) and then reverse and sprint until the next whistle. The next group of four players always starts on the second whistle after the previous group. The drill continues until a player reaches the opposite baseline and all players have run the floor. This is an excellent conditioning drill.

Coaching Points

- Each variation is done in one circuit (down and back).

- The first player in each line should come to a quick-stance position on the baseline and be ready before being required to move. Players should listen for the direction and the *go* command from the coach.

- Players should keep floor spacing equal side-to-side and down the court when initiating movement.

- Unless directed otherwise, subsequent groups of four begin moving when the previous group reaches the near free-throw line (about 15 to 18 feet [4.6 to 5.5 meters] apart).

- All groups move to the opposite baseline and re-form, with the first group of four in quick stance, ready to come back in the opposite direction.

- Review critical cues for starts, steps, stops, and turns.

LINE DRILL: QUICK JUMPS

Purpose: To develop basic jumping skills for rebounding and shooting.

Equipment: Half-court floor space (minimum).

Procedure: Players are in four lines on the baseline with the coach near the half-court line. One down-and-back circuit of quick jumps can be added. The first wave of players sprints forward from basic position on the *go* command. Whenever the coach gives a thumbs-up signal, players execute a quick stop into a quick jump. They continue to repeat quick jumps in place until the coach signals to run forward again with a hitchhiking sign. The first group sprints again as the next group starts from basic position on the end line. This pattern is repeated until all groups reach the opposite end line. The coach must be in front and visible so that all groups of players can see the signals. An alternate is to require three quick jumps at the free-throw line, the half-court line, and the opposite free-throw line. A regular power-rebound jump and chinning the ball (with both hands

CRITICAL CUE: The arms up, the hands above the waist.

under the chin) can also be done at the free-throw line, the half-court line, opposite free-throw line, and opposite baseline, resulting in four rebounds for each floor length.

Coaching Points

- Circle tight with the hands for quick jumps.
- Jump quickly with a pop, and land ready to repeat.

LINE DRILL: REBOUND JUMPING AND TURNS

Purpose: To develop jumping skills for rebounding situations.

Equipment: A ball for each line.

Procedure: The first person in each line steps forward with a ball. Using basic jumping techniques, players toss a ball in the air in front of them, pursue and capture the ball using the 2-and-2 rebounding technique, and chin the ball. The players' elbows should be up and out in order to protect the ball while they land in a quick stance. They should then execute a rear turn before stepping and passing to the next player in the line.

Coaching Points

- Coil and gather with the arms low; the arm explosion triggers the leg explosion for power jumps; capture and chin the ball.
- Rear turn: Lead with an elbow; turn on the PPF.
- Stay low and level.

LINE DRILL: QUICK STANCE, STARTS, STEPS, JUMPS, TURNS, AND STOPS

Purpose: To develop body-control movements by executing all skills properly, quickly, and at the right time. This is an ideal practice warm-up drill.

Equipment: Full-court floor space.

Procedure: Players stand in three or four lines on the baseline. The coach is positioned in the midcourt area and commands a half or full circuit of body-control moves. Players get in and maintain a quick stance, play, and stay low as they execute a variety of combinations directed by the coach. Coaches review basic body-control moves in this drill.

Coaching Points

- Emphasize the appropriate critical cues for the specific skills.
- Start all variations with an offensive quick stance.

LINE DRILL: STARTS, STOPS, AND TURNS

Purpose: This drill is designed to set the foundation of quick stance, quick starts, quick stops, quick turns, and passing and catching skills (ball added later) without the ball in a combination warm-up drill.

Equipment: Baseline area and floor space to the top of the key area.

Procedure: Players stand in four lines on the baseline with a minimum of two players per line. On the *ready* command, the first player in each line steps onto the court in an offensive quick stance (an imaginary triple-threat position) without the ball. To start the drill, coaches direct the drill as *direct drive, go* or as *crossover drive, go*. The first player executes a direct drive (long and low) with an imaginary dribble drive with the preferred hand for two dribbles and makes a quick stop (chinning the ball or staying in triple-threat position). Then the player executes a rear turn and an imaginary one-handed push pass (stepping and passing, exaggerating the follow-through). The next player in line is in a quick stance, with both hands near a respective shoulder, giving two spot targets for the imaginary pass. That player assumes the two-handed catch position with both feet in the air (ball in the air and feet in the air) and then repeats the direct-drive move. The coach then goes on to the crossover drive, dribble, and pass. For a right-handed player, the moves would require a crossover drive to the left side, a left-handed dribble, a quick stop, a rear turn on the PPF, and a crossover, imaginary one-handed push pass using the nonpreferred hand. Coaches should use starts, stops, and turns as a progression drill when the ball is added after teaching or reviewing passing and catching. The rule for nonpreferred body-control movement is three times as many repetitions as on the preferred side.

Coaching Points

- Passing: Pass with the feet on the floor; pass with a step; pass with a ping to a specific target; exaggerate the follow-through.

- Catching: Catch with the feet in the air; catch with a click (two hands and two eyes); catch in a quick stance.

- Emphasize the critical cues for starts, steps, stops, and turns.

chapter 2

Advanced Body Control

*"Basic basketball (the fundamental skills) is critical to success—
this includes learning to move without the ball."*

Fred "Tex" Winter, longtime Assistant Coach, Chicago Bulls and Los Angeles Lakers

One of the most difficult coaching tasks is to teach players to carry out actions that don't involve the basketball—the magnet of the game. An individual player on offense plays without the basketball over 80 percent of the time.

This chapter illustrates the importance of individual skills that do not involve possession of the basketball. Many coaches find that young players on offense are often "magnetized" by the ball and almost obsessively attracted to it (figure 2.1). Time must be spent teaching them that movement without the ball and proper offensive spacing and timing can be just as important as moves made with the ball in terms of setting up scoring opportunities. Coaches can help motivate players to carry out purposeful movement without the ball and to understand that proper spacing and timing are keys to successful team offense.

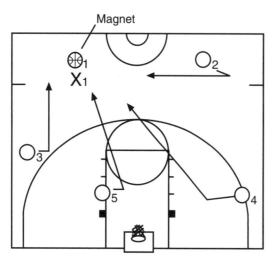

FIGURE 2.1 **Ball magnet and team spacing.**

Concepts of Moving Without the Ball

To move effectively without the ball, players must master and remember certain fundamentals on the court.

- Be alert and remember that all moves begin *on the floor*.
- Move with authority (distinct moves), balance, and quickness.
- Move with a purpose and with proper spacing and timing. Players must be aware of teammates' movements and maintain focus on the offensive strategies of the whole team.
- Read the defense and the ball. All individual movement, which is dictated by the team play situation, must be carried out in relation to the position and movement of the ball as well as the opponents' defense. Get open by moving to clear areas on the court for receiving passes.
- Communicate all cuts and moves by voice and with hands. Players cannot talk too much.
- Get open or get out. The primary purpose of movement without the ball is to get open to receive a pass from the ballhandler. Try to get open; if it is not possible, get out of the way. Keep proper spacing of at least 15 to 18 feet (4.6 to 5.5 meters) apart (12 to 15 feet [3.6 to 4.6 meters] for younger players and 18 to 21 feet [5.5 to 6.4 meters] for college or professional players).
- Get open in the perfect catching position—15 to 18 feet from the ballhandler. Ideally, this also will be in a floor position affording a player the option to pass, shoot, or dribble. Catch the ball facing the basket or catch the ball and then use a turn (pivot) to face the basket. Teach catch-and-face technique for offensive players in the frontcourt the following sequence: rim (look at the rim for the shot

and to see the whole floor), post (look inside to feed the post), and action (move the ball or dribble-drive to the basket). This sequence must become automatic and be executed very quickly in order. RPA (rim-post-action) every time players catch the ball.

- Be an actor. Movement without the ball is a continuous competition between offensive and defensive players. Keeping opponents guessing requires using believable fakes (and giving time for reaction) to bait the defenders and play the role of decoy.

- Lose the defenders. Move out of the defenders' fields of vision, and force them to turn their heads. Most defenders have their backs to the basket and their eyes on the ball, so offensive players should move behind them to the baseline and away from the ball (see figure 2.2). Cuts can best be made from this position where defenders cannot easily anticipate moves. This technique is especially effective against zone defenses that focus on the ball.

- Run through the ball. When moving to catch a pass, players should maintain the open position by moving toward and meeting the pass unless they are making a breakaway move ahead of the defender or a back cut behind a defender (figure 2.3). Beat the defender to the ball.

- Get close to get open. Because this rule goes against common sense, players make the mistake of trying to free themselves by staying away from a defender. It is actually more effective to stay close and then break away quickly to get open, as shown by O$_2$ and O$_3$ in figure 2.4. This effective move allows the offensive player to execute an *action* move that precedes and is quicker than the defender's *reaction* move. An effective fake-and-break V-cut or L-cut to get open is often a slow-to-quick action move.

- While applying all concepts, keep proper spacing (more than 15 to 18 feet [4.6 to 5.5 meters] apart unless cutting or screening) and make moves at the right time (better late than early).

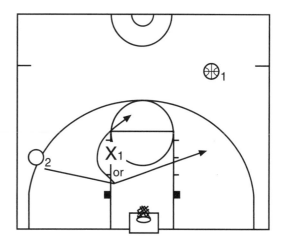

FIGURE 2.2 Lose the defenders (move out of the defender's field of vision).

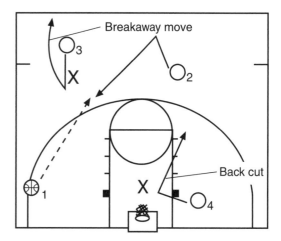

FIGURE 2.3 Run through the ball (meet the pass—O$_2$).

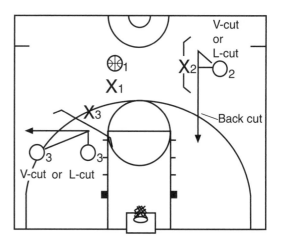

FIGURE 2.4 Get close to get open. O$_3$ moves close to X$_3$ and then makes a quick V-cut or L-cut move to get open to receive a pass. O$_2$ moves toward X$_2$, who overplays the pass from O$_1$, and O$_2$ then back cuts to the basket.

Basic Moves or Steps Without the Ball

Basic moves without the ball require that the player be deceptive in order to fool the defense. Players need to go slowly at first and be correct and then move progressively quicker until they can make game moves at game speed.

V-Cuts

Special purpose cuts or moves (quick steps) also include fake-and-break or V-cuts: basic zigzag or change-of-direction cuts that form the shape of a V. To execute a V-cut, place body weight on the foot opposite the desired direction of movement (sink the hips into the cut), point the lead foot, and step with that opposite foot. For example, *plant* and push from the right foot and *step* to the left with the left foot. Usually, one side of the V is the move to the basket, away from the basket, or to the defender. The other side of the V is the quick change-of-direction cut to get open. Beginners can also use short stutter steps during the fake (for balance) and then a quick plant-and-break step at a right angle. When teaching young players, use the term *fake-and-break* for the V-cut to get open. The first part of the V-move is toward the basket or the defender (the fake); it should be carried out slowly and quickly followed by the last part of the V (the break) to get open. On the break, both hands are thrown up in the direction of movement. The move is needed to catch the ball (communicate with hands that you are open) when players are using a screen or preparing for a shot. The break move is usually toward the ball but can also be toward the basket, as in O_2's back-cut move on X_2's overplay (figure 2.4 on page 25). The V-cut is a sharp change-of-direction cut from 60 to 90 degrees (called an L-cut).

Back cuts are important moves—15 to 18 feet (4.6 to 5.5 meters) away from the ball—that are used when defenders overplay the passing lane, as shown previously in figure 2.4. To execute this move, the cutter should get close to get open and make a slow-to-quick V-cut or L-cut move directly to the basket (rim cut) while communicating with the outside hand (the arm down, closed fist) on the fake, and the lead hand on the break (open hand, the arm horizontal). This move is shown clearly in figure 2.5 when the cutter moves from inside-out on a V-cut and is still over-played. The cutter needs to create enough space on the perimeter for the back cut by baiting the defender, at least to the three-point arc, while maintaining 15 to 18 feet of spacing from the passer. Players should *make* back cuts (hard and fast) but never *fake* back cuts; faking them usually confuses the passer and leads to a turnover.

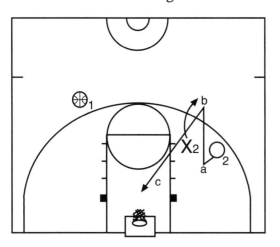

FIGURE 2.5 Backdoor cuts: *(a)* V-cut to get open; *(b)* bait defender and signal fake before back cut (outside fist closed and pointed down); *(c)* back cut to rim and signal open with the lead hand.

CRITICAL CUE:
Always *make* a back cut; *never fake* a back cut.

CRITICAL CUE:
Communicate cuts with the hands.

Front and Rear Cuts

These are types of V-cut moves made after a player has passed the ball to a teammate and wants to challenge the defense by cutting to the basket (making a rim cut) for a possible return pass. The pass-and-cut move—sometimes called *give-and-go*—is one of the most valuable offensive moves. The give-and-go was the first two-player offensive move that was developed in the game. It takes two forms: the preferred front cut, which allows the offensive player to receive the ball in front of the defender (an excellent scoring position), and the rear cut, which lets the offensive player cut behind the defender to gain an advantage going to the basket (figure 2.6). A front cut uses a V-cut to set up the defense, whereas a rear cut is a direct, straight-line cut used as a change-of-pace or slow-quick move. Both front and rear cuts are to the rim and end exactly in front of the basket. The front or lead hand on the cut is held out in front and horizontally to indicate the cutter's intention to the passer (communicate the cut with the hands), as shown in figure 2.7.

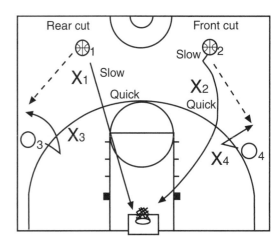

FIGURE 2.6 **Front and rear cuts—give-and-go basketball.**

FIGURE 2.7 **Communicate the cut with the hands:** *(a)* **front cut,** *(b)* **rear cut.**

Decoy Moves

Decoy moves are basic moves used to keep defenders busy, such as distracting defensive players from helping defend against a ballhandler or trap the ball. Teach players to be actors and distracters, misleading defenders with deceptive eye movements, physical bluffs, and other visual or auditory distractions.

Shot Moves

When the ball is in the air on a shot attempt by the offensive team, each offensive player should move to a rebounding position or go to a defensive assignment, depending on the position and role. Players need to make decisive moves when a shot is taken rather than standing and watching the ball. Spectators are ball watchers. But players should be movers and should always assume that the shot will be missed and that they need to rebound or get back on defense in order to do their jobs every time a shot is taken on offense.

Assigned Moves

Assigned moves are individually designated cuts in a system of play for special situations. Coaches make specific assignments for rebounding, jump balls, out-of-bounds plays, free throws, and set patterns. All players must carry out individual assignments properly, quickly, and at the right time. How well this is done is just as important as what is being done; spacing and timing of moves are essential.

Screen Moves

Setting and using screens to get a teammate open for a pass or a drive are unselfish team moves that are also essential skills of individual offense. Instruction in setting and using screens should not begin until secondary-school level (elementary-school players should concentrate on learning more basic moves and concepts without the ball).

Types of Screens

Screens can be classified according to location (on or off the ball), type of use (back screens [back to the basket] set behind or on the blind side of a defender and down screens [back to the ball] set in front of or to the side of a defender), and kind of body contact used to screen (front or rear of the body). See figure 2.8.

Coaches should develop their own theories of how screens should work: screening a certain spot or area on the floor (position screen) or screening the defender (player screen). A player screen is usually more effective in freeing the offensive player, but it may result in more fouls for illegal screens, or *blocks*. The authors prefer player screens: screen an opponent rather than a spot or a teammate.

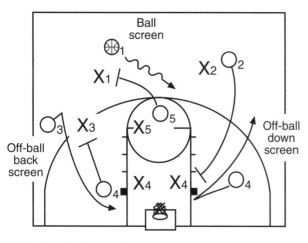

FIGURE 2.8 **Types of screens.**

Setting Screens

Setting a screen is a basic move: Players should use a noisy, quick stop, with the feet shoulder-width apart and the hands out of the screen (figure 2.9). The screen should be set perpendicular to the expected path of the defender and be forceful enough for the defender to see and hear it. Screening players should be loud, low, and legal—set with a quick stance after a quick stop—and capable of being heard when set and when the defender makes contact with it. Players should get low, be ready for contact, and play and stay low, sitting into contact. A legal screen includes correct position and legal use of hands. A down screen can be set skin-to-skin, but a back screen should allow at least one step for the defender to change direction. To avoid illegal hand contact, a player should use one hand to grasp the other wrist (usually of the shooting hand, for protection) and place the hands in front of the body over the vital parts. Against good defensive teams, the cutter is usually covered, but the screener is often open during a defensive switch or help.

Other tips include using down screens (toward the basket) when defenders are sagging, back screens (away from the basket) where there is pressure or defenders are overplaying, and flare screens (away from the ball and the basket) when defenders are collapsing inside. Be ready for contact and screen the defender. Players should alert teammates they are screening for by hand or voice signal.

CRITICAL CUE: Set loud, low, and legal screens.

FIGURE 2.9 Front screen: use a noisy quick stop with a wide base, keeping the arms out of the screen. *(a)* Men grab the shooting wrist over the groin area; *(b)* women cross the arms over the chest area.

Using Screens

The most difficult screening skill is to prepare the defender to run into the screen (players should use a teammate as a screen or obstacle) with a V-cut, usually started toward the basket as shown in figure 2.10. An important cue is to wait for the screen: Coaches can require the cutter to wait until the screener calls *go* as the user comes to the screen on a V-cut. This move is advocated by Tommy Lloyd of Gonzaga University. Other coaches insist that the cutter grasp the jersey or trunk of the screener before cutting. These techniques force the cutter to wait and read the screen.

Players should cut razor close so that they brush shoulders with the screener. On screens away from the ball, players should be in a low position with the hands up as they pass the screen, ready to receive a pass. Players should throw the hands up as they move past the screener on the break. Timing is crucial in effective screen plays: Players must wait for the screen to be set before making moves and read the defender's position to make the correct cut opposite.

When two players set and use a screen, they both are scoring options. The cutter reads the defender's position while waiting and then cuts accordingly to get open. For example, a defender trying to get through a screen causes a pop cut (outside shot) move with a reaction inside (a low cut) by the screener. The two scoring options are inside and low or outside and high

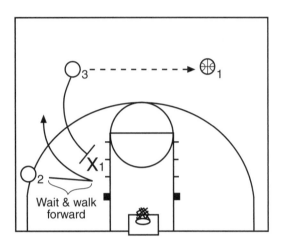

FIGURE 2.10 Using the screen. Wait (O₂) as the V-cut is made.

moves by the cutter and screener (in response to the cut). With less determined or skilled defenders, the cutter is usually open. With great defenders, the screener is usually open for the score.

On-the-Ball Screens

The pick-and-roll is a basic two-person play used at all levels. This play was a staple for one of the best inside-outside combinations in basketball history, Karl Malone and John Stockton of the Utah Jazz. Pick-and-roll occurs when a screen is set on the ballhandler. When an effective screen is used and defenders do not switch, the

dribbler is open for a shot (dribble-drive layup or set and jump shot), as shown in figure 2.11. The sequence occurs when O_1 V-cuts to get open as O_2 passes and sets the ball screen on defender X_1 (sprint to set the screen quickly). In this option, X_1 tries to fight through the screen (defenders do not switch assignments) but is impeded and O_1 is free for the shot (layup or set and jump).

When a screen (pick) is made on the ballhandler and the defenders switch assignments, the screener is open on a roll move to the basket. The pick-and-roll for the screener is shown in figure 2.12. When the ballhandler uses the screen, the screener makes a *half* rear turn and shuffle slides to the basket, keeping between the ballhandler and the original defender X_1. The screener should use a proper rear turn in order to maintain vision on the ball at all times. The ballhandler

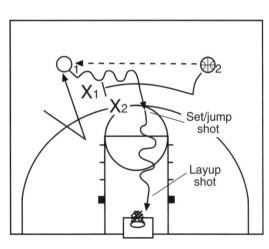

FIGURE 2.11 Pick-and-roll—defenders stay (no switched assignments).

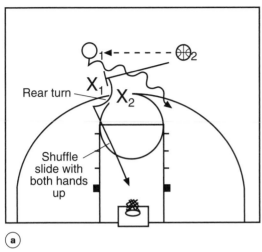
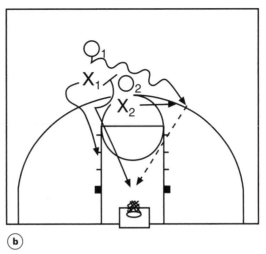

(a)   (b)

FIGURE 2.12 **Pick-and-roll—defenders switch.** *(a)* Screen (pick) set and rear turn on the left foot as the dribbler clears the screen on a two-dribble draw, *(b)* roll-pass to the screener rolling to the basket.

must make at least two dribbles past the screen to draw the switching defender X_2 (the dribble draw) and then make a pass (usually a bounce pass) to the screener on the roll move to the basket. On occasion, the defenders may double-team or trap the ballhandler. When that occurs, the screener should "pick and pop"—step back and outside for the return pass and the outside shot.

On all screen plays, two scoring options are always possible when an effective screen is made: the nonscreener is open if the defenders don't switch, and the screener is open if the defenders switch. Advanced players should be taught to look for both scoring options.

Another advanced option on all two-person screen plays is for the screener to slip the screen or fake the screen and cut to the basket as the defenders choose to switch defensive assignments in early anticipation of the screen. This option for on-the-ball screens is shown in figure 2.13.

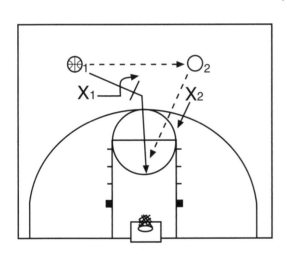

FIGURE 2.13 **Slip the screen.**

Off-the-Ball Screens

This type of screen is set *away from* the ball and occurs as a basic two-player pattern plus the passer. Off-the-ball screens are classified by the cutter's reaction to the defender's choice of combatting the screen:

• A *pop cut* is used when the defender attempts to fight through the screen (figure 2.14). O_1 passes to O_2 and screens away from the ball *on the defender* of O_3, X_3. O_3 gets an open shot *outside* if no defensive switch is made (option *a*). If X_1 switches defensive assignments, the screener O_1 gets the open shot *inside* by cutting (flashing) to the ball as the switch is made (option *b*). Players should communicate the cut with both hands up coming past the screen.

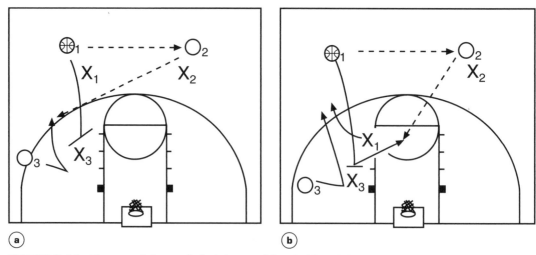

FIGURE 2.14 Pop cut: *(a)* no-switch defense, *(b)* switching defense.

• A *curl cut* is used when the defender trails the cutter around the screen (figure 2.15). In the first option, defense stays, and the cutter gets the open shot inside (curling to the basket). When the defenders switch, the screener O_1 gets the outside shot cutting to the ball (option *b*). Larry Bird, former Boston Celtic and Hall of Fame player, executed this screen cut to perfection. Players should communicate the cut with the inside (lead) hand forward when coming around the screen.

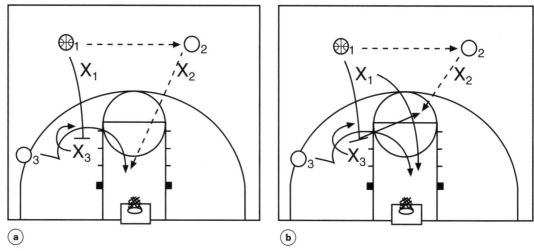

FIGURE 2.15 Curl cut: *(a)* no-switch defense, *(b)* switching defense.

• A *flare* or *fade cut* is used when the defender anticipates the pop cut (figure 2.16). When the defenders stay (no switch), the cutter is open by flaring away from the ball and outside (option *a*). The screener may reset the screen to pin the defender inside as the cutter pushes off the screener on the flare cut. When the defenders switch, the screener is open (option *b*) on the inside flash cut (slip) to the ball. The cutter communicates the U-cut (flare cut) by backing out with both hands up.

• A *back cut* is used when the cutter makes a pop cut and the defender fights through the screen (figure 2.17). In option *a* (no-switch defense), the cutter makes the pop cut, is overplayed, and reacts by making a cut to the basket using the back screen of O_1. The movement sequence for the cutter is to the basket (in), pop cut (out), and back cut (in) to the basket. When no switch is made, the cutter gets

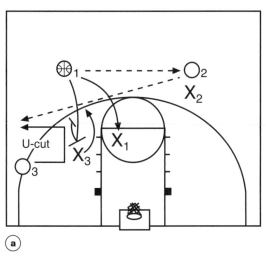

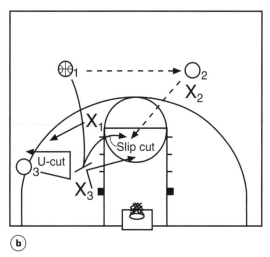

FIGURE 2.16   **Flare cut:** *(a)* no-switch defense, *(b)* switching defense.

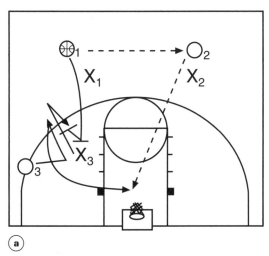

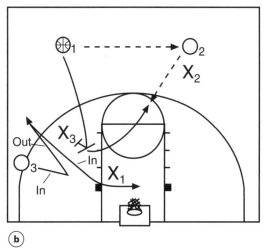

FIGURE 2.17   **Back cut:** *(a)* no-switch defense, *(b)* switching defense.

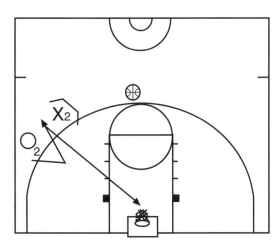

FIGURE 2.18   **Quick back cut.**

the shot inside going to the basket. In option *b* (switching defense), the screener O_1 gets the shot flashing to the ball outside as the switch is made. The cutter communicates the cut with a closed fist down on the outside hand as the out move is made. The back cut can also be done without the use of the pop cut: As the cutter waits while moving toward the screen, the defender anticipates the pop cut and cheats over the screen (figure 2.18). When the screener says *go*, the cutter makes a quick back cut directly to the basket with a front-hand communication for the layup. On the switch, the screener may slip cut to the free-throw lane area. An important reminder for players using a back-cut option is to *always* make a back cut and *never* fake a back cut.

CRITICAL CUE:
Make the back cut; never fake the back cut.

COACHING POINTS FOR MOVING WITHOUT THE BALL

- Use the floor when beginning a move.
- Move with authority.
- Move with a purpose.
- Read the defense and the ball and react.
- Get open or get out of the way; don't stand still.
- Know and use the perfect catching position (15 to 18 feet [4.6 to 5.5 meters] from the ball).
- Be an actor; take the initiative and use believable fakes.
- Lose the defender.
- Run through the ball (meet the pass).
- Get close to get open.
- Alert a teammate when setting a screen.
- Set loud, low, and legal screens; sprint to set a screen.
- Set a pick or screen at a right angle to the expected path of the defender.
- When using screens, wait for the *go* signal, use V-cuts or go to the screener, and brush past the screen (shoulder to shoulder or contact).
- Pick-and-roll and the two scoring options for on-the-ball screens.
- Off-the-ball screen cuts: pop, curl, flare, and back.
- Two scoring options on every screen: cutter and screener.
- Make the back cut; never fake the back cut.

TROUBLESHOOTING

Moves without the ball—where spacing and timing are critical—are considered *big picture* moves, advanced and difficult team plays that require patience and attention to detail. It is usually better to be too late than too early on most of these moves, especially cutting moves.

Movement mistakes occur when a player without the ball commits an error. Players need to focus their attention on recovery, call out for help from teammates when needed, and get in position immediately for the next play, especially when an offensive error results in a steal. Players should avoid making two mistakes in a row and learn to play through their mistakes. Mistakes are necessary for learning; analyze them and then forget them.

Drills for Moving Without the Ball

These drills are designed to teach players the most challenging moves, those without the ball. Players tend to be eager to develop ball skills and reluctant to drill on moves without the ball.

LINE DRILL: MOVE WITHOUT THE BALL

Purpose: To teach by simulation basic moves without the ball.

Equipment: Half court (minimum).

Procedure: The players should assume a basic four-line drill position on the baseline. The first player in each line moves down the court without the ball, imagining the ball to be in the center of the court (figure 2.19).

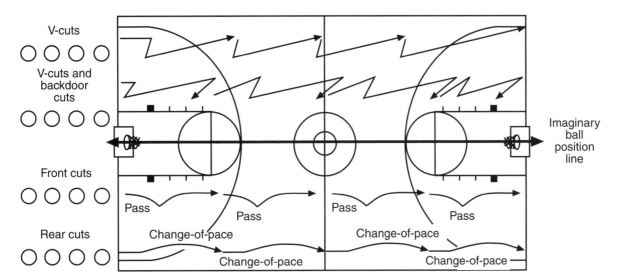

FIGURE 2.19   **Line drill: V-cuts, backdoor cuts, front cuts, and rear cuts without the ball.**

Options

- V-cuts to get open (designated to the basket and to the ball or to the defender and the ball): Repeated V-cuts, followed by quick stops to simulate catching the ball, are performed for the length of the court. Communicate the cut with the hands up.

- V-cuts to get open, followed by a backdoor cut: Players should use proper footwork and hand position. Communicate with the hands—up when getting open, the outside hand down and fist closed for the backdoor cut.

- Front cuts: A simulated pass to the center of the court is followed by a front cut (V-cut, move away slowly, fast cut to the ball) and a quick stop at the free-throw lines and the half-court line. Communicate with the inside hand across and up.

- Rear cuts: A simulated pass to the center of the court is followed by a rear cut (change-of-pace, slow to fast) and a quick stop at the free-throw lines and half-court line. Communicate with the hands up or the lead hand forward.

Quick stops are used at each free-throw line and at the half-court line. At the completion of each quick stop, players should challenge the imaginary defense by using a catch-and-face move—first a quick stop and then a pivot in order to face the basket and see the whole court.

V-CUT DRILL

Purpose: To teach players the basic moves without the ball in a 2-on-0, 2-on-2 situation.

Equipment: One ball per basket per group.

Procedure: The basic two-line formation for this drill is one line of guards or point position players out front and a line of forwards or wing position players on the side (i.e., two lines of outside players).

Options

- Use a forward V-cut to get open (fake and break) and, after receiving the pass from the guard, use a catch-and-face (the basket) move.

- Guard can make a front or rear cut to the basket (cut to the rim) to catch the forward-to-guard return pass and then go to the end of the forward V-cut line (give-and-go), or the forward can make a live-ball, dribble-drive move to the basket (figure 2.20a).

- Forward then rebounds the ball and passes to the next guard in line and goes to the end of the guard line.

- Figure 2.20b shows a forward backdoor move (advanced skill) performed during a guard dribble move. The ballhandler, dribbling toward overplaying defender, keys the backdoor cut, or the receiver, with the outside hand down, keys the cut. The forward backdoor cut should be made outside the three-point field-goal line; spread the defense and back cut.

The forward V-cut may be a fake to the basket and break to get open or to the imaginary defender (L-cut). When acceptable skill levels are reached, add two defenders and execute the drills in a 2-on-2 situation. Communicate cuts with the hands (figure 2.21).

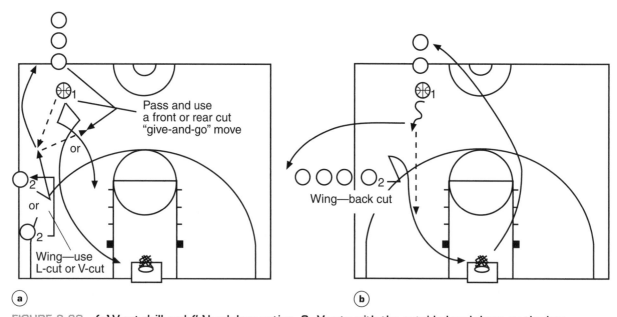

Pass and use a front or rear cut "give-and-go" move

or

Wing—use L-cut or V-cut

(a)

Wing—back cut

(b)

FIGURE 2.20 *(a)* V-cut drill and *(b)* backdoor option. O_2 V-cuts with the outside hand down as the key.

FIGURE 2.21   Communicate the cuts with the hands: *(a)* V-cut to get open, and *(b)* front or rear cut give-and-go (the lead hand).

PICK-AND-ROLL DRILL

Purpose: To teach players the screening and cutting options for on-the-ball screens.

Equipment: One ball per basket per group (four or more).

Procedure: Two lines of outside players 15 to 18 feet (4.6 to 5.5 meters) apart use the screening pattern of pass and screen the ballhandler's defender. The progression should be the following:

- 2-on-0: cutter (dribbler) scoring option alternating with the screener scoring option (roll or step outside for shot or pick and pop).

- 2-on-2: defense stays (score on the pick) alternating with the defense switches (score on the roll or step outside for shot or pick and pop).
  - Live offense and defense
  - Player rotation: offense to defense to the end of the opposite line
- 3-on-3:
  - Live offense and defense
  - Make-it-take-it (offense keeps the ball when they score); rotate when the defense stops the offense

3-ON-0 MOTION

Purpose: To teach both scoring options on screens away from the ball; two-ball shooting.

Equipment: Two balls per basket per group, six players preferred. Two passers (coaches or program assistants).

Procedure: The coach determines the cut at first, and then the cutters call the cut. Then two defenders are added, and the screener or cutters must read the defenders and cut accordingly while calling their cut (see figure 2.22).

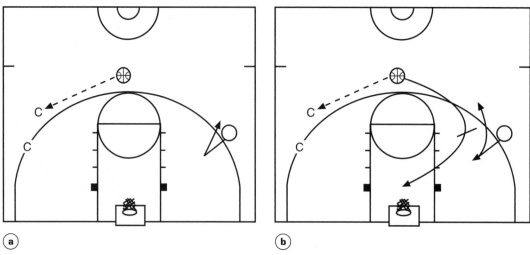

FIGURE 2.22   **3-on-0 motion drill:** *(a)* basic setup, *(b)* pass and screen away.

3-ON-3 MOTION SCREEN DRILL

Purpose: To teach players the screening and cutting options for off-the-ball screens.

Equipment: One ball per basket per group (six or more). Coaches can use two balls to pass on both scoring options.

Procedure: Three lines of outside players, 15 to 18 feet (4.6 to 5.5 meters) apart, use the options to pass and screen away from the ball: pop up, curl cut, flare cut, back cut. The progression should be the following:

- 3-on-0:
    - Pop cut (cutter cuts outside, screener cuts and slips inside)
    - Curl cut (cutter curls inside, screener pops outside)
    - Flare cut (cutter U-cuts outside, screener slips inside)
    - Back cut (cutter back cuts inside, screener pops outside)
- 3-on-3:
    - Defense stays (cutter options)
    - Defense switches (screener options)
    - Live offense and defense
    - Make-it-take-it (offense scores, they keep the ball)

Coaching Points

- Sprint to set a screen as the teammate is signaled.
- Cutter waits (verbal *go*) for the screen.
- Set screens that are loud, low, and legal.
- Signal cuts with the hands, and use verbal calls on all cuts.
- There are two scoring options on each screen.

chapter 3

Ballhandling

"Passing and catching are offensive team skills, while dribbling is an individual offensive skill; therefore the pass should be the primary offensive weapon."

Ralph Miller, Hall of Fame Coach

Ballhandling encompasses all offensive moves with the basketball—passing, catching, dribbling, shooting, individual moves, and rebounding. In this chapter's discussion, ballhandling includes only the skills of passing, catching, and dribbling.

The arm mechanics of the ballhandling skills of passing, dribbling, and shooting are almost identical—the arm and hand motion is the same for each skill. Passing and catching are the most important individual offensive fundamentals with the ball. Shooting can be considered as a pass to the basket and passing as a shot to a catching teammate. Dribbling, which can also be considered as a pass to the floor, is a secondary offensive weapon that should not be misused or overused, which is often the case. Players should pass first and dribble last.

Another ballhandling principle must be applied in order to achieve balanced development of ballhandling skills with the dominant and nondominant hands. Players need to work on the weak hand *two or three times* as much as on the strong hand.

Getting into triple-threat position (offensive quick stance)—where a player with the ball may shoot, pass, or dribble—should become automatic (see figure 3.1). In triple-threat position, the player with the ball *pits and protects* the ball (pulls the ball close to the armpit in order to protect it from the defender). Players should avoid dangling the ball away from the body; they need to keep their game tight. This protected area is also called the *shooting pocket*. Players should always use the catch-and-face move with the ball: catching it, moving it to triple-threat position, and then pivoting and facing the basket to see the whole floor (especially open teammates for possible partners for passing and catching). Offensive quick stance is attained with quickness and balance. Players must think quickly, move at top speed under control, and be ready to pass or catch first and dribble last. When players become ballhandlers, they should first look to pass the ball to a teammate (unless they are

FIGURE 3.1 **Triple-threat position (offensive quick stance with the ball):** *(a)* side view, *(b)* front view.

open for a scoring opportunity within their range) before choosing to dribble, which is the final option for moving the ball. The primary movement concepts of quickness and balance dictate the preferred order: passing before dribbling.

Passing and Catching

Passing and catching are the most neglected fundamentals in basketball. Players have to develop these skills in order to mount a successful team offense. Effective passing and receiving in the form of the scoring assist are measures of offensive teamwork and important tools for controlling game tempo on offense. An important measure of offensive team efficiency is the number of scores from assists (team plays from passing or catching) compared to scores from the dribble drive (individual plays). The team scores should always exceed individual scores.

Players who are good passers and catchers or receivers have an excellent chance to be important team members. In coaching, good passing tends to take the pressure off a team's defensive play and break down the opponent's defense. Because passing is the quickest way to move the ball and challenge the defense, it should be the primary weapon of offensive attack, thus applying the priority principle of balance and quickness.

Earvin "Magic" Johnson led his college and NBA teams to championships by becoming one of the greatest passers in the history of the game. John Stockton led the great Utah Jazz teams of the 1990s by doing the same thing. Steve Nash of the Phoenix Suns does the same thing today.

Convince players that passing and catching are primary offensive team plays; they are the most effective way of achieving the offensive objective—moving the ball quickly and getting it to an open player to set up a scoring opportunity.

CRITICAL CUE:
Get in triple-threat position, pit and protect the ball, and face the basket using a front or rear turn whenever you have the ball.

Passing Principles

Players need to look for the pass *before* dribbling. When catching, follow the rim-post-action (RPA) rule. When players catch the ball within the operating area of the offensive basket, they should catch and face the basket to look for the shot (rim), look to pass to an inside post player (post), and then move the ball (action). A player's first instinct is to dribble; continual emphasis on the shot and pass are required to overcome this instinct. Since dribbling is an individual skill, practiced each time a player touches the ball, a natural preference for it tends to develop.

Good passes can only be made when coaches also teach other fundamental elements of passing:

CRITICAL CUE:
See the whole floor, look to pass first, dribble last.

- Feet on the floor: Pass with the feet on the floor in most situations. Pass with a quick step for quickness (using the stepping foot).
- Quickness: The ball must be passed quickly (before the defender has time to react). The pass should be snappy and crisp, but not too hard or too easy. A quick step is usually made in the direction of the pass to provide added force. When a quick pass is thrown, a *ping* sound occurs. When the throw is too hard, the pass slaps loudly as it is caught; when the throw is too soft, no sound is

CRITICAL CUE:
Pass with the feet on the floor and a quick stepping foot.

FIGURE 3.2 **Getting open: Keep both arms up.**

heard as it is caught. The first passing guideline is to pass with a ping (i.e., a crisp pass, not too hard or too soft). This concept was made popular by Fred "Tex" Winter, longtime assistant coach for the Chicago Bulls and Los Angeles Lakers.

- A target: Each pass must be thrown accurately to a spot target (usually away from the defender). A raised hand away from the defender is commonly used as the target; players should have both hands up when catching, one target hand and the other arm up to ward off the defender (figure 3.2).
- Timing: The ball must be delivered when the receiver is open, not before or after. Pass with a ping at the right time. When learning to pass, exaggerate the follow-through.
- Deception: The passer must use deception to confuse the defender, who is reading the passer (especially the eyes) and anticipating the pass. Use ball fakes and keep *vision on the whole floor* as the passer sees the spot target.
- Shorten all passes (run through the ball) by meeting or coming toward the ball (unless on a breakaway).

CRITICAL CUE:
Pass to a spot target at the right time.

Passers should visually locate all teammates as well as defenders (see the rim of the basket in frontcourt, the net in backcourt), concentrating on the potential receiver without staring. This can best be done by surveying the whole floor area (broad focus) with the ball in triple-threat position. When they catch a pass, players should always be prepared to shoot when open (catch and face the basket) and within range; if unable to shoot, they should try to pass to an open teammate before dribbling (rim-post-action).

CRITICAL CUE:
Pass with a ping, not too fast or too slow.

Players must learn to give up the ball unselfishly by passing to an open player. Ballhandlers also can dribble drive and pass (penetrate and pitch); they can create an opportunity for an assist by making a dribble move that allows them to pass to an open teammate to score. When players are passing, the choice should be to make the easy pass through or by the defender. Teach players not to gamble on passes, to be clever, not fancy. Most of the time, a player using the dribble drive should use a quick stop before passing the ball at the end of the penetration or drive. This applies the rule of passing and stepping with feet on the floor. John Stockton, Gonzaga University and Utah Jazz All-Star player, became the all-time assist record holder in the NBA by making the easy pass (i.e., the simple play).

The most important passing principles are the following:

CRITICAL CUE:
Make the easy pass.

- Pass with the feet on the floor (use the stepping foot).
- Pass to a spot target at the right time.
- Pass with a ping (snappy and crisp) at the right time.
- Pass with deception.

Choosing the Correct Pass

The quickest passes are air passes. Simple geometry (the shortest distance between two points is a straight line) proves that the air pass is quicker than either the lob pass or the bounce pass, as shown in figure 3.3. Therefore, the air pass is the primary pass to use. All perimeter passes around the defense should be air passes.

Lob passes are used only when passing to teammates on a breakaway fast break, the lob allows them to run to catch up with the ball; when teammates are being fronted while playing a low post position; or when this is the best way to get the ball past a defender. The lob is always a slower pass.

Use bounce passes only when passing to players who are

- in the post position and are smaller than the defender,
- open on the baseline side,
- making a backdoor cut, or
- in an emergency situation.

Special Passing Situations

Situations related to passing include eliminating the pass across under the defensive basket; an interception there usually results in a score by the opponents. Other danger areas are along boundary lines and in court corners (figure 3.4). When a pass comes back out on the perimeter from the baseline, players should reverse the ball quickly to the other side of the court to test the defense and check for the opponents' alertness on the help side of the defense (test the second side or reverse [swing] the ball to make defenders move).

Types of Passes

In basketball, the type of pass used must fit the situation. For example, chest air and one-handed baseball passes are best used in open court or perimeter situations where speed is paramount, but the one-handed push pass is the preferred close quarters or backdoor pass.

Chest Pass

The chest pass, the basic air pass for effective, efficient ball movement when an offensive player is guarded loosely or in an open floor area, can be used for longer distances because the starting position for the pass is reached by moving the ball from triple-threat position to the center of the chest, close to the body, in a thumbs-up position. To throw the pass, a player then extends the elbows and pronates (rotates inward) the arms to a thumbs-down ending position. Players should push the thumbs through the ball to produce backspin on the ball. Players should also take a step forward to pass when there is time, but passing without stepping is quicker. Most of the time, step (quickly) and pass. On longer passes, the ball is rolled in a circular

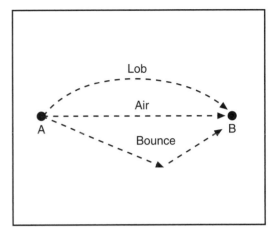

FIGURE 3.3 **Types of passes, their path and distance traveled.**

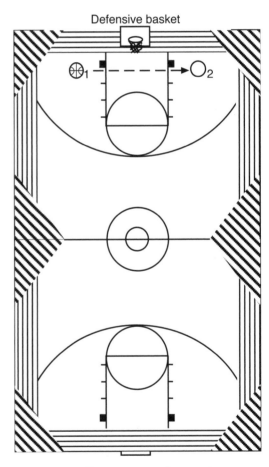

FIGURE 3.4 **Danger areas for passing or catching.**

CRITICAL CUE:
Chest pass—thumbs-
up to thumbs-down
position.

move—out, down, and toward the body—before release. The target of the pass is the throat (neck) area of the receiver who is stationary and defended from behind (aim for the face) and toward the receiver's outside hand (two-handed targets, see figure 3.2) when the receiver is near a defender.

Chest Bounce Pass

This pass is recommended primarily for backdoor moves and emergencies, when the passer must get out of a trap or when the defender is playing in the passing lane. Passing tips include making the pass to a target two-thirds of the way to the receiver and following through to that spot on the floor, as for a chest pass. The pass should be thrown hard enough that it bounces up to the receiver at hip level (usually about two-thirds of the way to the catcher). Starting with the ball in a thumbs-up position, passers should push the thumbs through the ball and follow through to a thumbs-down position (figure 3.5). The backspin is important in this movement because it increases the angle of rebound on the bounce pass, making it easier to handle. For power, players also may step forward (using the stepping foot) with the pass.

FIGURE 3.5 Bounce pass: *(a)* thumbs-up starting position (the target is a spot on the floor), *(b)* thumbs-down ending position (follow through to the spot) and catcher with the feet in the air.

Overhead Pass

When a player catches the ball, it is always moved quickly to triple-threat position (catch and face the basket). The ball can then be moved quickly overhead to pass over the defense. A valuable pass over the defense to reverse the ball to the second side of the floor (called a skip pass) is especially effective against zone defenses. The position of the ball allows the passer to show the ball and use pass fakes. Players need to keep the ball up, starting with and keeping the elbows locked or extended, and to throw the pass with the wrists and fingers; the ball should be overhead with little or no windup behind the head.

The technique involves starting with the thumbs back and then pushing the thumbs through the ball, finishing with the thumbs forward (figure 3.6). The overhead pass tends to drop, so the ball should be thrown to a high target (usually the receiver's head); the pass is hard to handle when dropping. For more power, players should step forward with the pass.

A distinction should be made between overhead passes for longer and shorter distances. The longer overhead pass usually occurs on a defensive rebound and outlet, a skip pass from one side of the court to the other (corner to opposite wing, wing to opposite wing, or other long pass or over-the-top situations). Shorter overhead pass instances include high post to low post or top-down perimeter to post passes and other perimeter pass situations, most often to the next receiver. Longer overhead

CRITICAL CUE:
Overhead pass: thumbs back to thumbs forward, the ball up, the elbows locked.

FIGURE 3.6 **Overhead pass:** *(a)* **thumbs-back starting position (the ball up, the elbows locked), and** *(b)* **the thumbs forward and the palms out (use the wrists and fingers, keep the ball up).**

passes necessitate a power step with the pass, full use of both arms and thumbs, and a complete follow-through. Overhead passes should be used as air passes, not bounce passes, because of the high starting position for the pass release.

One-Handed Baseball Pass

A baseball pass is used to throw a long pass (usually over half-court length) with the dominant throwing arm. Players should keep two hands on the ball as long as possible and use a stance with the body parallel to the sidelines and feet parallel to the baseline, and then they should plant the back foot, point and step with the front foot, and throw the ball from the ear, similar to a baseball catcher's throw. Proper follow-through includes carrying out a full pronation and extension of the arm, ending with the thumb down (figure 3.7). Players should throw this pass only with the dominant arm, using the other hand to catch the fake pass and stabilize the ball. The turning (pivot) foot on this pass is always the back foot, with the stepping foot as the front foot (an exception when using the PPF concept).

FIGURE 3.7 Baseball pass: *(a)* starting position: by the ear, both hands on the ball, *(b)* pull the string: the fake pass can be used from this position, and *(c)* pronate (the thumb down) on release.

One-Handed Push Pass

The one-handed push pass (flick pass), the most important offensive pass, is a quick pass used to pass through or by a closely guarding defender. This pass is used near defenders and at 15- to 18-foot (4.6- to 5.5-meter) distances. It may be an air or bounce pass and should be used from the triple-threat position; the key is the bent-elbow starting position (needed for power). The passer should work one side of the defender's body, especially past the ear, where the biggest gap usually appears, and make the pass above or below the defender's arms after finding an opening. Vertical fakes are used as players read the defender (figure 3.8). Players should fake low and pass high (air pass) or fake high (maybe a shot fake) and pass low (bounce pass), reading the defender's arm position and making short, quick fakes. The first look is always past the ear, using an air pass when the defender's arm is down.

When players move from the preferred side in triple-threat position, the ball is moved quickly (rip through) from side to side (pit to pit) to work the other side of the defender's body: a circle tight move, which is preferred to a high or low sweep for quickness and balance.

FIGURE 3.8 Push or flick pass: *(a)* use the triple-threat position to work on the side of the defender's body; when the defender's arm is down, pass high, near the hole by the ear, and *(b)* use vertical fakes (fake high, pass low) when the defender's arm is up.

Catching Principles

Catching the basketball requires a player to be ready. Potential pass receivers, in quick-stance position with both hands up, must be open and give a target at the right time.

Running through the basketball is another receiving rule that refers to meeting the pass unless the player is cutting to the basket on a backdoor cut or a breakaway situation. When defended, the receiver must move toward the ball until contact is made to ensure possession. Players should make a cut to finish running through the ball, about 15 to 18 feet (4.6 to 5.5 meters) from the ball (i.e., shortening the passing lane).

Players should catch the ball with feet slightly in the air whenever possible. The receiver should catch the ball with both feet in the air and then come to a quick stop with the ball in triple-threat (normal) or "chinit" position (under duress), ensuring

CRITICAL CUE:
Catch the ball with
the feet in the air.

body control, ball possession, and a quick return to quick stance (where either foot can be used as the pivot foot, the quick-stop advantage). Finally, all catchers should catch and face their offensive basket in order to see the whole floor and the rim (net).

Two-handed basketball is a good habit to develop in players. They should always catch the ball with both hands. Of the three methods of catching the ball, the first is with two hands up (thumbs together), used when the pass is near the middle of the body and above the waist (figure 3.9a). The second is with two hands down

CRITICAL CUE:
Catch with a click; use
both hands and eyes.

FIGURE 3.9 Catching the ball: *(a)* above the waist, *(b)* below the waist, *(c)* one-handed block, and *(d)* two-handed tuck.

(the thumbs apart), used when the pass is near the middle of the body and below the waist (figure 3.9*b*). The third method is the block and tuck, used when the pass is to either side of the body: Players block the ball with one hand and tuck it with the other; both hands should immediately be placed on the ball (figure 3.9, *c* and *d*).

As the pass is caught, the receiver should let the wrist and elbows give, which is sometimes called *developing soft hands*. Also, the eyes should be focused on the pass until it is in both hands. Players need to catch the ball with their eyes. The combination of catching with two hands and using both eyes is called *catching with a click*. When possible, the catcher should catch the ball with the wrist back and move to the shooting pocket (figure 3.10).

Finally, the pass catcher should meet the pass or shorten the passing lane by meeting or coming toward the ball to catch it with the feet in the air, except on a backdoor cut to the basket on defensive overplay. The important catching principles are the following:

FIGURE 3.10 **Catch the ball with the wrist back; be ready to shoot.**

- Catch passes with the feet in the air.
- Catch passes with a click (two eyes, two hands).
- Meet the pass; run through the ball.

COACHING POINTS FOR PASSING AND CATCHING

- Teach triple-threat position; pit and protect the ball while turning to catch and face up the floor.
- Help passers develop quickness, the use of a spot target, and proper timing.
- Teach players to pass with the feet on the floor and to pass with a ping.
- Teach players to pass and catch with two hands handling the ball as long as possible.
- Teach players to catch the ball with the feet in the air (ball in the air, feet in the air).
- Teach players to catch with a click (two hands, two eyes).
- Teach catchers to move the ball to the shooting pocket or chinning position.
- Teach players to catch and scan immediately to see the whole court (catch and face the basket or catch the ball with the feet facing the basket).
- Train catchers to be ready for bad passes and to stay in stance with the hands up and the body ready to move.

Communication of Passing and Catching

It is the responsibility of both passer and catcher to complete each pass, to strive for perfection, but to settle for success. Successful passes depend on communication, especially by the catcher. Every potential pass receiver should always be ready to catch a pass (quick stance with the hands up), to call the passer's name to show openness, and to communicate with the hands (both hands up when open, one hand inside for a curl cut, closed fist on the outside hand for a back cut). The passer must decide whether to make the pass. Some coaches prefer to have the passer call the catcher's name as the pass is made. Passers need to have eye and voice contact with catchers before and as the pass is made. Players cannot communicate too much.

CRITICAL CUE:
Catchers: Get open, be ready, call for the ball, catch the ball with the feet in air, and face the basket.

Dribbling

Dribbling is a touch, not a sight, skill. Players should learn to dribble up the court without watching the ball by focusing on the offensive basket (see the rim), looking over the whole court (using peripheral vision). Seeing the net in the backcourt allows the dribbler to see the whole court and open teammates. Seeing the rim in the frontcourt accomplishes the passing guide and gets players in the habit of looking for the shot every time they catch the ball (rim-post-action). The primary objective in the frontcourt is to create a move that allows a player to pass to a teammate for a score. When players are dribbling, this move might be a live-ball move, a basket penetration move past an opponent using the dribble drive to the basket, or ball movement by passing to get a teammate open. Dribbling is also an acceptable option, preferably for advancing the ball up the court when a pass is not available, maneuvering for a better position for a pass to a teammate, executing an offensive play or pattern, and getting out of heavy defensive traffic or a defensive trap situation (two defenders on the dribbler).

CRITICAL CUE:
Dribble *only* to make a live-ball move, penetrate the defense, get a teammate open, advance the ball, execute a play, or get out of trouble. Dribble with a purpose.

Dribbling Technique

Players should execute the dribble by first extending the elbow and flexing the wrist and fingers, dribbling with the wrist, hand, and a little forearm motion. The dribble is really a pass and catch to the floor. The fingers and pads of the hand control the ball (the ball should be kept off the heel of the hand); the fingers are spread comfortably and should be cupped around the ball (figure 3.11). Players should massage the ball, dribble it firmly, and stay low and sit into the game while dribbling. They should make the dribble a short pass for quickness.

Players should maintain maximum contact with the ball. The rules require the hand to stay on top of the ball: The dribble is legal as long as the hand does not leave its vertical position to get under and carry the ball or as long as the ball is not cupped by a large hand (figure 3.12). The ball must leave the dribbler's hand before the pivot foot leaves the floor when starting a dribble on a live-ball move.

It is strongly recommended that the quick stop be used to terminate the dribble (figure 3.13). This is the best method of avoiding traveling violations and protecting the ball while conserving critical time and space for passing or shooting. In traffic, players should pick up the dribble, use a quick stop, and chin the ball.

FIGURE 3.11 Dribbling: *(a)* use the fingers and the pads of the hands, *(b)* elbow extension and wrist and finger flexion to push the ball to the floor.

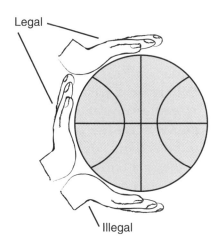

FIGURE 3.12 Dribbling rules: hand position.

Legal

Illegal

FIGURE 3.13 Terminate the dribble with a quick stop and chin (or triple-threat position).

When chinning the ball, players should get into a quick stance with the ball under the chin, with the fingers up and the elbows out and up (players make themselves big and protect their territory).

Players should learn to use either hand to dribble, developing the weak hand but using the preferred hand whenever possible. They should practice two or three times more with the nonpreferred hand. They always should use the dribbling hand away

CRITICAL CUE:
Dribbling is a touch skill; see the net and the whole court or the rim and half of the court.

FIGURE 3.14 **Closely guarded dribbler: Protect the ball with the body and the opposite hand, keeping tension on the legs and staying in quick stance (low or control dribble).**

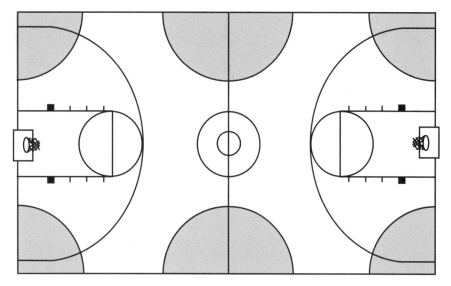

FIGURE 3.15 **To stay out of trouble, avoid the corners of the court when dribbling.**

from the defender when closely guarded and protect the ball with the body and the opposite hand (arm bar) when dribbling against a close defender. They should keep the ball low and to the side of the body and stay in a quick stance by sitting into their game (figure 3.14).

Dribbling Strategies

The general dribbling rule is that, when the ball is put on the floor, the dribbler should always be moving purposefully. On drives to the basket, the dribbler goes past the defender. The objective is to use one dribble to score in the frontcourt; bouncing the ball once or dribbling while not changing floor position (called *dropping the ball*) should be discouraged. A dribble penetration (*penetrate and pitch*) is best accomplished just after the player has received a pass, thus avoiding forcing the dribble into defenders who are prepared for the penetration.

A key guideline is for players to stay away from trouble while dribbling. Players should avoid dribbling into traffic (between two defenders); dribblers should keep alert for traps by watching for defenders and avoiding the corners of the court (figure 3.15).

Players should keep the dribble under control and conclude a dribble with a pass or shot, preferably after a quick stop (step and pass with the feet on the floor). A dribbler should use the right move at the right time and see the whole court as well as teammates and defenders.

Types of Dribble Moves

The right type of dribble should be used at the right time. A low or control dribble should be used around defenders when the dribbler is closely guarded, and a high or speed dribble should be used in the open court when a player is advancing the ball. All dribble moves should change directions at sharp angles.

Low Dribble. A control or low dribble is the first and easiest dribble to teach players. They should use a staggered stance—bent knees with the ball-side foot back. The opposite hand (*arm bar*) is used for protection from the defender—but not to push the defender back or hook the defender, only to protect the ball. The basic body motion is a sliding movement similar to defensive slides or short steps, running motion.

Players protect the ball by dribbling on the side of the body away from the defender, keeping the ball low and dribbling hard and fast near the back foot.

Power Dribble. An advanced version of the low or control dribble, the power dribble, is executed by using a sliding foot (step and slide or push-step) motion and low dribble so that the ball is protected by the front leg and the hip and front arm bar. The ball is dribbled below the knee, high near the back leg, as far away from the defender as possible. The dribbler advances up the court with push-step moves. As the player goes forward, the ball is near or in front of the back foot (figure 3.16*a*); as the player goes backward, the ball is near or behind the back foot (figure 3.16*b*). From this position, a player can use advanced dribble moves (described later), such as a pull-back crossover, a spin dribble, or a fake spin dribble, to create space and to attack the basket. Players should maintain vision up the floor over the lead shoulder: see the net (on the goal) in the backcourt or see the rim in the frontcourt, which allows the dribbler to see the whole floor.

Speed Dribble. For a speed or high dribble, players should push the ball out in front and run after it, keeping it ahead of them. The ball can be dribbled higher—near waist level—to attain more speed. The faster the movement is, the farther out in front and the higher the player should dribble the ball.

> **CRITICAL CUE:**
> Use a power dribble when using a dribble against extreme defensive pressure.

FIGURE 3.16 **Power dribble:** *(a)* shuffle forward, *(b)* shuffle backward.

Change-of-Pace Dribble. A change-of-pace dribble or dribble hesitation is accomplished by changing speeds from a low or control dribble in a stop-and-start motion. When slowing or stopping, dribblers should straighten up slightly to relax the defender. This move should be used to move past defenders who take the slow pace or stop fake. This is another slow-to-fast move to get dribblers in the clear and to keep them open.

On the change-of-pace or hesitation dribble, players can make it look like they are going to shoot or pass as they straighten up or hesitate. If players are within shooting range, they can fake pulling up for a jump shot; if out of shooting range, they should look to the other side of the court as if they are rising up to pass to that side.

Crossover Dribble. A crossover or switch dribble is a basic move used in the open court when there is sufficient room between the dribbler and defender and the dribbler has momentum to move by the defender (figure 3.17). Players should never cross over the ball in front of the legs on a stationary defender. They should attack one side of the defender and use the crossover dribble when the defender has stopped the initial attack. In this dribble, the ball is pushed low and quickly across the body. The proper technique is to push the ball from right to left (or vice versa) as a zigzag move or a V-cut from right to left (or vice versa) is made (figure 3.18). This move is used when the defender overplays the path of the dribbler on the ball side. Teach players to make the move before a defender gets too close (need room to cross over) and to explode past the defender as the move is made.

Head-and-Shoulders Move. The head-and-shoulders or in-and-out move is advanced. It is a dribble move to get around a defender using the preferred hand (figure 3.19).

FIGURE 3.17 Crossover dribble: *(a)* low dribble (one hand), *(b)* cross over low and in front of the body, and *(c)* low dribble (the opposite hand).

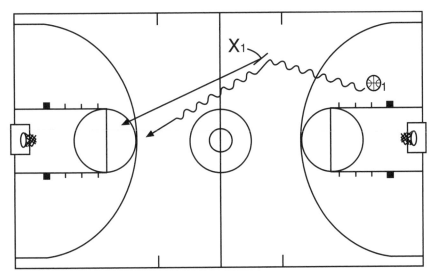

FIGURE 3.18 **Crossover dribble right to left; offensive zigzag pushing off the right foot, stepping with the left foot as the ball is crossed over (low and quick) from the right to the left hand.**

FIGURE 3.19 **Head-and-shoulders and in-and-out moves:** *(a)* weight on the right foot, dribble the ball on the right side, *(b)* zigzag on the left foot, head-and-shoulders fake to the left, and *(c)* move past the defender with the right foot.

Players should dribble the ball with the preferred hand and continue the move by a fake opposite with a zigzag move on the opposite foot as a head-and-shoulders fake is made to that side, keeping the ball in rhythm with the move. The move past the defender is made with the preferred foot. The rhythm is *right-left-right* to step by (when players are dribbling on the right side of the body) and *left-right-left* for preferred left-handers. The advantage of this faking move is that the dribbler can face and see the defense while executing a dribble move to get around a defender with the preferred hand. The sequence for a right-handed person is push from the right foot as the dribble is made; fake left with the left foot, head, and shoulders; extend the right foot with a long step forward and past the defender as the ball is pushed out in front; and step with the left foot and go to the basket and past the defender using hip contact to protect the ball.

Head-and-Shoulders Crossover Move. A head-and-shoulders crossover or in-out-in, another advanced move, is a dribble move to cross the ball over from the preferred hand to the other hand while the dribbler moves past the defender on that side while still facing the defense (figure 3.20). This move begins like the head-and-shoulders move. The crossover dribble is kept low and made across the body at the same time as the zigzag move is made from the preferred side to the other side. The footwork is *right-left-right-left*, in order to cross over from right to left and reverse when going from left to right. The dribble rhythm is timed with the footwork movement. The move must be made before the defender is close enough to reach the crossover dribble. This is the companion to the head-and-shoulders move. The sequence for a right-handed person is foot, head, and shoulders left; come back

FIGURE 3.20 Head-and-shoulders and in-and-out crossover moves: *(a)* weight on the right foot, dribble the ball on the right side, *(b)* zigzag on the left foot, *(c)* weight back to the right foot, *(d)* cross the ball over in front of the body from right to left, and *(e)* explode to the basket.

right (short step); take a short step with the left foot as the ball is crossed over in front of the body from right to left; and bring the right foot across and go to the basket past the defender.

Spin Dribble. A spin or whirl dribble is used for maximum ball protection when the ballhandler is closely guarded. During this move, the body is kept between the ball and defender as shown in figure 3.21. The disadvantage of this move is that the ballhandler briefly loses sight of portions of the court and of defenders and teammates and may be susceptible to blind-side traps or double teams. Spin dribble footwork

FIGURE 3.21   Spin or whirl dribble: *(a)* low dribble, *(b)* quick stop—rear turn, *(c)* pull the ball (keep it in the holster and tight to the hip), and *(d)* change hands and move past the defender.

CRITICAL CUE: Pull the ball to the hip on the spin dribble, keep it tight on the spin.

uses quick-stop, rear-turn pivot, and sharp-angled zigzag moves from right to left (or vice versa). As the 270-degree rear turn is made on the left (or right) foot, the right (left) hand pulls the ball with the pivot until the turn is completed, and the first step is made with the right (or left) foot. The ball is kept close to the body—the pull is similar to pulling a pistol from a holster. Have players pull the ball and keep it tight near the hip and leg to avoid the defenders' reach-around or slap-around moves. After the rear turn is completed, the ball is switched to the opposite hand and full court vision is regained. This move changes direction from an angle that is forward right to forward left (or vice versa) as the ball is changed from the right hand to the left hand (or vice versa).

Back Dribble.   The rocker dribble or back dribble move is used to back away from trouble, defensive traffic, or a trap. When dribbling with the right (left) hand, players should be in a low control or power-dribble position with the left (right) foot forward into trouble and then explode back (out move) in a sliding power-dribble movement to create space and get away from the defense. After players have reestablished a gap on the defense, any dribble move may be used to penetrate or go by the defender. The crossover dribble is especially effective following the dribble rocker or back dribble. The move is into the defender, back out, and then by the defender with a sharp-angled move. When players are crossing over in traffic, it is best to go between the legs or behind the back to protect the ball instead of using the front crossover, especially when facing a closely guarding defender.

CRITICAL CUE: Move in, out, and go by on the back dribble.

Pull-Back Crossover.   The combination of the power dribble (into trouble, traffic, or a trap), followed by the back dribble (out of trouble or to create a gap), and then the crossover dribble between the legs and advancing past one defender is an important advanced dribble move (figure 3.22). This move has the advantage of allowing the dribbler to meet defensive challenges successfully while seeing the whole floor. It also allows a less athletic ballhandler to compete well against aggressive, quicker defenders. The dribbler needs to go under control until trapped or in trouble, back

FIGURE 3.22   **Pull-back crossover dribble: (a) when in the trap, use a low control dribble.**

FIGURE 3.22 Pull-back crossover dribble: *(b)* Power dribble with sliding steps backward to get out of trouble, and *(c)* crossover and go by the defender to create space.

dribble out hard to create space, and then attack the other (usually outside) defender by crossing over with the ball and going by quickly (an in-out-by move).

Behind-the-Back Dribble. The popular behind-the-back dribble is used to change hands (usually from preferred to nonpreferred) and go past a defender who is overplaying on the right (left). This is done by changing direction slightly to the left (right) and going by on the dribbler's left (right). Plant the inside foot and step past the defender with the outside leg. As the left (right) foot is moved forward, the ball is moved from right to left (or vice versa) behind the back, coming up under the left (right) hand for a continuation of the dribble. Players can learn the coordination of the dribble and footwork by a stationary position side yo-yo V dribble (figure 3.23); players dribble with one hand back and forth with the opposite foot forward. When the ball is controlled from front to back, it can be moved behind the back as a step is taken with the left foot (figure 3.24).

  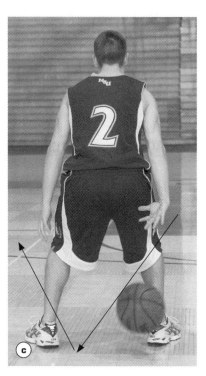

FIGURE 3.23 **Progression for behind-the-back dribble:** *(a, b)* front to back yo-yo (on the side of the body or front to back), *(c)* back yo-yo (side to side behind the back).

FIGURE 3.24 **Behind-the-back dribble (right to left hand) move:** *(a)* dribble with the right hand, *(b)* move the ball from right to left behind the back, and *(c)* continue dribble with the left hand, moving past the defender.

Between-the-Legs Dribble. The between-the-legs dribble is used to avoid overplay and to change the ball from one side (hand) to the other. When the ball is being dribbled with the right hand, it can be changed to the left hand between the legs when the left or right foot is forward (best with the right foot forward). This move is reversed for a left-hand dribble. The ball is kept low and crossed over between the legs with a quick, hard push across (the ball is snapped between the legs as the player steps with the other foot) (figure 3.25). Players can learn the coordination of the dribble and the footwork by walking forward slowly as the ball is crossed over between the legs during each step.

The move is really a one-foot quick stop on the outside foot as the ball is snapped between the legs and a sharp-angled step is made by the defender as the ball is switched to the other hand. The planted outside foot is then pulled past the defender to protect the ball. The between-the-legs dribble is the best dribble move to combat pressure, see the whole court, and move by a defender.

CRITICAL CUE:
Use a one-foot quick stop and then snap the ball on the between-the-legs dribbles.

FIGURE 3.25 **Between-the-legs dribble:** *(a)* dribble with the left hand and *(b)* push between the legs when one foot is forward.

COACHING POINTS FOR DRIBBLING

- ☐ Keep the head up. See the net and the whole court or the rim and the half court.
- ☐ Control the ball with the fingers and the pads of the hands.
- ☐ Massage the ball and dribble firmly; pass and catch to the floor.
- ☐ Around or close to defenders, stay low and protect the ball (sit into the game, keep tension on the legs, use arm bar).
- ☐ Use a quick stop and chin the ball when ending the dribble or pit and protect the ball, and be ready to pass after the quick stop.
- ☐ Pass first; dribble last.

Basic Ballhandling Drills

These drills involve ballhandling skills and are usually enjoyed by players. Coaches need to be insistent on quick and proper execution and timing. Players tend to learn to execute these skills at a slow speed and then progress to moves at game speed.

BALLHANDLING DRILLS

Purpose: To teach players to control the ball and become familiar with the ball—see it, hear it, and feel it.

Equipment: One ball per player and a 6-foot (1.8-meter) circle of floor space.

Procedure: Players spread out in their areas and execute the following drill options—working for proper execution first and quickness second.

Figure-Eight Speed Dribble: Start the drill with either the right or left hand. Start dribbling in and out between the legs in a figure-eight pattern. Start slowly and keep the ball as low as possible at all times. Players should gradually pick up speed after they begin to master the drill. There is no time limit to the drill, although 20 times around in 1 minute is excellent or 10 times in 30 seconds.

Blur: Start the drill with the legs about shoulder-width apart. One hand should be on the ball in front of the legs. Flip the ball in the air and reverse the position of the hands. Catch the ball in the fingertips and try to go as fast as possible for 30 seconds. The ball appears to sit between the legs if the move is executed properly. Assessment: Excellent: 81 to 100, Good: 61 to 80, Fair: 40 to 60.

Straddle Flip: Start with the legs shoulder-width apart, with the knees bent and the hands in front holding the basketball. Let go of the ball or flip it very slightly up in the air between the legs. Bring the hands to the back of the legs and catch the ball before it hits the ground. Flip the ball again in the air and bring the hands back to the front as quickly as possible. Drill as fast as possible without dropping the ball. Continue the drill for 30 seconds. Assessment: Excellent: 81 or higher, Good: 61 to 80, Fair: 40 to 60.

Rhythm: Take the ball around the right leg. Grab the ball with the left hand in front and the right hand in back. Drop the ball. Quickly reverse hands and catch the ball after one bounce. Move the ball back to start around the left leg. The opposite drill is to start with the ball in the left hand. Continue the drill for 30 seconds. Assessment: Excellent: 33 to 40, Good: 21 to 32, Fair: 10 to 20.

Double Leg and Single Leg: Take the ball behind the legs and around the front. When the ball reaches the right hand, spread the legs and take the ball around the right leg only. Close the legs and take the ball once around both legs and then open the legs and take the ball around the left leg once and then back to two legs again. The ball always moves in the same direction. Then start with the ball in the left hand. Continue for 30 seconds. Assessment: Excellent: 51 to 70, Good: 36 to 50, Fair: 25 to 35.

Around the Waist: Take the ball in the right hand and move it behind the back and catch it with the left hand; in one continuous motion, bring the ball around to the front to the right hand. Do the drill continuously for 30 seconds, as fast as possible. Execute the drill by starting with the ball in the left hand. Assessment: Excellent: 51 to 70, Good: 36 to 50, Fair: 25 to 35.

Around the Head: Place the ball in the right hand and, with the shoulders back, take the ball behind the head and catch it with the left hand and bring it around to the front to the right hand in a continuous motion. The opposite drill is to start with the ball in the left hand. Continue the drill for 30 seconds. Assessment: Excellent: 51 to 75, Good: 41 to 50, Fair: 30 to 40.

Figure Eight From the Back: Start with the ball in the right hand. Take it between the legs to the left hand; with the ball in the left hand, take it behind the left leg and between the legs to the right hand. The opposite drill is a figure eight from the front, which takes the ball from the right to the left hand through the front of the legs. Continue the drill for 30 seconds. Assessment: Excellent: 66 to 85, Good: 46 to 65, Fair: 30 to 45.

Figure Eight With One Bounce: Start with the legs shoulder-width apart and the knees bent. With the ball in the right hand, bounce it between the legs and catch it with the left hand behind the legs; with the ball in the left hand, bring it around to the front and bounce it between the legs and catch it with the right hand. The opposite drill is to take the ball behind the legs and bounce it to the front right and left hand. Assessment: Excellent: 41 to 50, Good: 31 to 40, Fair: 20 to 30.

LINE DRILL: PASSING AND CATCHING

Purpose: To teach passing and catching techniques and all basic passes.

Equipment: One ball per line and half-court floor space.

Procedure: Players are in four lines behind the baseline at one end of the court with the coach at the top of the key, directing the drill. The first player in each line starts at free-throw line distance facing the baseline as the first catcher (in a ready-to-catch stance). The ball starts with the player on the baseline. Passes are made as the passer quickly moves to replace the catcher. Critical cues are for players to pass with feet on the floor and catch with feet (slightly) in the air; passers to exaggerate the follow-through, pass with a ping, and pass to a spot; and catchers to give a target, catch the ball with eyes and both hands (catch with a click), and play two-handed. Be proper first and quick second. Suggested progressions are the following:

- Chest pass: air, bounce
- Push or flick pass:
  - Right side (air, bounce) or left side
  - Left side (air, bounce); go pit to pit quickly (circle tight) or right side
  - Read the defense; look by the ear first with air pass (fake high and pass low or fake low and pass high)
  - Passer passes and assumes defensive position (designated hand position)
- Overhead pass: catch, pit, and protect the ball; put the ball overhead
- Baseball pass:
  - Pass with the dominant hand only
  - Face the sidelines and step with the pass (move to the top of the key or a longer distance)
  - Fake the pass into the hand and then pass

TWO-PLAYER PASSING AND CATCHING DRILL

Purpose: To teach passing and catching with players using a push pass with either hand, after a dribble.

Equipment: One ball per pair and full-court floor space.

Procedure: Players are in four lines behind the baseline at one end of the court, with all players in the inside lines with a ball. The player pits the ball and executes a dribble drive with the hand opposite the partner, who moves parallel to the dribbler. The dribbler does a quick stop and a push pass to the partner with the closest hand if using either pivot foot. If using the PPF concept, a right-hander on the right side steps across to use the left-hand pass with the left PPF. On the left side, that player would step with the right foot (left PPF) and pass with the right hand. The partner catches the ball with feet in air and repeats the dribble-drive cycle. The catcher calls the passer's name before the pass is made. The complete sequence is shown in figure 3.26. The next pair begins their passing and catching sequence when the previous pair is 15 to 18 feet (4.6 to 5.5 meters) ahead (near the free-throw line).

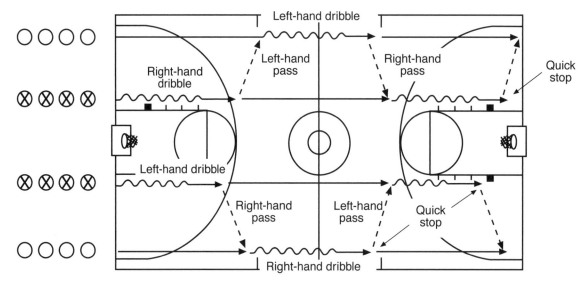

FIGURE 3.26 Two-player passing and catching.

2-ON-1 KEEPAWAY PASSING DRILL

Purpose: Teach passing-catching between partners who must pass by a defender.

Equipment: One ball per three players and floor space of 15 to 20 feet (4.6 to 6 meters).

Procedure: Players are grouped in threes; two offensive players 15 to 18 feet apart, with a defender between (figure 3.27). Defensive players rotate out each 30 seconds or when an interception is made. The following progression is recommended:

• the defender in position, designated hand position (up, down);

• the defender close to the passer, or away from the passer (teaches the passer to take the ball to the defender to take away reaction time); and

• live defense and offense.

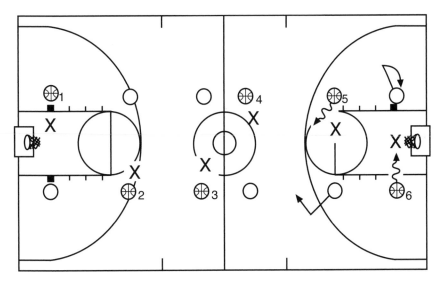

FIGURE 3.27 **2-on-1 passing.**

MOVING PAIRS PASSING

Purpose: To teach partner passing and catching skills while players are moving and playing against a defender.

Equipment: One ball and floor space of 15 to 18 feet (4.6 to 5.5 meters) in diameter per pair of players.

Procedure: Organize pairs of players with a ball and a court area: one passer and one receiver (figure 3.28). The receiver gets open, receives the pass with the feet in the air, quick stops, catches the ball, and faces the passer in a triple-threat position. The passer then becomes the next receiver. The drill involves continuous passing and catching. All passing and catching rules are practiced. For example, players pass with the feet on the floor and catch with the feet in the air. Another phase includes catch, dribble drive, quick stop, and pass. Catchers need to time their cuts to get open just before the passer is ready to pass the ball.

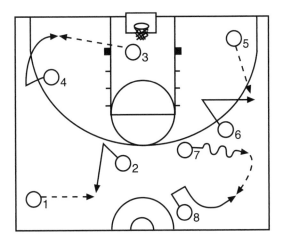

FIGURE 3.28 **Moving pairs, passing and catching.**

WALL PASSING

Purpose: To teach players passing and catching without a teammate.

Equipment: One ball per player and a wall space or tossback rebounding device.

Procedure: All basic passes can be practiced against a wall or a target. The tossback or passing rebounder, a commercial rebound device, is especially helpful for practicing this skill. It rewards a good pass by returning the ball on target and informs the athlete when an inaccurate pass is made. The following passes should be practiced: chest, bounce, overhead, baseball, and push. Players should pass the ball with the feet on the floor and catch the ball with the feet in the air. The tossback device can be used to increase speed and intensity gradually until a mistake is made (indicating learning). Players should work toward game moves at game speed.

LINE DRILL:
STANCE, STARTS, AND SKILL BREAKDOWN

Purpose: To teach players to carry out selected footwork skills from a quick stance and a quick start (direct drive, crossover drive).

Equipment: One ball per line, four lines on the baseline.

Procedure: First sequence, without the ball

- Quick start and quick stops at the free-throw line, the half-line, the opposite free-throw line, and the opposite baseline.
- Quick start and quick stop into a 2-and-2 rebound (at four locations).
- Quick start and quick stop after two imaginary dribbles, rear turn on PPF, step and imaginary pass to the next person in line.

Second sequence, with the ball

- Repeat variations with emphasis on a first step that is long and low (direct drive or crossover drive).

LINE DRILL: STARTS, STOPS, AND TURNS

Purpose: To teach players to combine dribbling, starting, stopping, passing, catching, and turning skills.

Equipment: One ball per line.

Procedure: The first player in each line is in an offensive quick-stance position with the ball (triple-threat position). On command, the player takes two dribbles forward past the free-throw line distance, does a quick stop, uses a rear turn on the PPF (nondominant foot), faces the catcher on the baseline (next person), steps and makes a push pass, and goes to the back of the line. The coach can designate any pass to be used and either direct drive or crossover drive when starting the play.

MASS DRIBBLING

Purpose: To teach the basic ballhandling skills of dribbling.

Equipment: One ball per player (or one ball per pair of players, one dribbler and a buddy coach) spread on a half court.

Procedure: Spread all players out in their own dribbling space, facing the court at the center circle area. Each player follows the coach's command to execute these dribble moves:

1. Stationary control and low dribble

- Right-hand control and low (command: *right low*)
- Change (right to left and vice-versa) (command: *change*)
- Left-hand control and low (command: *left low*)

2. Moving low and power dribble

- Right-hand low (command: *right low*)
- Right to left or vice-versa (command: *change*)
- Left-hand low (command: *left low*)
- Shuffle slide forward (command: *forward*)
- Shuffle slide backward (command: *back*)

Players should start with an overhead toss and trap the ball as it comes off the floor to begin the low dribble.

3. Rhythm push, pull (yo-yo)

- On the sides of the body (side yo-yo)
- In front of the body (front yo-yo)
- Between the legs laterally (side to side)

Coach commands should be given slowly at first to ensure proper technique at a slower speed and higher dribble; then command changes increase in favor of speed and a lower dribble until mistakes are made. Players should use the nonpreferred hand two or three times more often than the preferred dribbling hand. Coaching emphasis is for players to sit into the game (*stay low*) with the head up (*see the net*) and use a hard and low dribble (*pound the ball*), do it correctly and then faster until mistakes are made, and then go toward game moves at game speed.

FULL-COURT DRIBBLING

Purpose: To teach the ballhandling skills of dribbling.

Equipment: One ball per line (minimum) on a half court (minimum).

Procedure: Using the line-drill formation, players should form four lines on the baseline. The dribble moves of the drill are then practiced for one circuit. Players concentrate on maintaining eye contact with the net on the opposite end of the court. Coaches can also use two lines (the sidelines) to give players feedback on ball location, going by the position of the defender and by player location on the court. Cones can be spaced on the court to simulate defenders.

Options

- High or speed dribble: Players dribble down the court with one hand and then return dribbling with the other hand.
- Change-of-pace dribble: Players alternate high speed and low control dribbles down the court, using the opposite hand on the return.
- Between-the-legs dribble down the length of the court.

- Back dribble and crossover (pull-back crossover): Players dribble into an imaginary trap at the free-throw line, the half-line, and opposite free-throw line and finish with a quick stop and a ball chin at the end.

- Pull-back crossover repeated, three forward dribbles, two back dribbles, crossover, and go. Repeat the sequence over the whole floor.

- Players use a specified dribble and quick stop under control on the coach's signal.

- Zigzag or crossover dribble or spin dribble: Players dribble down court from a triple-threat position start in a zigzag, using V-cuts and a crossover or spin dribble.

- Two-ball dribbling (advanced): Players can dribble two balls while executing these selected dribble moves: low rhythm (both hands), low nonrhythm (both hands), high rhythm (both hands), high nonrhythm (both hands), high to low (right high and left low and vice versa). Players should start dribbling hard and low, then high, then alternate rhythm (one high, one low), then add changes of direction and speed, and, finally, use different combinations.

- The two-ball dribbling progression should be the following:
  - Stationary: low rhythm, low nonrhythm, high rhythm, high nonrhythm, high to low and reverse, windshield wipers (side yo-yo), front to back yo-yo.
  - Dribble on the move to half court (use all five combinations).
  - Dribble from half-line to baseline (use all five combinations plus change sides or hands with balls).

- Dribble drills
  - O-D Zag
  - 1-on-1 attack to score: Dummy D at top of key; add D hoop man; line D at top of key; add D hoop man
  - 1-on-1 full court (one player with two balls; one player with one ball): Goal is to get through the free-throw lane line

WALL DRIBBLING

Purpose: To teach ballhandling skills in a challenging format.

Equipment: Flat wall surface and two balls per player.

Procedure: Using a line of players per wall location (four or fewer), perform the following options using both preferred and nonpreferred hand dribbling against the wall.

Options

- One hand and one ball (left and right)
  - Pound
  - Around the world (circle pattern)
  - High to low
- Two hands or two balls
  - Pound
  - Around the world
  - High to low and low to high

- Two-ball stutter (nonrhythm)
- Two balls (one pound, one moving)
- Two balls (both circle)

BALLHANDLING BASICS

Purpose: To develop basic dribbling, passing, and catching skills.

Equipment: Basketballs, tennis balls, floor space.

Procedure

1. Taking infield: This is a favorite ballhandling drill from Baseball Hall of Fame shortstop Ozzie Smith. To adapt it to basketball, a player, with a tennis ball, should find a wall space and get into a low and wide quick stance with toes pointed slightly outward and about 20 feet (6 meters) from the wall. Player throws the ball against the wall hard 6 inches (15.2 centimeters) above the floor and catches the ball with a click (two hands, two eyes) as it caroms off the floor. The player gradually moves toward the wall to increase difficulty. Players should always throw sidearm during this exercise, not overhand, to protect the rotator cuff muscles.

2. Dribble and juggle: This drill is designed to work on nonpreferred hand dribbling and requires players to avoid watching the ball while dribbling. The player dribbles a basketball with the nonpreferred hand while tossing and catching a tennis ball. Players can increase difficulty by tossing the tennis ball higher and catching it in different ways and by adding various dribble moves while the tennis ball is in the air. Teaching tips are to get low and wide and pound the dribble hard. Players should keep control of the dribble at all costs, even when they lose control of the tennis ball; they should never give up their dribble.

3. Partner dribble and toss: Pairs of players talk to each other while dribbling with the nonpreferred hand and playing underhand toss and catch. Players should never give up the dribble.

4. Partner dribble and throw: Pairs of players throw the ball overhand to each other while dribbling with the nonpreferred hand. To increase difficulty, they should move away from each other in a random fashion.

5. Partner three-ball passing: Players can use two basketballs and one tennis ball or two tennis balls and one basketball. They pass to each other with a one-handed push or a flick pass, using the preferred hand to begin and then switching together to the nonpreferred hand to increase difficulty. Talking is critical. The ball is in the air, the feet are in the air on the catch, and the pass should be to the nonpassing shoulder of the catcher. The player who starts with two (of the three) balls starts the drill with the first pass.

6. Partner bad pass reaction: Pairs of players with one ball are 15 to 20 feet (4.6 to 6 meters) apart. They make sharp, crisp, inaccurate passes to each other. The catcher catches with a click and then captures and chins the basketball. The coach may also throw underhand (softball style) bullet passes to test catchers. The catcher should be in a quick-stance catching position. Players should catch the ball with the feet in the air, move the feet and get the body in front of the pass.

7. Partner back to the passer: Pairs of players use one basketball and space themselves 15 to 20 feet (4.6 to 6 meters) apart. The player without the ball has his or her back to the passer and is in quick-stance catching position. The passer

makes a crisp pass while calling the catcher's name. The catcher must catch the ball with both hands after making a quick jump turn to face the passer. The players exchange roles and repeat. They should pass as fast as needed to test their teammates. The catch should be with a click.

8. Pull-back crossover progression: With one ball, the player, starting in a stationary position with the foot opposite the dribbled ball forward, follows this sequence:

- Push-pull on right side, get a rhythm.
- Crossover to left side, repeat.
- Push-pull two or three times, crossover, repeat.
- Same move, but with a baby step, then do a lunge step forward.
- Two or three dribbles forward, two or three dribbles back, crossover, and repeat. Players should point the lead foot in the direction they are going.

chapter 4

Shooting

"The main thing on offense is that we get a good shot every time down the floor."

from *Pete's Principles*, Pete Carril, former Princeton Coach, now Naismith Hall of Fame Coach

Shooting is probably the best known fundamental skill in basketball—every player is interested in scoring. If given a basket and a ball, even a novice invariably dribbles and shoots.

Shooting, the fundamental skill that players enjoy and practice most, can be practiced alone. It is an action that produces immediate feedback. Most coaches contend that all players can become good shooters through long hours, days, and years of practice. Of course, great shooters must also possess special physical talents. Any player, however, can become a good shooter and an excellent free-throw shooter.

One of the two basic objectives of basketball is getting a good shot in order to score a basket. The other objective is preventing an opponent from doing the same. This chapter contains guidelines for teaching players how to get a good shot on every attempt and how to become better scorers (making a high percentage of shots taken) through physical practice (with proper technique) combined with mental practice to build confidence.

Field-Goal Shooting

CRITICAL CUE:
Game shots at game spots at game speed.

Players and coaches should realize that field-goal and free-throw scoring percentages are the most important statistical factor related to winning. Therefore, it is critical for players to build shooting confidence over time by careful preparation and by shooting with proper mechanics at game speed using proper mental techniques. Players cannot, literally, overpractice shooting (physically and mentally) as long as they are taking game shots at game spots at game speed in order to prepare properly for competition. Coaches cannot provide enough shooting time during team practice, so players need to understand the necessity of outside-of-practice individual shooting in order to reach shooting percentage goals.

General Concepts

Coaches should teach players to become scorers, not just shooters. Anyone can shoot, but considerable skill is required to score consistently in game situations. To maximize scoring-to-shooting ratio, players must learn when to shoot, when to pass, what their shooting range is, and from what spots on the court they can consistently make field goals. The recommended minimal percentage guidelines for all players are shown in table 4.1.

Practice goals should be set at least 5 percent higher than game goals because of expected slippage in shooting percentages that takes place during competition (table 4.1). Elite players who want to become great scorers need to set even higher goals.

Shooting percentages provide a bottom-line feedback measure for shooting effectiveness. Players need to pay attention to practice and game percentages; in particular, beginners and any players who are below the desired field-goal shooting percentages for their age group should adopt the shooting guidelines completely. Players should adopt one new idea to add to their game if they shoot near or above

TABLE 4.1 Desired Baseline Field-Goal Percentages

Grade level	Practice %		Game %	
	2-point	3-point	2-point	3-point
Elementary	35	n/a	30	n/a
Junior high school	40	n/a	35	n/a
Senior high school	45	35	40	30
College	55	45	50	40
Professional	55	45	50	40

the shooting percentage goals and always use percentages as self-feedback on practice and game shooting habits in order to assess status and progress. They must learn to play against the game—by setting scoring goals and by practicing game shots at game spots at game speed. Shooting percentages ensure that players can't fool the game or themselves when developing scoring skills.

Proper shooting technique can be developed only with sufficient basic skills and strength. Coaches can use a smaller ball and lower basket when teaching shooting skills to players in grades below 7 (ages 11 to 12 and younger). Proper mechanics can be learned early, in grades 4 through 6 (ages 9 to 11), and then applied readily to a regulation ball and basket. Young players should learn proper mechanics that can be easily carried out. This adjustment of equipment ensures that they will learn to shoot properly and build confidence more quickly.

Complete guidelines on modifying the game for younger players (including equipment recommendations) are available in a companion coaching book, *Basketball Skill Progressions, NABC's Handbook for Teaching* (Coaches Choice 2003) by Jerry Krause, Curtis Janz, and James Conn. This book also details what basketball skills to teach and when to teach them (i.e., a sequential, progressive approach). Even though some youngsters want to play with the big ball and the higher basket, they must be sold on solid progressions and correct mechanics at an early age. Using the big ball and the 10-foot (3-meter) basket too early in their learning can be harmful to their skill development.

Passing and catching and quick stops are the most important shooting fundamentals. Players should learn to get a shot by first moving to get open (use proper footwork). Then they must catch and face the basket in triple-threat position and be prepared to shoot (also footwork).

Teach players to attack and get shots as close to the basket as possible on a dribble drive. They should challenge the defense by probing for the basket—the ultimate shot is the layup.

Acronyms, such as BEEF and ROBOT, can be used to assist players in learning some of the key concepts of shooting. Younger players can learn proper shooting mechanics using the BEEF principle:

B—Balance, the most important foundation of every shot. The shot starts on the floor, before the player catches the ball, with proper footwork—with the knees bent and the feet ready first. Kevin Eastman, longtime college and professional coach, states the importance with the phrase "the feet make Js (jump shots)," which means that proper footwork is needed to make jump shots.

E—Eyes. To be accurate, players must pick up the target early (full focus for at least 1 second) and have a narrow focus on the spot target (the preferred spot target is the center of the back of the rim or the upper corner of the backboard rectangle); the "eyes make layups."

E—Elbow. Generally, players should limit all arm motion to a vertical plane, especially keeping the elbow up, in, and under the ball (except for pedestal-pocket shooting).

F—Follow-through. Players should use full extension of the arm (locked elbow), held for one count on a field goal or until the ball goes through the net on a free throw. The wrist is fully extended, with fingers pointed down (make a goose neck, put a hand in the cookie jar, or make a firm but floating parachute with one hand). The follow-through must be firm, but relaxed. The proper release angle is 60 degrees above horizontal. Finish high (release it high and let it fly). *Shoot up, not out* is the critical guideline for proper arch on the shot. Shooting high and soft is especially important on backboard shots. A 55- to 60-degree release angle on the shot produces an optimal entry angle into the basket of 45 to 50 degrees.

CRITICAL CUE:
Shoot up, not out.

John Bunn, a Naismith Hall of Fame coach and an educated engineer, advocated an optimal release angle of 60 degrees in his 1955 book, *Scientific Principles of Coaching*. He stated that the shooter should get as much arch as possible, consistent with his or her strength. He also found that more missed shots were short rather than long.

A new technology, Noah's Arc, has been developed to measure accurately and provide instantaneous feedback on the arc or basket entry angle for each shot. The shot or arc is filmed, analyzed, and logged into a computer; precise feedback on entry angle is provided to the shooter after each shot. In addition to heeding the coach's reminder to *shoot up, not out*, shooters can also use modern technology to assess their muscle memory. The optimal release angle of 55 to 60 degrees, translated into an optimal basket entry angle of 45 to 50 degrees, can be measured and provided to a player instantaneously. Studies have shown that a common problem with many shooters is a release angle and resulting basket entry angle that are too low. In fact, a basket entry angle of less than 35 degrees only produces a 9-inch (22.9-centimeter) window for the ball to go in, provided that it is exactly on line. This common problem can be addressed through coaching emphasis on a high 60-degree release angle or through practice using computer-programmed muscle memory data.

The arc conclusion is that players generally need higher arc on their shots that is consistent with their strength to produce accurate shots. Great shooters have consistent shots—start, finish, and arc. Each shooter must find an optimal arc (balancing accuracy and strength) in order to maximize the chance for scoring.

Players should also strive to become shooting ROBOTs—scoring machines:

R—A player is in effective scoring **r**ange (minimum practice goal of over 50 percent for two-point field goals and the equivalent 33 percent for three-point field goals) as well as shooting in rhythm (feel the shot).

O—A good shot requires that the shooter be **o**pen (no hand in the face).

B—A good shot is always taken on **b**alance. The shot starts from the floor, so players should get the feet ready. According to John Wooden, Naismith Hall of Fame player and coach, balance largely depends on footwork (and head position). Shooting can be evaluated by the position of the feet before and after shooting. The feet should land slightly forward—never back, right, or left—after the set or jump shot (about 6 inches [15.2 centimeters]). The head is a key to shooting balance; players should keep it slightly forward, especially before the shot.

O—Good shots are **o**ne-count shots where a player's feet are ready and the ball is shot in a single positive motion to the basket from the shooting pocket with hands ready (no two-count ball dip or swinging a leg unless needed for rhythm).

T—No **t**eammate has a better shot. Players should leave the feet and go up to shoot, and pass only when a teammate really has a better shot.

GENERAL COACHING POINTS FOR SHOOTING

- Shot starts on the floor—feet ready, hands ready (feet make jump shots).
- Offensive quick stance—weight on whole foot for quickness and balance, point shooting foot at basket.
- Full focus—early target on rim or backboard for 1 second (focus).
- Shooting hand—ball in whole hand, lock and load into shooting pocket.
- Bookend hand—on side, moves out and up on the shot.
- Release it high and let it fly—shoot up, not out, with a 60-degree angle of release above horizontal; thrust fingers through the ball to get backspin (feel).
- Full follow-through—firm but relaxed (field goal, 1 second; free throw, until the net).
- To build confidence, remember the makes, forget the mistakes.
- Use confident self-talk; focus (before the shot), feel (during the shot), and get feedback (*yes* or *swish* on made shot; shot location on missed shot) after each shot.
- Use quickness without hurrying. Be quick preparing for the shot, but don't hurry the shot.
- Maintain vertical alignment; keep the ball in the plane with the elbow in, up, and under the ball (unless using the pedestal shooting pocket). Players need to use a two-handed pickup to get the ball up and to the shooting pocket quickly.
- Use physical and mental practice (see, hear, and feel the perfect shot).
- Use the BEEF principle.
- Become a shooting ROBOT and apply the ROBOT concepts.
- Take game shots at game spots at game speed.
- Practice shooting from shots, the pass, and the dribble.

Building Field-Goal Confidence

After mastering the physical technique, players can concentrate on the mental aspects of shooting. Confidence is defined as the mental edge, built on careful preparation, that produces consistent success as demonstrated in practice and game competition. This definition implies that players can build shooting confidence by proper preparation that includes key elements of mental preparation and techniques.

The most important mental-edge techniques are shot preparation, shot execution, and after-shot skills:

1. Shot preparation: Players should pick up the spot target early and focus on it with narrow concentration for 1 second. Players must learn to ignore distractions and see only the ball and the net in their minds. This *full focus* is learned using the verbal prompt *focus*.

2. Shot execution: Studies have shown that skill improvement can occur when players become more aware of the feel of a shot from start (shooting pocket) to finish (full follow-through). During each shot, the verbal prompt *feel* reminds players to increase their awareness of the shot.

CRITICAL CUE:
Remember the makes, and forget the mistakes.

3. After-shot skills: Psychocybernetics research points to the importance of controlling self-talk after each shot to build confidence. When players are shooting, the feedback is "remember the makes and forget the mistakes." The process requires a shooter to emphasize and celebrate the shots that are made and to play down, with little emotion—to "analyze and forget"—the missed shots. Players should never be too hard on themselves over a missed shot. On a miss, a player is asked only to note the shot location and then continue with play. The verbal prompts are the following:
   - Made shot—*yes*, *net*, *swish*, or *money celebration*.
   - Missed shot—note shot location (*short*, *long*, *right*, *left*). Great shooters can be more specific.

CRITICAL CUE:
Focus, feel, feedback (*yes* on makes, *shot location* on misses).

4. Summary: During practice, players need to use the verbal prompts for each shot—*focus, feel, feedback* (*yes* on makes, *shot location* on misses). Confidence is built daily and requires many successes at high percentages over long periods.

Proper practice can make a shooter into a scorer—the secret of good shooting. Have players spend ample time shooting with proper form. Practice makes permanent (not perfect); therefore, players must learn to practice(physically and mentally) properly—game shots at game spots at game speed. They can use mental practice alone—3 to 5 minutes visualizing successful shooting situations and specific shots, imagining the look, sound, and feel of a perfect shot (see it, hear it, feel it). Players should repeat the cues *focus, feel, yes,* or *net* a minimum of 25 times daily as they visualize the perfect shot. The greatest progress can be made by combining physical practice with mental practice.

Shooting Mechanics

The specific physical techniques of shooting, called shooting mechanics, include the movements of the body, feet, and hands during shooting.

The movements are the same for the one-handed set shot and the jump shot. The essential difference is that the jump shot is executed by shooting the set shot just before the peak of a jump. Proper shooting mechanics should be taught and practiced. The medium arc shot (about 60 degrees at the angle of release) is the best compromise between the best arc for shooting (an almost vertical trajectory) and the available strength for accurate shooting. Most beginners shoot with a release angle lower than the optimal 60 degrees. With the regular side shooting pocket, the shooting foot, elbow, wrist, and hand are all in the same vertical plane with the basket as the ball is brought up past the face (figure 4.1). Hand and arm motions are the same on all set or jump shots—the power comes from the legs. Backspin on the ball produced by the finger thrust increases the angle of rebound off the rim (i.e., producing a more vertical bounce) and gives the shot a greater chance of going into the basket. It also stabilizes the flight of the ball. Players can produce backspin by thrusting the fingers through the ball on release.

In addition to these general points of shooting mechanics, players should be taught specific fundamentals such as maintaining proper body position, holding the ball, and executing the steps of the shot.

Balance With Feet Ready

A good shot starts with the feet ready (knees bent) and the dominant foot slightly forward and pointed toward the basket in a quick-stance or offensive triple-threat position (figure 4.2). The player's head is balanced and slightly forward, with the body generally facing the basket (the shoulders are not exactly square to basket—the dominant shoulder is slightly forward). Players should point the shooting foot at the basket and sit into the shot (the feet make Js). On pedestal-pocket shooting (explained later), the feet are square to the basket.

Footwork is the foundation of the shot that produces balance. Dan Hays, Hall of Fame coach from Oklahoma Christian University, uses a unique way to teach proper footwork for set and jump shots. Players stand with feet together and touching. The shooting foot is moved slightly forward so that the nonshooting toe aligns with the middle of the shooting foot. Then the shooting foot is moved laterally to a balanced feet-ready position for shooting.

Vertical plane

FIGURE 4.1 **Vertical plane shooting.**

CRITICAL CUE: The feet ready—the hands ready (the ball in the shooting pocket).

Target

When the ring of the rim is the target, players should focus on the imaginary center of the ring (the perfect target) or the best substitute for this imaginary spot, the middle eyelet loop on the back of the ring as viewed through the net.

FIGURE 4.2 **Shooting balanced:** *(a)* triple-threat position with the feet ready (front view), *(b)* triple-threat position with the feet ready (side view), and *(c)* pedestal pocket (square stance) with the feet ready.

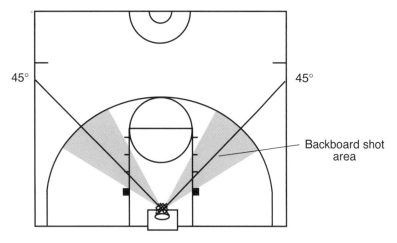

FIGURE 4.3 **Use the backboard target at a 45-degree angle.**

CRITICAL CUE: Full focus—early target (the rim or the backboard).

Because accuracy tasks require a spot target, most misses are short, and most made shots are near the back half of the basket, the back of the rim is the preferred spot target. Some coaches prefer the front of the rim. For angled shots (45 degrees with the backboard), players can use the upper corner of the backboard rectangle as the spot target. Coaches should remind shooters to hit that backboard target on the way down in order to have the same arc on ring and backboard shots (which tend to be too low or flat). On a rim or backboard shot, players should pick up the target early with a full focus of one count. The best court areas to shoot the board shot are shown in figure 4.3. The rim shot and the backboard shot should both have the same arc on the shot; generally, the top of the ball on a medium range shot is the same height as the top of the backboard. Player guidelines are *release it high and let it fly*, shoot *high and soft* with backspin (especially on backboard shots), and *shoot up, not out*.

The eyes should be kept on the target at all times (except to follow the flight of the ball after release, as a weekly drill to check proper backspin, as described later).

Shooting Hand

The next step is for the shooter to grip the ball properly. The fingers of the shooting hand should be spread comfortably, with the ball touching the whole hand except the heel (figure 4.4). The angle between the thumb and first finger is about 70 degrees (not 90 degrees). Players should form a V, not an L, between the thumb and index finger. Players (facing the coach) can hold up the shooting hand and spread the fingers as much as possible (90-degree angle) but then relax the hand slightly (thumb and first finger in a V) and put the ball onto the whole hand by placing the ball in the shooting hand while holding the palm up in front of the body (figure 4.5). When handling the ball, players can move it to shooting position by grasping the ball with both hands on the side and then rotating the ball so that the shooting hand is behind and under the ball. This technique is called *locking and loading* the ball into the shooting pocket.

This technique places the shooting hand in the same position for each shot for consistency: The shooting pocket is always in the same starting position.

To lock and load the ball into the triple-threat shooting pocket (the same starting position for each shot), players should first place the ball on the whole hand in front and to the side of the body (figure 4.5a). Then the nonshooting hand grasps the shooting hand wrist in order to lock it into the starting position (4.5b). The nonshooting hand is then placed on top of the ball or the hand in order to load the ball into the shooting pocket (figure 4.5c).

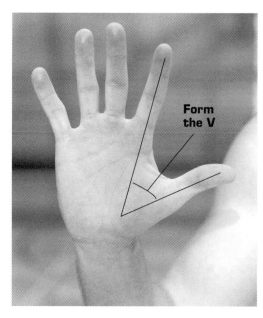

FIGURE 4.4 **Proper shooting hand grip: use the whole hand, except for the heel (the finger and thumb at 70 degrees, forming a V).**

CRITICAL CUE: The hands ready— the ball to the shooting pocket.

FIGURE 4.5 **Lock and load: (a) the ball in the whole hand, (b) lock the wrist in, and (c) load the ball into the shooting pocket.**

FIGURE 4.6 **Regular side pocket—the elbow up, in, and in front of the wrist, vertically balance the hand.**

After moving the ball into shooting position, the shooter should bend the wrist back and load it in, forming an L at the wrist and at the elbow (see wrinkles on the back of the wrist). Set the ball on the hand and hold an imaginary tray with the shooting hand. This position for the side shooting pocket is shown in figure 4.6. The locking and loading technique ensures that the starting position is the same on each shot for consistency.

The elbow (the L) is kept up, in, and in front of the wrist (figure 4.6). Beginners may have a lower starting elbow position, but the elbow should still be in front of the wrist and above the shooting foot. Younger players tend to drop the ball too low to gain momentum, pull the wrist in front of the elbow, and, in the process, develop an inefficient shooting mechanic. Shooting power comes from the legs; the arm shooting mechanics stay the same. The most common error that players make with the shooting hand or arm is having the elbow out when the shooting foot is pointed at the basket and when they are using the armpit or shoulder shooting pocket. Elite players may modify the pocket by moving higher. This *pedestal pocket*, as a middle shooting position, is described later.

Balance or Bookend Hand

The balance (or bookend) hand is only used to steady the ball, not to shoot it. The *bookend* term, which more properly describes the position and function of the nonshooting hand, was first developed by Dan Hays of Oklahoma Christian University. The bookend hand is kept on the side of the ball to avoid thumb drag; it does *not* guide the ball. As the shot is released, the bookend hand is moved *slightly* up and out of the way and then finishes in a vertical position off the ball, with the fingertips at the level of the wrist of the shooting hand. The elbow remains slightly flexed. Common errors of the bookend hand are the thumb push (to shoot the ball), the heel pull (to hold under and drag the ball), and rotation of the off hand with the shot (it should be a stationary guide). These errors can be caused by extending the nonshooting elbow during the shot. Figure 4.5c shows the correct shooting-pocket position and the position of the bookend hand. The position of the bookend hand can also be described as pointing that thumb at a right angle to the shooting thumb.

CRITICAL CUE:
The bookend hand on the side—move it off the ball and up slightly before release, keep the balance elbow bent. Point the thumb back with the fingers up in a vertical position.

Coaches can illustrate the concepts of the whole hand and locking and loading without the ball by asking players to place the shooting hand in front of the body (palm up) and spread it to the whole-hand position. Players should imagine that a ball is sitting on the hand, as shown in figure 4.7a. Then they should grasp the shooting hand wrist with the nonshooting hand and rotate it in until it won't rotate any further (locked in position, as in figure 4.7b, but without the ball). Finally, they should place the balance hand on the shooting hand (palm to palm) and load the imaginary ball into the final shooting pocket (as in figure 4.7c). All this can be done without a basketball in order to ensure that players understand the feel of the same starting position on each shot (the shooting pocket). The shot can be simulated by pushing the elbow button, shooting the imaginary ball, and holding the follow-through.

FIGURE 4.7 Locking and loading (without the ball): *(a)* grip with whole hand, *(b)* lock the shooting wrist or rotate in, *(c)* load the shooting hand with the nonshooting hand, *(d)* push the elbow button to shoot up, release the imaginary ball, and hold the follow-through.

Release

Shooting up and over by pushing the elbow button, as shown in figure 4.7*d*, requires thrusting the fingers up and forward through the ball or snapping the wrist. Players should visualize shooting out of the top of a glass telephone booth or over a 7-foot (2.1-meter) defender. Backspin is produced when the fingers *thrust* the ball up and over (push through the ball and snap the wrist) (figure 4.8). The ball comes off the index and middle fingers last.

Backspin produces a soft shot that can hit the rim, slow down, and bounce in. The backspin keeps the ball around the shooting target. Players can check the backspin weekly by shooting a vertical shot without a target or following the flight of the ball after the release of a regular shot. Players should *not* develop the habit of watching the ball; they should focus on the target instead.

The proper release angle is about 60 degrees above horizontal. For most players, the release angle is too low, which decreases the size of the available target from above and lowers shooting percentage. Coaches should guide players to *release it high and let it fly* (*shoot up, not out*).

A common shooting problem centers around the arc of the shot after its release. Lower arcs tend to reduce the available entry area of the ball as it passes through the rim. Thus, many players struggle with attaining an optimal shooting arc. The higher the arc is, the greater are the muscle forces needed to propel the ball, resulting in more forces and less accuracy. Players and coaches should be aware of attaining optimal release angle and shot arc with a smooth, rhythmic release that uses minimal forces. The shot with a 55- to 60-degree angle of release produces an optimal basket entry angle of 45 to 50 degrees.

The Importance of Arc in Shooting

Here is how the ball sees the hoop as it enters the basket (the basket entry angle):

1. Coming from an angle of 90 degrees from the horizontal, the target area is 100 percent.

2. Coming from an angle of 51 degrees from the horizontal, the target area is 55.6 percent.

3. Coming from an angle of 31 degrees from the horizontal, the target area is 33.3 percent. (For a clean shot, the minimum entry angle is about 35 degrees.)

4. Coming from an angle of 20 degrees from the horizontal, the target area is 22.2 percent.

5. Coming from an angle of 9 degrees from the horizontal, the target area is 12.2 percent.

Studies at the University of Calgary have shown that the recommended range for the ideal release angle is between 52 and 55 degrees. To shoot at an angle higher than 55 degrees requires extra velocity or ball speed, which has a detrimental effect on accuracy. Because of learning slippage, the best compromise between force on the ball and accuracy is an optimal release angle of 55 to 60 degrees.

This principle applies more easily to pedestal-pocket shooting from an overhead or a middle starting spot. As the ball is pushed up (not out) from the pedestal pocket, the ball is thrust up and over with the fingers touching the ball last to produce ball backspin (figure 4.9).

> **CRITICAL CUE:**
> Release it high and let it fly (release the ball high, up, and over, at 60 degrees with backspin).

Follow-Through

The final step in shooting is full follow-through with complete elbow extension (lock the elbow), arm pronation or turnout, and wrist flexion (controlled relaxation). Players should visualize making a goose neck, putting their fingers in a cookie jar, putting a hand in the basket, or making a parachute with a firm floating hand and holding that position (figure 4.8). The hand and fingers are firm but relaxed. A full follow-through ensures that the ending position is the same for each shot.

Shooting skill is first built on proper mechanics and technique as described earlier. Players must develop correct technique as a physical foundation for the shot:

> **CRITICAL CUE:**
> Full follow-through and hold it (field goal, one count; free throw, until *net* or *swish*).

- Feet ready for balance.
- Ball into shooting pocket (same starting point); use whole hand grip (form the V), lock and load the ball (two-handed pickup), bookend balance hand.
- Release and full follow-through (same ending point); shoot up at 60 degrees (not out), hold follow-through.
- Balance at the end of a shot—head forward.

FIGURE 4.8   High release and follow-through (55- to 60-degree release angle).

FIGURE 4.9   Pedestal-pocket shooting—shoot up.

Types of Shots

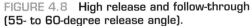

Although the basic mechanics of shooting are found in the set and jump shot, they are also applied in close shots (including layups) and long shots (like the three-point shot). The same mechanics are used in post player shots as well.

Layups

All players should learn to shoot both left- and right-handed layups while jumping from one foot. The technique is to jump from the left leg when shooting right-handed and from the right leg when shooting left-handed. A high jump is made by stamping on the last step to minimize the forward long jump and to maximize the high jump. Coaches should have players use the backboard whenever possible; exceptions may be the baseline dribble drive and the dunk shot. The dunk shot should be used only when a player can dunk the ball without strain and defensive traffic is minimal.

Approach.   Attacking or accelerating to the basket is a positive approach that players can use readily. When a player is shooting a layup, the attack move is made by taking the ball up in a two-handed pickup motion (bring the free hand to the ball when dribbling, chin the ball near the shooting shoulder—usually opposite the jumping foot—and keep the ball chest high on the side away from the defender). Use a two-handed pickup (see figure 4.10*a*) to pit and protect the ball away from the defender. Players should keep the ball away from the hip and avoid dangling the ball away from the power position (near the upper chest or shoulders). The two-handed pickup and chin move is used to prevent players from rocking the cradle (figure 4.10, *b* and *c*) and exposing the ball to the defender as it is brought across the body. The last dribble is timed with the last jumping step on the inside foot when the player is using a dribble-drive move; this is often called an opposition move when a player shoots a right-handed layup with a jump from the left foot (opposite foot) as shown in figure 4.11. On a left-foot jump, the right (or opposite) knee drives up toward the basket (like a knee on a string with the same side elbow). Coaches should teach beginners to use a gallop move with a layup. For a right-handed dribbler and shooter, the last one-two gallop move is with the right foot and the left foot as the jumping foot, in that order. The final layup shooting reminder is for players to pick up the target early (usually the backboard) and focus for at least one full second; eyes make layups.

CRITICAL CUE:
One-foot layups: Opposition, two-handed pickup, high and soft shot on the backboard.

Jump. The opposite knee (to the jumping foot) is then raised high when the player is jumping (figure 4.12) and straightened just before the peak of the jump. Other tips include using the backboard to your advantage, shooting softly with a feather touch (shoot high and soft), and focusing on the ball and the target. For one-foot jump layups, coaches can teach the primary overhand, or push, (palm facing

FIGURE 4.10 Shooting the layup: *(a)* two-handed pickup, *(b, c)* avoid rocking the cradle.

FIGURE 4.11 Layups—opposition move.

FIGURE 4.12 Overhand, or push, layup.

FIGURE 4.13 Underhand, or scoop, layup.

target—figure 4.12) and the underhand, or scoop, layup, which produces a softer shot and is executed with the shooting hand palm up (figure 4.13).

Power Layup. This layup is really a quick stop with the player facing the baseline into a two-foot layup. The quick stop is made for power and balance and is used in traffic or under defensive pressure when control and power are needed. The power layup is a slower but stronger move than the one-foot jump layup. On approaching the basket, the shooter lands facing the baseline or backboard with feet pointed to the baseline in a quick stop (one-count landing on both feet). See figure 4.14. The player chins the ball on the outside shoulder away from the defense and explodes vertically from both feet to the basket to shoot (hand facing or hand under) a one-handed layup off the backboard.

Three-Point Shots

Shooting the three-point shot requires some adjustment. Three-point shooters must develop a sense of where the line is without looking down (respect and know the line). Long shots produce long rebounds, and rebounding teammates must adjust accordingly. Knowing the time and score in a game is important for all shots, but especially for the three-point shot (the trey). This shot should only be attempted as the player is moving toward the line with a quick stop or after a plant and pivot (figures 4.15). These movements provide the greater force needed for this shot and allow beginning players to take it without straining. Emphasis should be placed on

CRITICAL CUE:
To shoot the trey, get power and momentum from the legs, and emphasize full follow-through with elbow in line (regular pocket).

FIGURE 4.14   **Power layup: *(a)* quick stop, *(b)* power shot.**

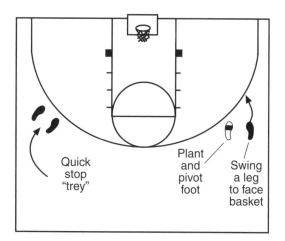

FIGURE 4.15   **Footwork for the three-point field goal.**

getting momentum from bending the knees more for extra power from the legs, using the elbow L, and on releasing the shot on the way up with a full follow-through. For most players, the three-point shot is more of a set shot.

Homer Drew of Valparaiso University teaches his players to get the three-point field-goal shot from the pass in six ways, including the following:

- inside-out passes,
- offensive rebound—pass out,
- penetrate and pass (pitch),
- fast break to the trey,
- skip pass (with or without a screen), and
- screen and fade-and-flare.

Pedestal-Pocket Shots

Modifications can be made for players with higher strength levels (especially core and upper body) and inside players who shoot most of their set and jump shots closer to the basket. For an in-depth treatment of these techniques, see *The Perfect*

Jump Shot by Scott Jaimet (Elemental Press, 2006). These recommendations are a departure from shooting techniques described previously and may not be suitable for most players, but they have the advantages of high arc, added balance, symmetry, and increased relaxation during shooting. This technique is for elite players with high levels of upper-body strength.

Jaimet advocates a focus on four important factors: balance, rhythm, extension, and symmetry. The one-handed set or jump shot described in the previous section depends heavily on shooting rhythm, full extension, and balance. Balance depends primarily on footwork but is more challenging with the ball's shooting pocket on one side of the player's body. The shift of the ball to a position directly overhead and near the middle of the body facilitates balance. This overhead or forehead shooting pocket is the pedestal-pocket position. Players should grip the ball, form a V with the shooting hand, and then lock and load the ball to the pedestal pocket with a two-handed pickup, as shown in figure 4.16. The whole hand is always placed under the ball on the shooting pocket on the traditional side or the more centered pedestal pocket. Players should always lock and load the ball into the shooting pocket with a two-handed pickup. The pedestal pocket is a balanced trigger point where the shot should be initiated. From there, the player takes the shot up toward the basket (not out) by pulling the trigger or folding the tent (figure 4.16c). The middle or pedestal-pocket position has the distinct advantage that the player shoots up, not out, thus preventing the most common error in

CRITICAL CUE:
Lock and load into the pedestal pocket with a two-handed pickup.

CRITICAL CUE:
The ball overhead vertically between the eye and the ear in the pedestal pocket.

FIGURE 4.16 **Pedestal-pocket shooting: *(a)* grip ball and form the V, *(b)* lock and load to form the tent, full focus—see under the tent, and *(c)* fold the tent and hold the follow-through.**

CRITICAL CUE:
Right angles at the elbows and the thumbs at right angles on the ball (pedestal-pocket shot).

shooting—closing the available entry area into the basket because of a lower arc on the shot.

When players are using the pedestal pocket, the position of the arms and feet must also be modified. The shooting hand (under the ball) and bookend hand (on the side) are placed similarly on the ball. The feet are in a more parallel stance, and both elbows are pointed outward in a balanced, relaxed position to form a tent (the elbows at the base and the ball at the peak and in the pedestal pocket, see figure 4.16b). The forearm and upper arm form a right angle (90 degrees) at the elbow. Another advantage of the pedestal pocket is that the shooter can more readily pick up the shooting target early and get a full focus on the target without visual obstructions from the arms or the ball. Players should form the shooting tent and put the ball in the pedestal pocket, above the head and between the eye and ear. Coaches should emphasize that the elbows should be at eye level and the arms at right angles at the elbows. Having the ball in the pedestal pocket and the elbows high makes it easier for players to shoot the ball up (not out). When players shoot from this trigger spot, the arms are fully extended (the shooting arm at the elbow and the wrist) with a full follow-through that is firm but relaxed for *pulling the trigger* and *folding the tent* as the ball is thrust upward and released at the peak of the jump (or on the toes for the set shot).

Note the symmetry of the feet and arms when players are using the pedestal-pocket shooting technique (figure 4.16). The body faces the basket directly in a balanced, symmetrical position before, during, and after the shot. The complete sequence of the pedestal-pocket shot is shown as follows:

1. Use a quick stop (or plant and turn) into a balanced quick and square stance, facing the basket. Sit into the shot and square to (face) the basket; grip the ball with wrist wrinkles (figure 4.16a).

2. Grip the ball with wrist wrinkles and use a two-handed pickup in a tight arc to move the ball quickly to the pedestal pocket—form the tent (figure 4.16b). Lock and load the ball into the pedestal pocket; put the ball in the trigger spot with thumbs forming a right triangle.

3. Use full focus on the target for one full count (see the target through the V under the tent) while jumping with full extension.

COACHING POINTS FOR PEDESTAL-POCKET SHOOTING

- Face the basket with the shoulders square to the basket and the feet parallel in quick stance. Sit into the shot; use the legs for power.
- Lock and load the ball in a tight arc into the pedestal pocket. Use a quick two-handed pickup with wrinkled wrist.
- Form the tent with the elbows out and the ball at the trigger point. Arms, elbows, and thumbs should be at right angles. Use full focus on the target early (the back of the rim or the upper corner of the backboard rectangle).
- Jump with full extension; straight up or slightly forward.
- Pull the trigger to shoot up (not out) with full follow-through; fold the tent to shoot.
- Land in a balanced quick stance.

4. Release the ball at the peak of the jump, with full follow-through (figure 4.16c). Pull the trigger and fold the tent (make a parachute and hold it for one count).

5. Land with balance slightly in front of the takeoff spot.

Post Power Shot

The power shot, an adaptation of the power layup for post players, is the most basic scoring move for players with their backs to the basket. It is used when the defender plays on the side (side fronting) position (figure 4.17). The offensive post player gets in a position on the post line, as shown, and the pass is made to the baseline hand in this case (pass leads to a score). After catching the ball (capture and chin, as shown in figure 4.18a), the offensive player maintains contact with the lower body and seals the defender with

FIGURE 4.17 **Low post—side front defense.**

FIGURE 4.18 **Post power shot:** *(a)* catch and chin the ball, *(b)* half rear turn to seal the defender.

FIGURE 4.19 **Power shot:** *(a)* bounce and hop, *(b)* quick stop and chin.

a half rear turn or leg whip (figure 4.18*b*), immediately followed by a two-handed, two-foot bounce and hop move with the ball and to the basket. Figure 4.19 shows this move with the one dribble taken from a two-handed chinit position near the lead foot as a two-foot jump is made with a quick-stop landing. The post player lands facing the baseline and shoots a power shot by exploding up to the basket or backboard from the chinit ball position (figure 4.20).

The post power shot can be used in two ways: without the dribble (only leg whip), when the player is catching the ball in the lane, and with the dribble, bounce, and hop (two feet to two feet move) when the player is catching the ball outside the lane. Both shots, called angle baskets, allow the offensive player to use a body position advantage to make a post-player angle move to the basket.

Post Hook Shot

The preeminent player who used the post hook shot was Lew Alcindor (now Kareem Abdul-Jabbar), who played at Power Memorial High School (New York City), UCLA, and in the NBA, where he developed and mastered the *skyhook*. His Los Angeles Lakers coach, Pat Riley, described his post hook shot as "the most awesome weapon in the history of any sport."

Players in the United States used to dominate the world by learning to play with the back to the basket and using size and position. The skyhook fits Kareem perfectly because it is an act of faith by an extremely driven, willful person. As Jabbar states, "Everybody wants to see the ball as they let it go, to have it on-line from the start." But the post hook shot won't allow players to see the ball as they release it from behind and then over the head. As Kareem describes it, "It requires triangulation and rhythm, touch and repetition." The lesson is that the post hook shot requires faith, willpower (a strong mistake mentality), and considerable practice (Wolff, 2002).

Sometimes called the baby hook or modern hook shot, the post shot is used by players who receive the ball in a low post position with the back to the basket. The best location for a post shot is just outside the free-throw lane near the block (figure 4.21). This low to medium post position is just outside the lane, near the first or second free-throw lane spaces. The post player generally locates on or near the post line, a straight line between the passer and the basket.

On receiving a pass with the back to the basket in the post, the player should capture and chin the ball with two hands. The offensive player in the low post area should have the ball in the two-handed power position under the chin (chinit). Any player receiving a pass should be in quick-stance position and chinning the ball. The footwork for the post shot involves making a partial rear-turn pivot into the lane, using the baseline foot as the pivot foot. The other foot is used to step into the lane as far as possible in a balanced position facing away from the basket. Ideally, this foot is parallel to the baseline. When the nonpivot foot hits the floor, the pivot foot is raised as the knee is lifted high and rotated to face the basket, as in a normal layup. The ball is then moved from the chinning position past the side of the head, pushed overhead, and released with full arm extension (elbow locked) and pronation. This move is led by the inside elbow. The complete post shot sequence is shown in figure 4.22 and includes these essential steps:

FIGURE 4.20 **Power shot: explode to the basket.**

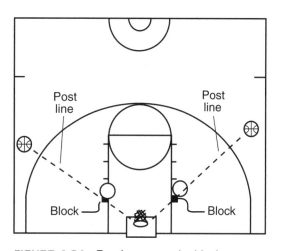

FIGURE 4.21 **Posting up on the block.**

FIGURE 4.22 The post shot: *(a)* posting up—two-handed targets ready to receive the pass (in this case, the pass is to the left hand because the pass leads the post player to a scoring move toward the middle), *(b)* meet and chin the ball—use the quick stop when possible, *(c)* step into the lane, with the stepping foot parallel to the baseline, *(d)* protect the ball on the outside shoulder, *(e)* take the ball up and over the head, *(f)* follow through, face the basket, and assume that the shot will be missed, with the hands up.

- Post up with two-handed targets—sit into the stance (figure 4.22*a*).
- Catch and chin the ball; capture and chin the ball to the power position—possession is more important than position (figure 4.22*b*).
- Make a partial rear turn using the baseline foot as the pivot foot, and step into the lane with the stepping foot parallel to the baseline (figure 4.22*c*).
- Move the ball up and over the head with full extension and pronation of the arm, and keep the ball close to the body until the release (figure 4.22*d*).
- Rotate and shoot the post shot (figure 4.22*e*).
- Land in quick-stance position and assume that the shot will be missed; put both hands up and assume a quick stance for a possible offensive rebound (figure 4.22*f*).

Post Jump Hook Shot

A variation of the post player hook shot, the jump hook is a simpler shot than the post hook shot, requires less skill, is easier to teach, and has a quicker release. All players can be taught this shot, which can be used close to the basket and can be shot over taller defenders.

The teaching progression for the shot is as follows:

1. Shot mechanics (preferred and nonpreferred hand) in front of basket facing the sideline (home base). This is shown in figure 4.23 as the player shoots from a

CRITICAL CUE: Jump hook: Point inside shoulder at basket, release ball overhead, complete full follow-through.

FIGURE 4.23 **Jump hook:** *(a)* starting position and *(b)* ending position (without jump).

Basketball Skills & Drills

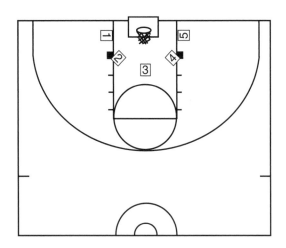

FIGURE 4.24 **Jump hook—five spots.**

deep crouch or wide-stance position, with the ball on the outside shoulder chin location, to a shot directly overhead. Emphasis is on the overhead release, with full arm extension and wrist snap, and the inside elbow or shoulder is pointed at the basket. Nonpreferred hand repetitions are taken two or three times more than preferred hand shots.

2. Jump hook from home base (with the jump)—release the ball on way up near the peak of the jump and come down in a ready position with the arms up (assume a miss).

3. Jump hook—right and left hand from five spots (baseline, 45 degrees, home base, 45 degrees, baseline), as shown in figure 4.24.

4. Jump hook at five spots over dummy defenders or shooting pad (both hands up).

5. Power move to the middle—one dribble power move to home base (in front of the basket or in the lane) and jump hook (figure 4.25) or home base, shot fake, and jump hook (figure 4.26).

6. The final version of jump hook shot is to catch the ball in the air and turn, landing in the lane, (i.e., the pass to the post player is made into the free-throw lane). As the pass is made, the post player catches the ball with both feet in the air and turns to see the basket as the nonshooting shoulder is pointed at the basket. The ball is chinned near the shooting shoulder. The jump hook is shot from a two-foot power jump and released directly up from the shooting shoulder with a locked elbow and flexed wrist follow-through. The sequence is catch and turn, jump hook up and over, land in quick stance, and assume that the shot will be missed.

FIGURE 4.25 **Power move to the middle:** *(a)* post player catches the ball with the defender on the baseline side, *(b)* power move to the middle—rear-turn seal.

FIGURE 4.25 Power move to the middle: *(c)* power move to the middle—bounce and hop to home base, *(d)* jump hook from home base in front of the basket.

FIGURE 4.26 Shot fake—lock the legs, 1-inch (2.5-centimeter) shot fake, keep the heels down.

Shot Fakes

Being prepared to shoot by having the feet and hands ready (triple-threat position and shooting pocket) allows the player with the ball to be quicker and more aggressive offensively. It also prepares players to use the complement of the shot—the shot fake.

Proper technique for the shot fake is for players to take the ball (from the pit or triple-threat position or pedestal pocket) quickly and vertically (vision is kept on the shooting target in a quick 1-inch shot fake). The body stays in quick-stance position as the player makes a short, quick vertical fake upward with the ball with the eyes on the basket. Players should give the fake time to work rather than rushing into the move. The shot fake can be used when players are facing the basket, when they have their backs to the basket, or when they are executing a jump hook. A test of the shot fake is whether the player's heels stay down on the floor and the legs stay locked in a crouched or explosive position. Players need to stay in the stance as they use a shot fake (figure 4.26 on page 95).

Free-Throw Shooting

Field-goal and free-throw percentages are the number one statistical factors related to winning. Players and coaches need to realize the importance of scoring, to know correct shooting techniques, and to practice these skills properly. Free-throw shooting is especially critical for the following reasons: it is a mental as well as a physical technique (confidence is important), the game stops during the skill, and little improvement has been seen in free-throw percentages for over 35 years (NCAA Basketball Trend Statistics, 2006). Free-throw shooting is truly a team skill that each player should be able to master, at least to national averages, regardless of age level or gender.

Teams should practice free throws in proportion to their importance in games; 20 to 25 percent of scoring, shots taken, and games decided happens at the free-throw line. For practices evenly divided between defense and offense, 10 to 12 percent of total practice time should be spent on free throws. Ten percent of 60 minutes is 6 minutes, so a minimum of 5 minutes per hour—the 5-minute free-throw rule—should be spent on free-throw practice for every hour of practice or game time during the season as well as in the off-season.

Game percentage goals, as shown in table 4.2, should be set relative to age. These measures indicate whether players should adopt the book guidelines completely or adapt them to improve free-throw shooting. Practice standards should be 5 percent higher than game goals because of slippage in normal game performance.

> **CRITICAL CUE:**
> Spend 5 minutes per hour on free-throw practice.

> **CRITICAL CUE:**
> Groove the shot first; then compete (against goals, defenders, and situations).

Free-Throw Technique

In free-throw technique, the key differences from field-goal shooting are making an alignment on the dot or spot (foot position), having a set ritual, pausing at the bottom of the shot, and exaggerating the follow-through. Players should keep the free throw simple and the same each time. The complete free-throw technique is shown in figure 4.27.

Players should know how a good shot looks, sounds, and feels and eventually be able to shoot free throws with their eyes closed. A shot should be executed with controlled tension—not too relaxed or too tight. The important physical mechanics are the following:

- **Find the spot:** Align on the center of the free-throw line each time—the shooting foot, elbow, hand, ball, and eye are aligned in a vertical plane with the basket. The shooting foot should be in the same spot every time and pointed toward the basket or slightly to the left of a line perpendicular

TABLE 4.2
Desired Free-Throw Percentages

Grade level	Practice %	Game %
Elementary	55	50
Junior high school	65	60
Senior high school	75	70
College	80	75
Professional	85	80

FIGURE 4.27 **The free throw:** *(a)* align and get down on the spot with body weight forward, *(b)* focus for one full second, and *(c)* use a full follow-through (hold until the net).

to the free-throw line. Place the toe of the dominant or lead foot (the right foot for right-handers and the left foot for left-handers) in the exact center of the free-throw line. Hardwood courts have a nail hole at the center for measuring purposes. On other courts, mark that spot. Put the lead foot near the center and point the lead foot at the corner of the backboard on the same side (right foot, left backboard edge and vice versa). Place the other foot in a comfortable position, with feet shoulder-width apart in a balanced, staggered stance. The open stance at the free-throw line is preferred to the parallel or square stance. Being slightly open relaxes the shoulder muscles and puts the shooting arm directly in the vertical plane to the basket. For a pedestal-pocket shooter, the eyes and the ball should be centered on the dot or spot, with the feet in a closed, square stance (figure 4.28).

CRITICAL CUE: Get on the spot or dot.

- **Full focus:** The focus should be on the center of the ring or the center eyelet at the back of the rim. A player should focus on the target and think *nothing but net* or *make the defense pay for fouling*. The focus on the target should begin early and be held for one full second (focus, feel, feedback mental approach).

- **Bounce at the bottom:** At the bottom of the shot, the player should pause for an instant of physical and mental calm and focus and then bounce at the bottom for rhythm. After the pause, all motion should be up and over toward the basket. This is called a one-piece shot,

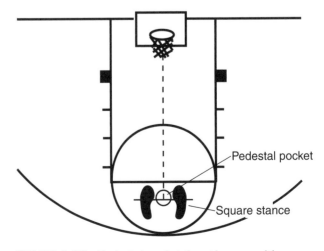

FIGURE 4.28 **Pedestal-pocket free-throw position.**

CRITICAL CUE: Full focus—pick up the spot target early and hold it for 1 second (the back of the rim is preferred).

with all positive motion toward the basket. Players should keep the shot simple and eliminate down and up motions, replacing them with simpler positive motion.

• **Ritual:** A ritual should be developed for the complete shot. Coaches should help each player do the same thing the same way every time—it is much easier to groove a pattern that is always the same. A deep breath just before the shot should always be part of the ritual (breathing in through the nose and out through the mouth). Players should include the same grip on the ball. Most players put their fingertips across the seams of the ball. They should be slow and deliberate with the ritual while keeping it simple; it is sometimes best to eliminate dribbling from the ritual. Finally, a verbal prompt of *nothing but net* is used to clear the mind.

• **Full follow-through:** Full extension and pronation are keys to the follow-through. The shooter should come up on the toes—get power from the legs. The upper arm should be 55 to 60 degrees above horizontal on the follow-through. Release high and hold the follow-through until the ball hits the net. Put a hand in the basket.

COACHING POINTS FOR FREE-THROW SHOOTING

- ☐ Keep the shot simple and the same—simplify the motion and do it the same way each time.
- ☐ Groove the shot daily (e.g., take 20 shots and record the number of makes).
- ☐ Compete (e.g., 1 shot, bonus, 2 shots, 3 shots)—make every shot a game shot in the player's mind and set competitive shooting goals.
- ☐ Record—keep written records and practice at 5 percent higher than game goal.
- ☐ Take the time—spend 5 minutes per hour on free throws for every hour of practice or play.

COACHING POINTS FOR PHYSICAL TECHNIQUE

- ☐ Find the spot—get on the dot in the same way each time, with the same alignment with the lead foot on the nail hole.
- ☐ Perform a ritual—make it simple and the same each time; include a deep breath (in through the nose and out through the mouth), the same grip on the ball, and a verbal prompt to clear the mind and get a mental picture of the expected outcome.
- ☐ Bounce at the bottom—a positive motion to the basket (one-piece shot) with rhythm (bounce two or three times).
- ☐ Use a full follow-through—firm but relaxed hold until the ball hits the net (keep body weight forward; stay in the shot).

COACHING POINTS FOR MENTAL EDGE

- ☐ Ritual—for comfort and confidence (use verbal prompt *nothing but net* to clear the mind, deep breath, and same ball grip). See and say *net* to form the proper mental picture.
- ☐ Full focus—early target pickup, preferred middle spot on the back of the rim for 1 second.
- ☐ Feel—say *feel* during the shot and become more aware of the shot from start to finish.
- ☐ Feedback—after every shot, remember the makes (celebrate with *yes*) and forget the mistakes (analyze and forget them using verbal prompt for shot location: *short, long, right, left*).

Come up and finish on the toes or jump slightly forward. Stay in the shot and keep body weight forward with the hand in the basket.

Free-Throw Confidence Building

Players can develop confidence in free-throw shooting with a gradual, long-term approach using specific mental techniques, including the previously described ritual. Players need to groove their techniques early in practice and during the season by shooting consecutive free throws properly, picking up the spot target early, and using full focus (verbal prompt *focus*) for 1 second. Coaches can teach players to concentrate on every shot using positive thoughts, such as making the opponents pay for every foul, thinking *net* or *swish* (shots that hit only *net*), and seeing the net ripple as the ball goes through. Shooters develop shot awareness by using the verbal prompt *feel* during each shot. A positive shooting attitude also is developed by celebrating successful shots and evaluating missed shots using proper feedback (verbal prompts: *yes* on makes and *short, long, right,* or *left* on misses). The shooter blocks all negative thoughts and uses only the positive. Confidence is developed from careful preparation and demonstrated skill in competition. Players need to shoot free throws in competitive situations, to make every shot a game shot.

Elementary school age players should use a smaller ball, lower baskets (8 feet [2.4 meters]), and a shorter free-throw line (9 feet [2.7 meters]). Junior high school players should shoot from 12 feet (3.7 meters) at a basket set at a height of 9 feet (see *Basketball Skill Progressions*).

Shooting Drills

Coaches should be creative in developing shooting drills that are sequential, progressive, and include all of the basics of shooting: footwork and balance drills without the ball, spot shots, shots from a pass, and shots from the dribble. Emphasize correct execution first and then game shots at game spots at game speed.

LINE DRILL: SHOOTING ADDITION

Purpose: To teach shooting in a simulated game situation.

Equipment: Half court (minimum), four balls (minimum).

Procedure: Form groups of players in four lines in the baseline formation. This is a form shooting exercise without the ball or a defender (the ball is added later). Players should execute a quick stop in shooting position after jumping from the foot closest to the basket. Later, the drill may be done using a ball and an underhand spin pass or a dribble.

Options

- Straight line—shots are taken without a target at the free-throw lines and the half-court line and the opposite baseline, with players focusing on the basket at the opposite end of the floor.

- Offensive zigzag—a shot is taken at the location of each change-of-direction spot. Most movement should be lateral to make it easier for players to select the foot closest to the basket.

TROUBLESHOOTING

Following are some common shooting errors:

Problem: Off balance shots, with side drift or moving backward on the shot.
Correction: Proper footwork (feet about shoulder width, sit into the shot) with balance is the antidote. Balanced quick stops or stride stops (plant and turn or pivot) correct this problem.

Problem: Low arc shots.
Correction: The shooting pocket is too low or too far in front of the body (dangling the ball). Raise the side shooting pocket or use the centered pedestal pocket. Shoot up, not out, to shoot up and over the basket, not at the basket.

Problem: Late target pickups.
Correction: Use full focus and early target sighting. Sight the target while dribbling or right after catching the ball (*focus*).

Problem: Poor alignment or direction problems.
Correction: Shooters need to face the basket with either a slightly staggered stance (side shooting pocket) or parallel stance (pedestal pocket). With the regular side pocket, check the vertical stance alignment of the ball and the shooting hand, shooting elbow and shoulder, and shooting foot and knee. With the pedestal pocket, be sure the trigger spot is centered overhead and that the arms and the body are symmetrical.

Problem: Slow release on the shot.
Correction: This is often caused by players using a slow ball pickup to the shooting pocket (side pocket), dangling the ball low, locking and loading to the pocket too slowly, or making the down and up motion in shooting (a two-count shot). Quicken this move, tighten the arc to the shooting pocket, and make the shot a completely positive motion toward the basket. Eliminate the dip, bend the knees more, and sit into the shot.

Problem: Rushing the shot.
Correction: This is usually caused by players not focusing on the rhythm of the shot. They should take game shots at game spots at game speed—but be quick and not hurry, as advocated by Hall of Fame player and coach John Wooden.

Problem: Inconsistency.
Correction: This is often the result of shot to shot changes in technique. Every shot should have the same starting or trigger point and ending point (full follow-through). Players should groove the shot so that it becomes automatic.

Problem: Slow to build confidence.
Correction: Coaches should reteach the self-talk (*focus, feel, feedback*) shooting technique. Insist on game shots at game spots at game speed. Apply the BEEF and ROBOT shooting principles.

- Straight line with shots called by the coach—players in groups of four begin on the *go* command; the next four players begin when there is 15 to 18 feet (4.6 to 5.5 meters) of space between them and the preceding group. The coach designates a basket to the side of the court (use the intersection of the sideline and the half-court line). Players move forward under control in the basic position until the coach gives the *shot* command. Then each player on the court simulates catching a pass with a quick stop or shooting off the dribble and makes a shot to an imaginary basket. On the *go* command, all players continue up the court until the coach throws another imaginary pass. Players must be ready to shoot with balance and control at any time, shooting to the right going down and shooting to the left coming back.

- Line shots with the ball—the first four players start together and use proper technique to shoot four imaginary shots (the free-throw line, the half-court line, the opposite free-throw line, and the opposite baseline with the ball). Players shoot at the opposite basket and then shoot as though the basket were to the side. With the basket to the side, they hop from the basket-side foot and land facing the basket. With the ball, they catch and turn in the air to face the side and then shoot. Players can shoot from a pass to themselves (two-handed underhand spin pass with backspin thrown at the location of the intended shot). Then players can shoot from a dribble. The shot is taken with a high 60-degree arc slightly in front of the shot location—the follow-through is exaggerated and held until the ball hits the floor. No target is used; coaches should emphasize shooting up and holding the follow-through until the ball returns to the floor.

LAYUP PROGRESSION SHOOTING

Purpose: To teach players progressively to shoot game-type layups properly and quickly.

Equipment: One ball per player (when possible), one basket per 12 players.

Procedure: The coach should use as many stages of the progression as appropriate to the age or skill level of the players.

Layup Progression

- Line drill—no ball, carry the ball, dribble the ball. Layup at the free-throw line, half-line, opposite free-throw line, and opposite baseline. Exaggerate the follow-through.

- Carry the ball in pickup position, using the outside chin spot for the ball; shoot a one-handed layup.

- One line dribble in layups—each player with a ball (six per basket). Start in live-ball quick stance and use appropriate direct or crossover drive and dribble from the wing position. Emphasis—early target, opposition, two-handed pickup, high jump (rebound the player's own shot before the ball hits the floor)—can add dummy defender or cone halfway to the basket.

- Two-line layups (12 players with three balls per basket).

  - Dribble in and the opposite line rebounds
  - Pass from the opposite line

Note: a progression on layups from a pass is to carry the ball in a shoulder and chin position as each player gallops into the basket.

Dribble chase layups: Players form pairs, each with a ball. The player with the ball stands behind the baseline and outside the free-throw line. The partner (the catcher) is the outlet between the free-throw line and the half-line. The passer uses a baseball pass to the outlet catcher, who receives the ball, faces up floor, and speed dribbles to the other end for the layup as the original passer chases the dribbler down from behind (cannot foul but can go for the ball. This occurs in pairs at opposite ends simultaneously; half of the groups are at each end. Rotate clockwise and then change to counterclockwise to ensure ample practice with the nonpreferred-hand dribble and layup.

Two-minute team layups: Use four coaches or program assistants as passers located at the top of the key level just outside of the free-throw lanes. Divide the team or group into two lines located behind each baseline under each basket on the full court. Start with two balls and add two more later. The sequence is the following: the first player in line gets a make or misses a layup and outlets to the coach on same side while fast-break sprinting to the other basket in the sideline lane. Then the player receives the ball back, near the half-line, from the first coach, passes on the move to the second coach, receives the return pass for the layup, and goes to the back of the line at the opposite end of the court. The player at the opposite end does the same actions simultaneously (two balls going). The coach may add two balls for higher skill levels.

Coaching Points

- One-foot layups—opposition (jumping foot and shooting hand).

- Two-foot layups—power up from a one count or a two-foot quick stop.

- Two-handed pickup and chin on shoulder away from the defender—the balance hand drives or picks the ball up to the shoulder (prevents rocking the cradle).

- High jump, not long jump (stamp hard on last step).

- Early target—hit it high and soft, use the board almost all of the time.

FIELD-GOAL PROGRESSION

Purpose: To self-teach progressively the skill of shooting with a warm-up drill that provides a player with feedback needed for improving shooting in all basketball situations. Some form of field-goal progression needs to be used daily by all players to reteach or review physical and mental techniques.

Equipment: One ball per player (when possible), basket, or two players per ball (a partner can act as a coach).

Procedure: Each player takes a ball and reviews shooting according to this progression. Five repetitions of each of the options are carried out each time.

Options

- Two-handed *ball slaps* develop the feel of having the ball in the whole hand. Place the hands on the side of the ball, toss the ball up slightly, and *slam* the hands against the ball while catching it five times. Players should do this each time they pick up a basketball and enter the court.

- One-handed arm swing to the shooting pocket, shoot, and retrace (without ball). Players may also use the bookend hand. Repeat five times.

- TV shooting without ball—player on the back with the shooting elbow on the floor and an imaginary ball on the horizontal hand (like a TV tray). Shoot vertically and hold the follow-through. Repeat five times.

- TV shooting with ball—same as the previous option but with the ball. The ball must be shot at least 6 feet (1.8 meters) up (ensure full follow-through). Hold the follow-through for 1 second and then catch the ball coming down. Repeat five times.

- Wall or backboard shooting without a basket target—start with the ball in the shooting hand and the open hand facing up (form the V), lock and load into the shooting pocket, place the bookend hand up but not touching the ball, and then shoot up and high on the wall or the backboard.

- Form shots, or shoot it straight shots, are one-handed vertical shots without a target that start with the ball in the player's hand in a palm-up position. The player shooting the ball aligns the shooting foot on any line on the floor, rotates the ball into the shooting pocket with the balance hand off the ball and slightly to the side in a vertical position, shoots with good thrust (for backspin), snaps the wrist, holds the follow-through until the ball hits the floor, and checks where the ball bounces (on or near the line to see if the player is shooting the ball straight and 6 to 8 feet [1.8 to 2.4 meters] in front of the player to ensure he is shooting up, not out). Five repetitions are taken.

- Close to the basket shots or soft touch, or killer, shots are taken with a target (the rim and the backboard). Remind players to practice from the inside out, starting close to the basket and gradually moving out. *All* shots are *inside* the free-throw lane. A minimum of five shots are taken per spot (higher goals for intermediate and advanced).

- The circle shots drill emphasizes footwork: each player moves in a circle, carrying the ball with two hands held chest high (pit and protect the ball), using proper quick-stop footwork (hop from basket-side foot, the player lands with the feet aimed at the basket and ready to shoot, and shoots a short shot) while shooting at five spots inside the free-throw lane, as shown in figure 4.29. After five shots are taken moving clockwise, each player shoots five shots moving counterclockwise. Shots taken at 45 degrees are board shots (spots 2 and 4); rim shots are taken at spots 1, 3, and 5. No dribbling is allowed—circle shots focus on having the feet in position and the hands ready to handle the ball. Rotate the circle after every shot. When players are moving clockwise, the proper footwork is to hop from the basket-side foot in order to land with the feet ready to shoot from a quick stop, facing the basket with the dominant foot forward and the hands ready (ball in shooting pocket). Counterclockwise motion is done by hopping from the left foot; clockwise movement uses hopping from the right foot.

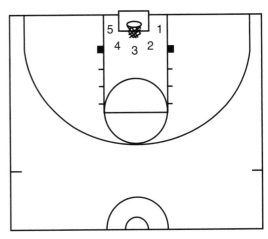

FIGURE 4.29 **Soft touch or circle shot spots.**

Another version of a footwork drill that can be used as a warm-up is simple and quick and encompasses pass pickups and footwork for shots from a pass as well as footwork from a dribble. The Hays footwork drill, developed by Dan Hays at Oklahoma Christian, is carried out from elbow to elbow at the free-throw lane (could be from side to side anywhere near the free-throw lane, 15 to 18 feet [4.6 to 5.5 meters] apart). The shooting footwork from a pass version begins at the left elbow; the player faces the opposite sideline and, using a two-handed underhand pass to herself with backspin, tosses the ball near the opposite elbow and moves toward the pass while performing proper footwork (hop from basket-side foot and land with a quick stop facing the basket). The player snaps the ball to the shooting pocket with a two-handed pickup move. The player picks up the spot target early, uses the verbal prompt *focus*, and tests body balance by using a short, quick shot fake (legs bent and locked, heels down) but does not shoot the ball. Then the player faces the opposite sideline, uses the bounce pass to herself at the height of the chest or the shooting pocket, and repeats the pass footwork, going from right to left. Now the hop foot is the right foot. This process is repeated 10 times; 5 to the right and 5 to the left. This action simulates, in a warm-up, catching the ball and being ready to shoot from a pass with balance and quickness, moving to the right or to the left.

Follow with 10 repetitions of shooting from a dribble using the outside-hand dribble; the right hand goes from left to right and the left hand goes from right to left. The focus is on making a good self-pass (the last dribble) as the players hop from the basket-side foot. The last dribble is a hard dribble that gets the ball to the shooting pocket accurately and quickly (dribble pickup) at the same time as the basket-side foot is used to hop into a quick stop. No shot is taken, but a shot fake is made as a balance check.

CRITICAL CUE: Use field-goal progression daily—five repetitions of slaps or slams, form shots, and soft touch or close shots. Shots from the pass and the dribble should also be used during each practice.

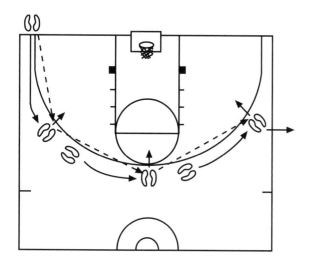

FIGURE 4.30 **Pass or dribble pickups.**

• Shooting *from a pass* involves players tossing a high, two-handed underhand pass to themselves in a desired spot and using proper footwork to land in triple-threat position, facing the basket and ready to shoot. Shots from a pass are preceded by the pass pickups footwork drill around the three-point field-goal line (clockwise and counterclockwise). No shots are taken—the focus is on footwork and using a shot fake to check balance (figure 4.30). On pickups, the ball is snapped quickly into the shooting pocket from a two-handed pick or grab. When receiving a pass or on completion of the dribble, players must get the ball quickly into shooting position. Players should make a pass to themselves, hop from the basket-side foot, land facing the basket with the feet ready, use a shot fake to test balance, and then repeat the sequence.

• Shooting *from the dribble*—from a triple-threat position, 15 to 20 feet (4.6 to 6 meters) from the basket, a player makes a dribble-drive move to the left or right, makes a quick stop, and shoots from a desired spot. Preliminary work should be done on pickup technique. The footwork for shots from the pass and the dribble is identical. With a dribble, the last *hard* dribble occurs as the basket-side foot is used to hop into a quick stop facing the basket (with the lead foot forward). Coaches can have players take the last dribble with either hand, jumping from the opposite foot with a quick stop at the same time and landing in the triple-threat position. Players go from baseline corner to baseline corner, tracing the three-point arc using proper footwork and practicing the dribble pickup technique (snap the ball into shooting position) prior to actually taking shots from the dribble. Players should practice the technique with clockwise and counterclockwise motion. Players should dribble with the outside hand, hop from the basket-side foot as the last hard dribble drives the ball into the shooting pocket (two-handed pickups), land facing the basket with a quick stop (with the feet ready), use a shot fake to test balance, and then repeat the sequence.

SOFT TOUCH OR KILLER SHOOTING

Purpose: To review shooting mechanics and build confidence in players by shooting on a regular basis (recommended as a warm-up for each practice).

Equipment: One ball and one basket per player. Not more than four players per basket.

Procedure: Soft touch or killer shots are taken at five spots (five shots at five spots) with specific goals appropriate to skill level. For example, beginners might shoot or make one shot at each spot (two backboard shots at 45 degrees and three rim shots—corner, middle, corner); see figure 4.31. The mental goal is to develop the habit of full focus (pick up target early and see or hold for one count). Intermediate players might be able to make two or three shots at each spot; advanced players could set a goal of only swish shots at the five spots (make three or make up to five in a row). Of the two soft touch options—one-handed and two-handed—either or both are used, but especially the one-handed version, in which the player goes to the spot, places the ball in the whole shooting hand (the palm up), locks and loads the ball into the shooting pocket, places the balance or bookend hand to the side of the ball (not touching), and shoots the shot. Coaches can emphasize these points: have the feet ready, sit into the shot, put the ball in the shooting pocket, use full focus (verbal prompt *focus*), and execute a full follow-through. Each player goes through the checklist to review the basics on each shot.

The same drill of five shots in five spots can be done with the use of the balance hand added. The essential four steps of field-goal progression should be performed each time that a player steps on the floor to practice. Every time a player picks up a basketball, it's an opportunity to relearn shooting (the essential slams, form shots, Hays footwork drill, and soft touch).

Players should always use soft touch shooting to apply mental practice and use verbal prompts (*focus, feel* [during shot], *feedback* [after shot, *yes* or *net* on makes; shot location on misses]).

GROOVE IT SHOOTING DRILL

Purpose: To evaluate shooting effectiveness and range.

Equipment: Ball, basket, and court area.

Procedure: At any spot or shot, shoot and make a minimum of 5 out of 10 shots (preferably, 7 out of 10 shots) with that move and from that location. The preferred spots or shots are shown in figure 4.31.

Options: To groove the shot at each spot, start at five locations outside the arc with a live ball.

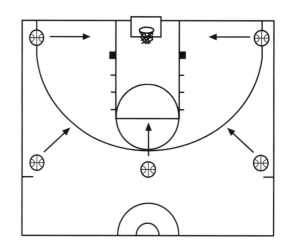

- Pass right and left—repeat a set of 10 shots until reaching the goal for made shots.

- Use a shot fake and dribble right and left with proper footwork; shoot sets of 10 shots until the goal is met.

FIGURE 4.31 **Groove shooting spots.**

- Face away from the basket in front of the five spots at 10 feet (3 meters) from the basket. Toss a two-handed underhand self-pass at 12 feet (3.7 meters), use a two-handed pickup and a PPF rear turn to face the basket, and shoot using mental edge technique (*focus, feel, feedback*). Players should keep track of their personal records for consecutive makes at each spot.

PAIRS OR IN-AND-OUT SHOOTING

Purpose: To teach shooting in a 2-on-0 game simulation drill that covers all shooting situations.

Equipment: Basket and one ball per pair of players (players can also work in groups of three or four).

Procedure: This continuous competitive shooting drill, shown in figure 4.32, incorporates all of the principles of movement: passing and catching, shooting, and offensive rebounding. Players are grouped in pairs (there may be one or two pairs per basket). The basic rules are as follows:

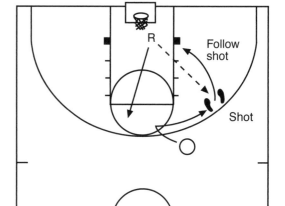

- All pairs begin on the coach's command, starting with the passer under the basket with a ball; a teammate gets open for the shot, calls the passer's name, and receives a pass for the shot.

- Shooters rebound their own shots until a basket is made (always assuming that the shot will be missed) and then gain possession to pass to a teammate for a shot.

FIGURE 4.32 **Pairs shooting: one pass.**

- The receiver must always get open and call the passer's name.

- Passers make a quick, on-target pass at the right time to a teammate for a good shot and go quickly to another location near the edge of their shooting range, ready to move only when a teammate has scored and has possession of the ball.

Options

- Groove: each player gets open and shoots for 30 seconds while a teammate rebounds; players take turns shooting and rebounding, changing roles every 30 seconds.

- The shooter makes five baskets and switches positions with a teammate.

- The 10-scores game to 10 made baskets (or 5) involves players moving with shots from a pass and from a dribble.

- The coach designates the type of pass (push, overhead, air, bounce) and type of shot (regular or shot fake and shot). This drill is excellent for practicing passes with the nonpreferred hand (passers can use only this pass to increase repetitions with the nonpreferred hand).

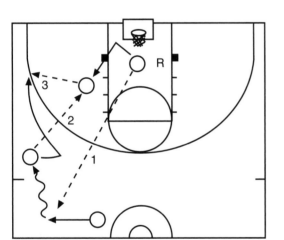

FIGURE 4.33 **Pairs shooting: three passes.**

- Pressuring the shooter involves the rebounder passing and making a poor defensive closeout while applying some type of false pressure (go by, shout, hand in face, contact) after the pass to the shooter. The defender cannot block or alter the shot or foul the shooter. At least once a week, use the variation of having defenders pressure shooters with hands up to help shooters develop the greater arc needed for shooting over defenders.

- Three-pass shooting involves shooting from an outlet pass (passer posts up), a pass to post (passer cuts), and a return pass for shot (figure 4.33).

- The *beat the star* variation places shooters in competition with a designated star shooter with a rebounder partner. The game begins with one free throw and continues with players shooting set or jump shots. Scoring rules for free throws give challengers 1 point for successful shots and 3 points for the star on misses; challengers score 1 point for successful field goals and the star gets 2 points for misses. The game can be played to 11 or 21 points.

MAKE-IT-TAKE-IT ROW SHOOTING

Procedure: To teach the skill of shooting in a self-testing format adjusted to standards set by the coach.

Equipment: Basket and one ball per player.

Procedure: All tasks in this drill are self-testing and require the player to meet effective scoring standards. All moves are to be carried out consecutively without rest to practice shooting in game situations.

Players make dribble-drive layup moves from left and right corners (with a foot on the sideline), each hash mark, and the top of the key. They are allowed only one dribble and must make three baskets in a row from each spot. Frontcourt players with the ability to dunk the ball must do so by dribbling only once. The objective is to cover the greatest distance possible with a layup scoring move. After each row of three shots is made, the player earns the right to shoot free throws. The percentage goal must be met on free throws (four out of five for college players; three out of four for high school; two out of three for junior high) or the player repeats the move and free throws.

Advanced Options

* Shoot from a spot with a selected move until two shots in a row are missed.

* Consecutive swish—shoot from a spot with a selected move until a swish shot (the ball hits the net only) is made two shots in a row.

* Forty-point scoring—start three different scoring moves from five different spots along the three-point line: on the baseline on both sides, the wing on both sides, and the top of the key. The first shot is a three-pointer from a spin pass. If the player makes it—3 points. The second shot is a quick one-dribble pull-up jump shot worth 2 points. The third shot is a drive after a shot fake and a power layup at the basket—2 points. Players finish with five free throws—1 point each. A perfect score is 40 points; 7 points per five spots and 5 points per five free throws.

* Three-point contest—shoot five three-point shots from the same five spots as the 40-point scoring drill. Players get 1 point for every shot made, except for the fifth shot (2 points). A perfect score is 30 points.

INDIVIDUAL DRILL FOR GROOVING THE SHOT

Purpose: To teach players to self-assess the mechanics of the shooting hand and the balance hand while increasing shot range.

Equipment: Ball, basket, and teammate or coach to rebound and provide feedback.

Procedure: Player shoots along a straight line directly in front of the basket moving toward the free-throw line and the half-court line. Start in close at about 6 feet (1.8 meters) in front of the basket and in the free-throw lane. Place the ball on the whole shooting hand (held horizontally facing up). Using only the shooting hand, rotate and move the ball to the shooting pocket (lock the wrist in and bend the wrist back—place the ball on the shooting tray or form an L). With the bookend hand directly to the side of the ball (but not touching), shoot a high arching shot and hold the follow-through for one full count. Continue moving away from the basket while using correct form. Players can find their effective range (over 50 percent) quickly.

This drill is also a good check of vertical plane alignment of the shooting hand, elbow, and shoulder (keep the ball straight) as well as using the legs for power. Keep the shot the same with the arms; get lower for power. The partner can help the shooter check position and mechanics. The balance hand should finish high. As the shooting elbow is locked and the wrist is flexed for follow-through, the fingers of the balance hand should be vertical at the lead of the shooting wrist. The pedestal-pocket shot with both hands can also be used, often at much closer distances.

FIELD-GOAL CORRECTION DRILL

Purpose: To focus on specific problem areas with shooters.

Equipment: Ball, basket, and coach.

Procedure: Focus on one problem at a time: footwork, balance, shooting hand, balance hand, or follow-through. Practice from inside-out: 3 feet, 6 feet, 9 feet, and 15 feet

(.9, 1.8, 2.7, and 4.6 meters) from the basket. View the shooter from the side and from behind.

Options

- Footwork and handwork—players move right and left carrying the ball in the shooting pocket, use a quick stop to shoot, and then dribble right and left to shoot.

- Balance—check head and foot position before and after the shot; head straight or toward the basket (not left, right, or away).

- Shooting hand and balance hand—check shooting hand at start (elbow in and L, wrist L) and finish (60-degree release, hold follow-through firm but relaxed). Check balance hand at start (side of the ball, vertical or right angle to the backboard and the floor) and finish (pull slightly off the ball, the elbow stays flexed, the shooting hand above the balance hand, fully extended, or the fingertips of the balance hand at the level of the shooting wrist).

- Swish game (plus three, minus two)—count a swish shot as 1 point, a make that hits the rim is 0, and a miss is –1. A score of +3 wins the game and a score of –2 loses; the winning and losing scores can be modified according to skill level.

- Do a consecutive swish—players shoot until they fail to swish two shots in a row, keeping track of row swishes.

- Shoot until two or three are missed in a row—record the number of field goals made.

FREE-THROW PROGRESSION

Purpose: To provide players with a daily drill designed to reteach and review free-throw shooting fundamentals during each practice period.

Equipment: Ball, court area, and basket.

Procedure: The free-throw progression drill is always the same and consists of the following parts, each with a learning reminder:

1. Five slams—as players pick up a ball, they grab the ball and slap or slam the ball hard with both hands simultaneously on the sides of the ball.

Learning Reminder

- Shoot the ball with the whole hand—spread the fingers and form a V with the thumb and first finger. Feel it.

2. Five form shots on any spot without a shooting target. Put the shooting foot perpendicular to any line on the court (e.g., the sideline) and at any spot, and shoot five free throws using perfect technique. Hold the follow-through until the ball hits the floor.

Learning Reminders

- Find the shot.
- Get a ritual.
- Bounce at the bottom.

- Use a full follow-through (exaggerated).
- Shoot up, not out.
- Use the legs for power, up on the toes.
- Keep body weight forward.

3. Shoot at least 10 soft touch, or killer, free throws. From a position 6 feet (1.8 meters) in front of the basket, shoot free throws with complete physical technique. When the coach or the player is satisfied with proper technique, add the mental edge technique for confidence building. Set appropriate goals for free throws made from 5 makes to 8 or 9 makes, to 10 swishes, depending on the skill level.

Learning Reminders

- Apply the four physical technique essentials.
- Add mental edge technique (*focus, feel, feedback*).

4. Go to the regular free-throw line and shoot free throws with perfect technique. Use all of the correct physical and mental techniques to groove the free throw; use these techniques in competitive situations.

Learning Reminders

- Use all physical techniques.
- Use all mental techniques.

FOUL-SHOT GOLF

Purpose: To teach players to shoot free throws with competition against self or others.

Equipment: Ball and basket.

Procedure: Start at the foul line and play 18 holes. A birdie (1 point) is earned for each swish. On a made shot (0 points), par is made. If the foul shot is missed, a bogie (–1 point) is earned.

Players get three shots at a time, or a round of three holes, until all players have taken a round. The game is over after six rounds. The player with the highest score wins.

KNOCKOUT SHOOTING

Purpose: Practice shooting in a competitive situation.

Equipment: Two balls and three to eight players per basket.

Procedure: Form one line at a selected distance and spot. The first player shoots and rebounds his own shot and, if the shot is made, passes back to the next teammate in front of the line without a ball. If the shot is missed, the player follows and rebounds the shot. If the next shooter makes the shot first, the player is knocked out—to run a lap, sprint to the opposite wall and back, or some other penalty before returning to game. Play for 1- to 3-minute periods. The coach can also set up the game with permanent knockout until a final winner is determined.

ROW PLUS FREE-THROW SHOOTING

Purpose: To provide competitive shooting practice.

Equipment: Ball and basket.

Procedure: Any player may compete against the game by selecting a move, shot, or situation and practicing it until a number of field goals are made in a row and a free throw is made, coupled to the goal. This approach to shooting practice is modified from that taken by many great offensive players, one of the most notable being Bill Bradley, who used this approach in high school (Crystal City, MO), college (Princeton University), and professional (New York Knicks) basketball to become one of the best offensive scorers in the game.

For example, a player might select a left move, consisting of a shot fake or a dribble drive, with a pull-up jump shot at 15 to 18 feet (4.6 to 5.5 meters), starting at the top of the key. The goal might be two in a row plus a throw. That player replicates the move and shot at game speed until two field goals are made in a row. The player must then follow with a made free throw before going on to another move or shot situation. If the free throw is missed, the player must start over and repeat until that goal is met (two in a row plus a free throw). Elite players might use goals as challenging as five in a row or more plus a free throw to compete against the game.

FOOTWORK AND FIELD GOALS (OR FREE THROWS)

Purpose: To provide competitive shooting practice.

Equipment: Ball, basket, and half-court playing area.

Procedure: Goals can be set for this game as consecutively made shots (field goal or free throw) or to avoid two consecutive misses over a period of time (e.g., 3 minutes) or for a given number of attempts (10, 15, or 20). The player with the ball may select any field-goal situation (shots from a pass or shots from a dribble) and any move (pull-up jump shot, layup, or runner). A free-throw situation could also be selected.

The competing player begins the drill facing away from the baseline, positioned directly under the basket in the triple-threat position. Using a shot fake, the player executes either a direct drive or crossover drive move (any live-ball move) for two dribbles, to get as far past the three-point line as possible, and then terminates with a controlled quick stop. On landing in a triple-threat quick stance, the player executes a PPF rear turn to face the basket in triple-threat position. At that time, the player either tosses a two-handed underhand pass to a shooting spot (shoots from a pass) or uses a shot fake and a dribble-drive or live-ball move (shoots from a dribble) into a competitive move (a layup or a pull-up jumper). The player assumes that every shot is missed and either retrieves the made shot out of the net or follows the missed shot until it is made. On two-handed capturing and chinning the ball from the net, the player, who is now facing the baseline, executes a PPF rear turn to face away from the basket in a new direction and repeats the cycle. The sequence is as follows: capture and chin the ball, use a live-ball move away from the basket for two dribbles, use a quick stop, execute a PPF rear turn to face the basket, shoot from a pass or a dribble, do a completion move, be ready for a possible rebound, and repeat.

During the drill, the player needs to use all live-ball moves and the whole half court—drive to the corner, the wings; guard the out-front position. A goal number of repetitions (10 to 20) or row field goals may be set. If the player is doing footwork and free throws, the drill terminates each time the player quick stops and executes PPF rear turns to face the basket. At that time, the player goes to the free-throw line. The drill continues again after a free throw is either made or missed. A lot of footwork with the ball can be practiced in a short time. Up to four players can do the drill at once on each basket.

MENTAL PRACTICE DRILL FOR FIELD-GOAL AND FREE-THROW SHOOTING

Purpose: To teach players to use automatic verbal prompts, shooting rituals, and self-evaluation to build shooting confidence.

Equipment: Ball and basket.

Procedure

1. Mental practice shooting—carry out at least 25 perfect shots daily in a quiet, focused place.

   - Field goals.
   - Verbal prompts—*focus* (the back of the rim target), *feel* (the shot from successful start to finish, from shooting pocket to held follow-through), and *feedback* (*yes, net, swish,* and *money* on made shots). There are no misses in the mind to analyze and forget.
   - On backboard shots—*focus* (high), *feel* (soft), *feedback* on make.
   - Visualization—every shot is perfect in the mind; see it, hear it, and feel it. Players should paint the perfect picture in their minds.
   - Free throws.
   - Verbal prompts—see and say *net* or *swish* (or *nothing but net*) during the preshot ritual (e.g., bouncing ball, focus, feel, feedback [*yes* or *net*]).

2. Soft touch with mental practice—on each soft touch or close shot, use verbal mental practice prompts.

   - Rim shots—focus, feel, feedback (*yes* or *net*).
   - Backboard shots—focus high, soft, feedback.

3. Mental practice personal record test—chart status and progress weekly. From a 12- to 15-foot (3.7- to 4.6-meter) distance, shoot as many shots as possible in 5 minutes to attain the greatest number of consecutive makes in that time.

   - Rim shots—move from the baseline around the court to the opposite side of the free-throw lane on the baseline. Keep track of consecutive makes in 5-minute periods in two situations.
   - Use a two-handed underhand toss to the 12-foot (3.7-meter) spot; catch facing away from basket. Using the PPF, face and focus, shoot (*feel*), and use feedback while repeating. Time and record for 5 minutes (personal record for doing catch-and-face).
   - Use a two-handed underhand toss to the shooting spot while catching and landing facing the basket, and then use verbal prompts (*focus, feel, feedback*) while shooting. Record the number of consecutive makes in 5 minutes (personal record for facing the basket).
   - Backboard shots.
   - From the 12- to 15-foot (3.7- to 4.6-meter) distance on the 45-degree angle with the backboard, players should go from side to side (two spots) while

shooting backboard shots from two situations: catch and face, followed by face and shoot. Use verbal prompts on each backboard shot; focus high, soft (*feel*), *yes* or *net* (feedback). Record the number of consecutive makes in a 5-minute period.

- Catch and face (personal record for the backboard)—land facing away from the basket, turn and face, and shoot (personal record for facing the backboard). Record the 5-minute personal record.
- Land facing the basket and shoot (personal record for 5-minute periods).

chapter 5

Outside Offensive Moves
Playing the Perimeter

"Drive and dish (penetrate and pitch), pass and catch, and create scoring chances for teammates should be the definition of a point guard."

Jerry V. Krause

Any discussion of individual offensive moves should begin with the reminder that basketball is first and foremost a team sport. Although every game situation provides opportunities for individuals to use offensive moves, the player with the ball must coordinate offensive moves closely with four other players. Coaches need to place limitations on individual offensive moves to ensure that players use their strengths.

Outside moves are offensive moves around the perimeter of the court while players are facing the basket. The four types of individual outside moves are the following:

- live-ball moves (when the offensive player with the ball still has a dribble available),
- dribbling moves (when the offensive player is in the process of dribbling),
- dead-ball moves (made at the completion of the dribble, when a player has used the dribble and stopped, in possession of the ball), and
- completion shots (shots taken after a dribble).

Proficiency in live-ball moves should be coupled with the development of quick, controlled dribble moves that are used with a purpose. All live-ball moves and dribble moves should result in a pass, a dead-ball move, or a completion shot. This chapter describes live-ball and dead-ball moves. Dribble moves and completion shots are described in chapter 3, Ballhandling, and chapter 4, Shooting.

Fundamentals of Live-Ball Moves

CRITICAL CUE:
Start live-ball moves from the triple-threat position facing the basket.

All live-ball moves begin from a basic position, with the player in offensive quick-stance or triple-threat position (can shoot, pass, or dribble) facing the basket. Players should be in their effective shooting range. They should get into position by catching the ball with the feet in the air and landing with a quick stop facing the basket (i.e., catch and turn in the air). The alternative is to catch and face—the player catches the ball with both hands, uses a quick stop facing away from the basket, and makes a pivot (turn) in triple-threat position to face the basket (using the nondominant foot as the PPF whenever possible). Players should especially explore live-ball moves as they catch the ball (on the catch).

Players should always protect the ball and keep it close to the body in a power position (pit and protect the ball), using the body as a shield. They provide this protection in triple-threat position (figure 5.1) by keeping the ball near and under the shoulder with the dominant hand behind the ball (wrinkle wrist position and bent elbow), during a live-ball move by dribbling the ball on the side opposite the defender, by using a catch-

FIGURE 5.1 Triple-threat position: *(a)* side view and *(b)* front view.

and-face technique (chinit and pivot to triple-threat position) in defensive traffic (figure 5.2), and by avoiding dangling the ball with the elbows locked or extended. Dangling the ball means danger—players lose arm quickness with the ball, power to protect the ball, and may lose the ball to a defender (figure 5.2*c*).

Conserving time and space with balance and quickness is a basic guideline for outside moves with the ball. All moves should be quick and made in a straight line toward the basket whenever possible. The offensive player should make slight shoulder contact with the defender while moving past on the dribble drive (figure 5.3) and then use quick shot and pass fakes while maintaining a quick stance. The live-ball

FIGURE 5.2 **Catch and face—protect the ball:** *(a)* catch facing away from the basket; *(b)* pivot (turn) to face the basket using the PPF; *(c)* don't dangle the ball.

move (using the dribble drive past a defender) should be made with a quick first step, long and low, past the defender in a straight line toward the basket. A catchy phrase for players to remember during dribble drives by the defender on a live-ball move is *shoulder to knees, feel the breeze*. It is important to get the head and shoulders by the defender's trunk. Then, on contact, it is a foul on the defender. This technique is called *winning the battle* of the first step.

The attack-the-front-foot or hand rule is applied when the defender is in a staggered stance (see figure 5.3). The most vulnerable part of the defender is the front-foot

FIGURE 5.3 Direct drive: *(a)* attack front foot, *(b)* side view, defender in staggered stance (left foot forward), *(c)* defender must pivot to cut off move, then player has hip contact with defender (win the war) on second step.

or the front-hand side because the defender must pivot before angling back to cut off the dribble penetration of the offensive player. So the offensive player should be aware of the defender's front foot and hand and use a live-ball move to that side of the body whenever possible. The dribble drive *war is won* when inside hip contact is made with the defender to prevent recovery on the drive.

The player should attack the basket on the dribble drive by accelerating to the basket under control. *Now or never* means that the live-ball move is best made immediately after the player receives a pass, before the defense can adjust, and while the defense is moving (drive against momentum or in the opposite direction of the defender). If in doubt whether the dribble drive is open, the driver should pass the ball (pass first, dribble last).

The primary objective of any live-ball move in the power zone is to score a layup with one dribble (more than two dribbles are seldom needed). Players should read the defense to anticipate chances to use a controlled dribble drive as a reaction to a defensive adjustment. Learning to get by the defender and control the dribble drive well enough to permit a last-second pass to an open teammate or a pull-up for a shot, helps players challenge the defense even more. Penetrate and pitch is an excellent perimeter move needed by all perimeter players. Players using the dribble drive are looking for the options of the layup, the pass when a help defender appears (using a quick stop first), or a pull-up jump shot or completion move if another defender is waiting at the basket.

Permanent Pivot Foot Moves

These moves should be used when a permanent pivot foot (PPF) is used for all live-ball moves. The left foot should be used for right-handed players and vice versa. The following moves to get by the first defender should be taught as basics: the direct drive, the hesitation move, the rocker step, and the crossover drive.

The PPF approach to footwork is preferred for perimeter moves because it is simpler and easier to learn than using either pivot foot. Players can attain greater skill levels because of fewer choices and moves to be learned. In addition, on the two primary live-ball moves (the direct drive and crossover drive), driving success occurs on the second step with the more comfortable and quicker preferred side, and on the first step to the slower, less comfortable and nonpreferred side. With the direct drive, the battle is won on the first step (head and shoulders by the defender) and the war is won on the second step when hip contact is made on the defender (lock in the defender with inside hip contact). For the crossover drive (to the nonpreferred side, which is normally slower), the battle and the war are both won on the first step as the driver gets the head and shoulders by the defender at the same time as inside hip contact is made on the defender. The key to live-ball moves is the long and low first step (*shoulder to knees, feel the breeze*).

Direct Drive. This is a drive past the defender with the dominant foot. The right-handed player should drive past the defender's left side, taking the first step with the right foot (and vice versa for the left-handed player) by establishing triple-threat position in a staggered stance and pushing off the pivot foot without a negative step. The quick long and low move is taken with the stepping foot straight to the basket, as the ball is pushed to the floor, and in front of the lead foot before the pivot foot is lifted. Finally, a step is taken past the defender with the PPF to attack the basket.

The breakdown count consists of the explosion step with the dominant stepping foot (down) and the player pushing the ball ahead to the floor on the dribble drive (figure 5.3). Playing rules require the ball to be out of the hand before the pivot foot is lifted (American rules). For international play (FIBA rules), the ball must hit the floor on the first dribble before the foot is lifted, which requires a longer and lower first step.

Hesitation or Step-Step Move. This is a secondary dominant-side move that is executed by establishing the triple-threat position and making a short jab step at the defender and basket with the dominant foot. If the defender doesn't react to the jab step, a second long and low explosion step, as a direct-drive step, can be made past the defender. The breakdown count consists of a jab step with a short pause (slightly forward and down), a long and low explosion step (go move), and a dribble drive initiated by pushing the ball ahead to the floor as hip contact is made (figure 5.4).

FIGURE 5.4 Hesitation or step-step move: *(a)* short first step, *(b)* long and low second step past the defender, and *(c)* near hip contact with the defender.

Rocker Step. Another dominant- or preferred-side move is the rocker step: a direct-drive jab fake and return to triple-threat position, followed by a direct-drive move. The sequence is to establish triple-threat position, make a direct-drive short jab step, and then return to triple-threat position where a shot fake may be used to lure the defender forward. When the defender moves toward the offensive player in reaction to the return to the triple-threat position, the offensive player should then make a direct-drive move. The rule is to drive against a defender's momentum. The breakdown count consists of a jab step (down), a move rocking back to triple-threat position (up), a long and low explosion step against the defender's momentum (down), and a dribble drive (go) started by pushing the ball ahead to the floor (figure 5.5).

FIGURE 5.5 Rocker step: *(a)* jab fake (down), *(b)* return to triple-threat position with shot fake (up), and *(c)* take a long and low first step past the defender reacting to the shot fake (down).

Crossover Drive. The basic countermove to the opposite side, when the defender overplays the dominant side, consists of establishing the triple-threat position and then crossing the dominant foot over to the other side of and past the defender while keeping the ball close to the body and swinging it across (circle tight) at the same time. The ball then is taken from the nonpreferred triple-threat position and is pushed ahead to the floor with the player's nonpreferred hand to begin the crossover dribble drive. The dominant foot is pointed toward the basket. Players should keep the pivot foot stationary while the crossover step is made with the same stepping foot. The breakdown count consists of triple-threat position, swinging the dominant foot over to the other side (long step) as the ball is snapped over from pit to pit while placing the nonpreferred hand behind the ball (circle tight), and pushing the ball ahead to the floor on the dribble drive (figure 5.6). The ball should be moved across the body (pit to pit) high in the chest area. Some coaches prefer the high sweep and low sweep, but this is too slow and takes the ball too far from shooting or driving position. Some coaches also teach a jab step to the preferred side to set up the crossover, but this move is slower and tends to make the reaction crossover move lateral rather than toward the basket.

The direct-drive and crossover moves are the basic live-ball moves that are sufficient for most players to combat most defenders. Beginners can usually depend on one basic go-to move (direct drive) and one countermove (crossover), with the secondary moves being the rocker and hesitation to the preferred side (the side most players are more comfortable using).

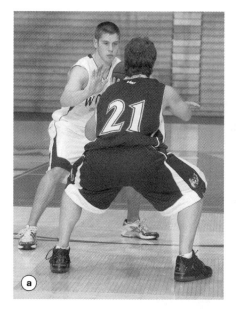  

FIGURE 5.6 **Crossover drive for the left-hander:** *(a)* triple-threat position (jab), *(b)* bring the ball to the nonpreferred side (circle tight), and *(c)* move with a long and low stepping foot past the defender (the left foot).

Moves With Either Pivot Foot (Advanced)

These moves can be taught when either foot is used as the pivot foot in live-ball moves. Both right- and left-handed players should be able to establish a pivot with either foot using this method.

Direct Drive With the Direction Foot.   This move, used to dribble drive past a defender, consists of making the explosion step with the foot on the side the player is driving. The sequence is for players to make a quick stop facing the basket and, when driving right, to use the left foot for a pivot foot and take an explosion step past the defender with the right foot. Also, when driving left, players should step with the left foot, using the right foot as the pivot foot. The ball is pushed ahead on the floor on the dribble drive. The breakdown count consists of taking a long and low explosion step, with the foot on the same side as the dribble drive (right foot to the right side, left foot to the left side), and pushing the ball ahead to the floor to start the dribble drive. The ball must be out of the hand before the pivot foot leaves the floor. The disadvantage of this move is that hip contact on the defender occurs on the second step.

Direct Drive With the Opposite Foot.   This move is used to drive past a defender on either side by using the opposite foot to step across and shield the ball as a long and low direct drive is made. The opposite-foot drive is executed by making a quick stop facing the basket and, when driving right, stepping past the defender with a left-foot explosion step and pushing the ball ahead on the dribble drive. The breakdown count consists of taking an explosion step past the defender, with the foot opposite the side of the dribble drive, and pushing the ball ahead on the floor for the dribble drive (figure 5.7). This move has the advantage of getting the head and shoulders by and making hip contact on the defender during the first step.

FIGURE 5.7   **Live-ball move for either pivot foot—direct-drive move with the opposite foot:** *(a)* **to the right with the left foot,** *(b)* **to the left with the right foot.**

Crossover Drive.   Players can also learn a countermove using either foot as the pivot foot (fake right, cross over left with the left pivot foot; or fake left, cross over right with the right pivot foot). This is carried out by making a quick stop facing the basket, making a jab step and crossover with the same foot to the opposite side (swinging the ball across and close to the body), and finally pushing the ball ahead to the floor and starting a dribble drive. The breakdown count consists of a jab step, a crossover step with the same foot while bringing the ball across the body, and a dribble drive started by pushing the ball ahead to the floor (figure 5.8).

FIGURE 5.8 **Either pivot foot for a live-ball move—crossover drive: *(a)* crossing over from right to left (jab right), *(b)* crossover drive left past the defender.**

Fundamentals of Dead-Ball Moves

These maneuvers are used at the completion of a dribble move when the quick stop is made within 10 to 12 feet (3 to 3.7 meters) of the basket. Dead-ball moves can be used when players are moving either left or right, but they must be within close shooting range for the moves to be effective. Players in possession of the ball should avoid dead-ball situations whenever possible unless a pass or shot is anticipated. In other words, the live dribble should be maintained.

Dead-ball moves using either pivot foot should be made after a quick stop, either from a pass or, more commonly, at the termination of the dribble. Remind players to see the whole court as the quick stop is made in order to read the defense and make a proper decision quickly.

Jump Shot.   Players should execute a quick stop and take the jump shot with balance and control (see chapter 4). The quick stop allows the shooter to slow momentum, go straight up, and land slightly forward of the takeoff position.

Shot Fake and Jump Shot.   Players should make a quick stop and follow with a believable shot fake (eyes on the basket; a short, quick 1-inch [2.5-centimeter] vertical fake). With vision on the basket, the player moves the ball up slightly (1 inch), while maintaining a quick stance with the legs locked and the heels down, and then quickly follows with a jump shot.

Step-Through Move Into One-Foot Layup (Advanced).   The advanced move past either side of the defender to shoot a layup after a quick stop (with or without a shot fake) is another attacking option. Players should make a quick stop facing the basket, followed by a shot fake to get the defender out of quick stance unless the defender is already overcommitted. When going to the right, take a step past the defender with the left foot (or with the right foot when going left) and shoot a right- or left-handed running layup or a post shot. The breakdown count consists of a shot fake, a step past the defender with the opposite foot, and a layup shot (one-foot or power).

Crossover Step-Through Move (Advanced).   This advanced countermove, used to step past a defender by faking one way and going the opposite way for a layup or a post shot, is done by making a quick stop facing the basket, taking a jab step with either foot, a crossover step, and a move past the defender with the opposite foot to attempt a layup or a post shot. The breakdown count consists of jab step, crossover move, and layup or post shot (figure 5.9).

Step-Through Move Into Power Shot or Layup (Advanced).   Even though the step-through and jab-step moves can be legally used to get layups, they are sometimes called traveling by officials. To prevent this call, players can use a step-through completion move and finish the move with a two-foot power shot so that the pivot (turning) foot leaves the floor at the same time as the stepping foot, as shown for a right-handed player in figure 5.10. Coaches should take every opportunity to educate and inform officials about this move before their players use it.

Spinner (Advanced).   A pivoting rear turn and layup or post shot is most effective from a dead-ball quick stop at right angles to the baseline when the player is stopped by a defender in the direct path. Coaches can teach this advanced move by having a player make a quick stop facing the opposite sideline at the free-throw lane while chinning the ball, make a rear turn on the pivot or turning foot closest to the basket, and shoot a layup (one-handed or power layup) or a post shot. The breakdown count consists of a using a quick stop, making a rear turn, stepping past the defender to the basket with the opposite foot, and shooting the layup or post shot (figure 5.11 on page 126).

COACHING POINTS FOR OUTSIDE MOVES

- Visualize the defender and learn to read and react to the defender.
- Develop a go-to move and a countermove.
- Use game moves at game speed.
- Develop balance and quickness during all moves.
- Go at top speed under control.
- Make legal moves.
- Execute moves correctly and then correctly and quickly. Do them right first and then speed up until mistakes are made; then strive for game moves at game speed.

FIGURE 5.9 Crossover step-through move: *(a)* quick stop, *(b)* jab step toward the defender with the left foot, *(c)* crossover move (right pivot foot), and *(d)* layup or post shot.

FIGURE 5.10 **Crossover step-through move to a power shot:** *(a)* quick stop, *(b)* jab step, *(c)* crossover move with the right pivot foot, and *(d)* power shot or jump hook from two feet.

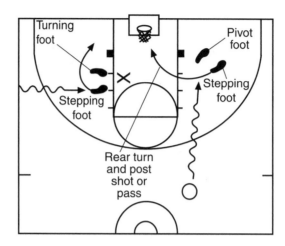

FIGURE 5.11 **Spinner steps—from wing-middle dribble or guard-side dribble.**

TROUBLESHOOTING

Problem: Poor execution when learning.
Correction: Demonstrate again and slow down to get proper execution first.

Problem: Trouble executing moves with the non-preferred side.
Correction: Practice two or three times more often with these moves.

Problem: Traveling violations on perimeter moves.
Correction: Reteach the rules of movement and footwork as boundaries of performance.

Problem: Ballhandling skill difficulties with perimeter moves.
Correction: Prescribe added practice on passing and catching, dribbling, and basic ballhandling.

Problem: Challenges with perimeter moves when defenders are present.
Correction: Develop sequential progressive practices—players should use slow but correct moves first, get a rhythm, gradually increase speed until mistakes are made (acknowledge, understand, learn from), and execute game moves at game speed. Coaches can add dummy defender for all situations and, finally, add live defender(s) with all variations.

Perimeter Drills

These drills should be adapted to a coach's style of play and to situations encountered by perimeter players in that style of play. As always, they should be sequential and progressive.

Guidelines for Perimeter Drills

1. When working alone, use an underhand spin self-pass before moves, always face the basket in triple-threat position with a live ball.

2. Respect the three-point arc. Keep the feet behind the arc or penetrate for a pull-up shot or finish at the basket.

3. On all layups, go for net or swish shots; mix up power and one-foot layup completions.

4. Precede all drives by a shot fake.

5. Tighten your game; increase balance and quickness for game moves at game speed.

WARM-UP FOR PERIMETER PLAYERS

Purpose: To provide perimeter players with a warm-up for fundamental skills.

Equipment: Two balls per player, tennis balls, half court with basket.

Procedure: Spend 1 minute on each of these exercises.

1. Dribbling sequence: one ball, two balls, dribble and juggle, pullback crossover sequence.

2. Imaginary defense with talk: on-the-ball, off-the-ball, off-the-ball to on-the-ball, post defense and blockout, and transition.

3. Moving without the ball: offensive pass and cut, screen and slip, screen cuts, offensive rebounds, and transition.

4. Fast-break package sprints: without the ball.

5. Shooting progression: field goal and free throw (see chapter 4).

6. Fingertip push-ups and stretching, especially a long and low drive stretch for the groin and hyperextension of the wrist for shooting.

7. Ballhandling sequence: around the body, the arms, and the legs.

Coaching Points

- Use imagination to simulate game moves.
- Do things right, and then do them quickly at game speed.
- Become a detail player.

LINE DRILL: LIVE-BALL, DEAD-BALL, AND COMPLETION MOVES ADDITION

Purpose: To teach players live-ball and dead-ball moves and to review dribble moves.

Equipment: One ball per line of players, full court.

Procedure: Form four lines of players on the baseline. No defenders are placed on the court. Each circuit should eventually include a beginning live-ball move, a dribble move in the middle of the court, and a dead-ball or completion move at the far basket (figure 5.12).

There are two other line drill options. Put the first player in each line at the free-throw line extended, with the next player in triple-threat position with a ball. The ballhandler passes to the opposite player at the free-throw line and closes out to play defense. The catcher makes a 1-on-1 move past the defender; use dummy closeout first (overplay left, then overplay right). Live closeout is the next progression. The penetrator passes by the defender to the opposite player and then becomes the closeout defender.

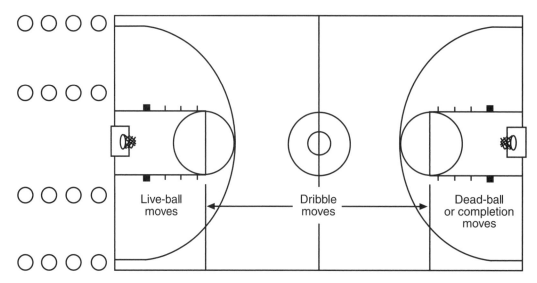

FIGURE 5.12   Line drill: individual outside moves.

The second option is for the first player in line to use a live-ball move, quick stop at the free-throw line, and catch and face (using a rear turn). Then that player makes a crisp, one-handed push pass to the next player in the line. Finally, the passer becomes a closeout defender to the catcher, who makes a live-ball move around the defender. Repeat the action.

OUTSIDE MOVES USING A SPIN PASS

Purpose: To develop skill in using outside moves.

Equipment: Basket and one ball per player, half-court area.

Procedure: Players practice live-ball moves and completion or dead-ball moves from a simulated passing and catching situation. Players use the two-handed underhand spin self-pass to begin the drill in all primary offensive locations and situations. The sequence is first to spin self-pass in spot locations near the edge of the three-point field-goal line, catch the ball on the first bounce with the feet in the air, and land facing the basket. Apply RPA technique. Players should catch and face the basket every time they handle the ball by using the quick stop and the pivot, and then attack the basket. Set goals—two or three in a row with a move, make three to five baskets with a specified move, etc. Coaches should evaluate moves—only perfect practice makes perfect. Use PPF (basic) or either pivot foot (advanced) technique for developing footwork. This self-monitored drill makes it possible to practice appropriate live-ball, dribble, and dead-ball or completion moves using the basic principles. A tossback training device, partner, or coach passer may be used in conjunction with the spin pass technique to simulate passing and catching situations used with the outside moves.

Options

- Catch and shoot—spin pass to self and take a quick but unhurried, balanced shot.
- Catch and quick drive—spin pass to self, V-cut away, catch and face from pass to self, dribble drive, and finish.
- Catch and one dribble pull-up jump shot.

- Catch, shot fake, and one dribble pull-up jump shot—quick, short shot fake (1 inch [2.5 centimeters]) with quick stance (the legs locked and the heels down).

- Catch, pass fake, and shoot—only move the arms and the head on the pass fake. Keep the pass fake short and quick—stay balanced.

- Catch, pass fake, drive, and shoot (may designate a completion move).

- Catch, jab step, and shoot—create space for the shot—stay balanced and use a short jab step.

- Catch, jab step (hesitation or rocker), drive, and shoot.

- Catch, one dribble, change direction, and shoot—attack the basket on initial dribble, change direction (crossover, spin, behind the back) to continue penetration and finish.

- Spend extra repetitions with moves to the nonpreferred side.

CLOSEOUT: 1-ON-1, 2-ON-2, 3-ON-3, 4-ON-4

Purpose: To practice all outside moves by perimeter players.

Equipment: One ball and one basket per group.

Procedure: Form a line of players under each basket off the court. The first player steps under the basket with the ball and is the defender. A line of offensive players is placed 15 to 18 feet (4.6 to 5.5 meters) away, facing the basket. The defender makes a crisp air pass (with the feet on the floor) to the first player in the offensive line and then closes out to defend that player. The drill begins as soon as the pass is made for both offense and defense. The perimeter offensive player should catch the ball with the feet in the air and facing the basket, read and react to the defender's actions, and apply fundamentals to shoot or make an outside move.

Players may rotate to the back of the opposite line each time. Play make-it-take-it or any arrangement of their choice. The drill may also be run as a 2-on-2 option (figure 5.13) that then becomes a teamwork competition with on-the-ball and off-the-ball play. The passer guards the ballhandler on the first pass.

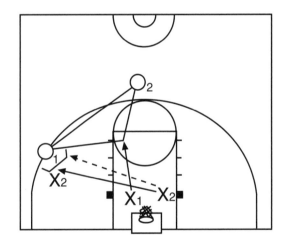

FIGURE 5.13 **2-on-2 closeout.**

1-ON-1 DRILL

Purpose: To provide a variety of 1-on-1 competition for perimeter players.

Equipment: One ball and one basket per group.

Procedure: 1-on-1 competition allows each offensive player the chance to evaluate the effectiveness of perimeter play in all situations: live-ball, dribble, and completion moves.

1-on-1 Starting 15 to 20 Feet (4.6 to 6 Meters) From the Basket

- Have a limit of two dribbles.

- Begin with a move to get open—V-cut or L-cut—and then use catch and face.

- Make-it-take-it.
- Play games to five baskets.
- Use a 5-second limit to make a move or limit to two dribbles.

1-on-1 Starting Near the Half Court

- Use a cut to get open and then catch and face with the ball.
- Use dribble moves to go by the defender.
- Use a completion move to score, usually a layup or a jump shot.
- Use a teammate or coach for a passer.
- Add a second hoop defender in the lane (first defender operates back to the free-throw line).

1-on-1 Completion Moves That Are In the Lane

(The defender allows a pass. Or use the manager or program assistant with the Air Dummy Defender.)

- Make a move from the perimeter and catch the ball facing the basket in the free-throw lane.
- Score with a completion move (jump shot, step-through layup, crossover layup, spinner move). This move is made without a dribble.
- Alternate games to five or make-it-take-it.

1-on-1 From Offensive Positions

Have the players receive the ball at the locations of the fast-break or set offense.

PARTNER PENETRATE AND PITCH DRILL

Purpose: To practice live-ball moves and passing to a teammate for a score at the completion of a dribble drive.

Equipment: Two players, ball, and basket (can have three pairs per basket).

Procedure: Partners start 20 to 25 feet (6 to 7.6 meters) from the basket, spaced 15 to 18 feet (4.6 to 5.5 meters) apart; point-wing or guard-forward and forward-forward combinations (figure 5.14).

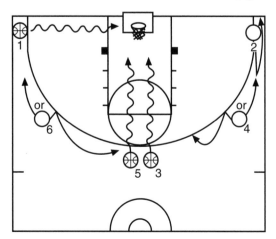

FIGURE 5.14 **Penetrate and pitch drill.**

The ballhandler starts with a live-ball move into a dribble drive. The potential catcher partner times a cut to be open when the passer is ready to pass and with proper spacing. The guard-forward partners use the cutting options of sliding away (drift) or filling behind (crack back) into the driving path. The cutter looks for completion shots to the basket or outside shots—medium range or three-pointers. The penetrator or passer passes (pitches) to the partner or fakes the pass and shoots the shot. The forward-forward partners are on opposite sides of the floor. The penetrator drives the baseline and passes along the baseline and, using the baseline hand, executes a push pass to the partner catcher, who slides (drift or baseline release) to an open position toward the baseline on the opposite side of the floor (baseline release). Except for the baseline release pass, which is a bounce pass, all other perimeter passes are air passes.

PARTNER PASSING AND SHOOTING

See chapter 4 for the descriptions of a variety of shooting drills after individual outside moves. An example is using one, two, or three passes. Make six field goals on one pass, six field goals on two passes, and six field goals on three passes.

TIMED LAYUPS

Purpose: To practice ballhandling and layup shooting in a competitive situation.

Equipment: Ball, free-throw lane, basket, and timing device.

Procedure

V layups: Start drill on the right elbow at the free-throw line in triple-threat position, dribble drive to the basket, and shoot a layup; use two hands to grab the ball out of the net and do a right-handed dribble past the free-throw line to the left elbow and a left-handed dribble continuous for the left-handed layup, two-handed grab and left-handed dribble past the free-throw line to the right elbow. Repeat as many times as possible for 30 or 60 seconds. Count the number of made layups for the personal record.

Reverse-V layups: Same drill, but cross the rim to shoot a layup on the other side of the basket with the appropriate dribbling hand. For example, start at the right elbow; use a left-handed dribble to cross in front of the basket, and shoot a left-handed layup. Then use a right-handed dribble past the free-throw line to the left elbow and reverse back to the other side. Time for 30 or 60 seconds; record the layups made as a personal record. This drill is a good way to finish a perimeter workout.

PERIMETER GAME

Purpose: For players to practice all of the perimeter moves with the ball in a competition against themselves and their own personal record.

Equipment: Ball and half court, two or three players per basket.

Procedure: This drill can be done from three spots (wing, top of key, wing) or five spots (add both baseline corners). Rules: All layups must be clean (swish) to be worth 2 points. Mix power layups and one-foot layups. On swish set or jump shots, the player gets a bonus point. Call out the score on *every* shot attempt, made or missed. Put back all misses, even though they don't count. Use free-throw swish rules (swish or net = +1, make but hit rim = 0, miss = −1). The moves are the following:

1. Three field goals
2. Middle drive to cross rim
3. Baseline drive to rim (toes to baseline on power layup)
4. Middle drive to pull-up jump shot
5. Baseline drive to pull-up jump shot
6. Middle drive to quick stop, step across, power shot (or runner)
7. Baseline drive to quick stop, spinner or power shot
8. Middle drive and hop back shot
9. Baseline drive and hop back shot

10. Middle drive, hesitation or rocker off hop back, to rim

11. Baseline drive, hesitation or rocker off hop back, to rim

12. Jab step to three field goals

13. Free throws (four)

Top score = 64

Repeat at all three or five spots.

Coaching Points

- On power layups, point all toes to the baseline.
- Properly and quickly execute the fundamentals of the game for the welfare of the team.
- Be a practice player first.
- Game moves at game speed—practice and play with the intensity and poise of a championship team player.

chapter 6

Inside Offensive Moves

Playing the Post

"Get the ball inside first—take the ball inside or to the baseline.
Place pressure on the defense to foul. Post play is a key to success."

Dean Smith, North Carolina, Naismith Hall of Fame Coach

Most coaches and players recognize the importance of establishing an inside game with a post player receiving a pass near or inside the free-throw lane area. This inside game can serve several useful purposes. It can produce the high-percentage shot—the scoring opportunity close to the basket. The inside game also can increase opportunities for the original three-point play (inside score plus a foul shot)—post players in a congested inside area are difficult to defend and are often fouled when attempting a shot. When the ball is passed to inside post players (pass penetration), the defense is forced to collapse in order to contain them. Passing the ball back outside to teammates can create outside shot opportunities (the trey).

The underlying concept in this chapter is an emphasis on another key element of the scoring objective—getting the ball inside for a higher-percentage shot and forcing the defensive team to respect the inside game in order to open up outside shooting opportunities, especially the three-point field goal.

Post Play Fundamentals

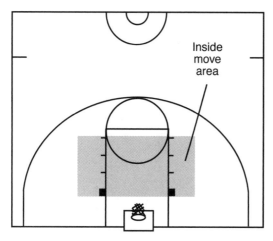

FIGURE 6.1   **Inside move area—the low to medium post.**

Post play is the key to building the offense from the inside out. Playing the post is a skill that requires a minimum of ballhandling and can be learned readily by players of all sizes with sufficient practice time and patience. All players should learn postup skills because advantage matchups occur. Good post players get open for high-percentage shots by developing a variety of inside moves, considered back-to-the-basket scoring moves, usually from a low or medium post position (figure 6.1). Post players need to learn how to get open, stay open, catch the ball safely, and score simply.

Penetrate.   To be successful, the offensive team must penetrate the perimeter of the defense on a regular basis by taking the ball inside using the dribble drive (penetrate and pitch, drive and dish) or the penetration pass to a post player. The objective of offensive penetration is to create the opportunity for a shot taken as close to the basket as possible, usually inside the free-throw lane, or to force the defense to collapse and open up the outside shot. Penetrate the defense with the pass or the dribble. This principle can dramatically increase efficiency in team offense, partly by drawing more opponent fouls.

Backboard Shots.   Offensive players should use the backboard when shooting after most inside moves, especially when shooting from a 45-degree angle, using a power move, or in an offensive rebounding situation. Backboard shots are higher-percentage shots than rim shots for inside play where control and congestion are common. The rule is "when going to the glass, use the glass," unless the player is dunking the ball. The margin of error is greater when the backboard is used as a shooting target. Chapter 4 discusses the use of the backboard as a shooting target (shoot it high and soft).

Assume the Miss. Since inside players are stationed close to the basket, they can be primary rebounders. Because the shooter can best gauge the exact location and timing of the shot, a post player using an inside move always assumes that the shot will be missed and prepares to rebound from a quick stance with the elbows out and the arms and hands extended above the shoulders (i.e., 2-and-2 rebounding with the hands up). An inside player can also block out a defensive opponent, when possible, or at least make a rebounding move to the middle of the lane for a primary rebounding spot.

CRITICAL CUE:
Assume a miss on every shot.

Everyone Is a Post. All players are post players. Although some of the best inside players have been medium and large people, technique is more important than size. A more critical factor is relative size—each player should be able to post up a defender of similar size or smaller and to develop basic post moves. Cliff Hagan was a 6-foot, 4-inch (193 centimeters) center at Kentucky who was inducted into the Naismith Basketball Hall of Fame as a player. In addition, many undersized post players like the physical play in the post area.

Create Contact. The inside area, which is frequently congested, offers considerable physical contact. Inside offensive players should *create* contact (post up on defenders to make open space for passes) and use their bodies to control defenders. Players must learn to initiate contact with the hips and upper thighs while maintaining balance and stance. Stay low with a wide base, and keep the feet active in a quick stance. Generally, defensive players are allowed to take one defensive position and then post players create contact to keep them there.

CRITICAL CUE:
Get low and wide, create contact when on offense in the post area.

Hands Up. Passing to inside players is difficult and challenging, and the margin for error is small because of congestion and time constraints. Thus, inside players always should be prepared to receive a quick pass from a teammate by using the post stance: having both hands up as contact is created (figure 6.2 on page 136). Sit into the stance, create contact with the defender, use the legs and the lower trunk, and then give two-handed targets for the passer with both hands up (the upper arms horizontal with the shoulder, the forearms nearly vertical, and the hands slightly forward of the elbows so you can see the backs of the hands).

Patience. Many large post players are late developers and may have poor self-image as a result of their size and relative lack of coordination. The prescription is coaching time, patience, and regular practice (repetition, repetition, repetition). George Mikan, NBA player of the first 50 years, spent hundreds of hours with his coach, Ray Meyer, during his college years at DePaul University. His workouts focused on footwork, ballhandling (passing and catching), shooting, and coordination drills.

Post Skills

Coaches should get players into a post-player stance. The inside or post player must develop the ability to assume an exaggerated basic position, with a wider than normal base, a low center of gravity, the elbows out, the forearms vertical, the upper arms parallel to the floor as extensions of the shoulders, and the hands up and slightly forward with the fingers spread and pointing to the ceiling (figure 6.2). Post players should provide a two-handed target for passers. The hands are kept up and ready.

FIGURE 6.2 **Post player's basic stance:** *(a)* front view, *(b)* side view.

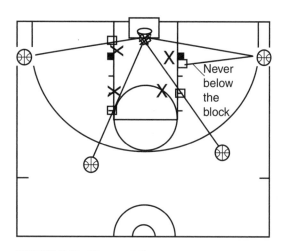

FIGURE 6.3 **The post line.**

Posting up should take place on the post line (defined as the straight line through the ball or the passer and the basket). The post line is shown in figure 6.3. The inside player should attempt to get open inside or just outside the free-throw lane, on or near the post line. Establishing position on the post line shortens the distance the pass travels from the post feeder. Ideally, the post player should be posted up with the shoulders square (at right angles) to the post line, "showing numbers" to the passer (i.e., the passer should be able to read the jersey number when passing to the post player). Keep the passing lane open by showing numbers to the passer and moving the feet (active feet or footfire) while creating lower-body contact on the defender. Use the posterior as radar bumpers. This rule applies in all situations except when defenders are fronting (playing between the passer and the post player).

The post line should be used whenever possible to shorten the passing lane except when the passer is in the corner; then the lowest foot of the post player should be on or above the block in order to have space for a baseline scoring move. Low post players sometimes start on one side of the post line to force defenders to defend them on one side or the other.

Getting Open in the Post

The post player needs to get open on the post line between the passer and the defender whenever possible by using a V-cut and swim move, stepping into the defender, and using a rear turn to seal the defender (place the turning foot between the defender's legs), or stepping across the near leg of the defender (sit on the defender's leg or fight the front foot) as contact is created. See figure 6.4. The offensive post player uses proper footwork to post up and then maintains contact and takes the post defender further in their set direction (i.e., defender high—move her higher; defender low—move her lower; defender behind—move her toward the basket; and defenders in front—move them away from the basket).

Getting open at the right time and staying open are primary tasks of the inside player. Because post play is a constant 1-on-1 battle, players must learn to *create contact* and stay open. Once the defender has taken a position, inside players should make contact to keep the defender in place. They should keep their feet active and use the whole body to work in a half-circle move (figure 6.5). The hips and buttocks (the lower trunk) are used to sit on the defender's legs or body and to maintain contact.

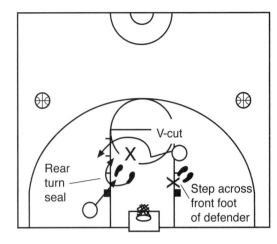

FIGURE 6.4 **Getting open in the post.**

Catching the Ball Inside

Post players must want the basketball. They need to build confidence in teammates that they will get open, catch the ball safely when it is passed to them, and score simply inside when open or pass outside when they draw two defenders.

Maintain contact in order to feel and seal the defender (use radar bumpers, not the arms or hands). The post player should also be able to locate the defender by reading the pass. The passer feeding the post player should pass to the hand target away from the closest defender. The placement of the pass

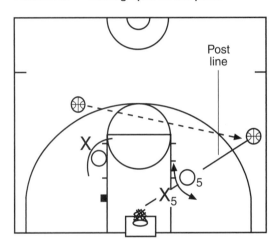

FIGURE 6.5 **Half-circle move: keep open by saddling up on the defender and showing numbers to the passer.**

helps the post player locate the defender—the pass leads to the score. Keeping the passing lane open is one of the toughest tasks for post players. Players must keep their feet active and maintain contact until the ball hits the receiver's hand—show numbers to the passer (face the passer).

Post players must step into the pass and meet the ball and still hold their position by catching the ball with two hands, with both feet slightly in the air (when possible), and then executing a quick stop (except when fronted). Possession always takes precedent over position, even though position is necessary to get open. Coaches should train players to focus on the ball until it hits their hands. When players catch a pass, they must protect the ball by using the chinit technique—the elbows out and up, the fingers up, the ball under the chin (or from shoulder to shoulder)—which keeps post players from dangling the ball and allows good ball protection.

The lob or ball reversal can be used when post players are fronted. When the defender establishes a ball-defender-post (fronting) position, two techniques are recommended. The first is an over-the-top lob pass (figure 6.6), where the passer shows the ball (go from triple-threat position to overhead), uses a check pass to read the help-side defensive coverage, and then quickly throws a pass over the defender to the junction of the backboard and the rim. The post player, maintaining quick stance

FIGURE 6.6 Lob pass over the defender: *(a)* both hands up—contact with the rear end and hip, *(b)* use a check pass *(pull the string)* to test the help-side defender's reaction, *(c)* two-handed capture and chin catch with a power move.

and keeping both hands up (the palms facing the passer), faces the baseline and establishes contact with the defender using the hips and buttocks (radar bumpers). The post player waits until the ball is overhead before releasing to catch the ball with two hands, the palms facing the ball. Care must be taken to maintain contact with the lower body and not push off with the arms (especially the forearm). The second technique is to use ball reversal to the high post or help side. If a defender is fronting on one side of the court, the ball may be reversed (second side) as the defender is sealed off and the post player steps to the ball (figure 6.7).

Taking Out the Defender

Inside players must learn to take the defender out of the play automatically. If post players are defended on the low side, they should take defenders lower (if defended on the high side, take them higher); if fronted, they should make lower-body contact while facing the baseline and take defenders away from the basket. If played behind, they should step into the lane before posting up with a V-cut or a rear turn. The idea is to allow defenders to take a position of choice and then take them further in that direction and pin or seal them in that position by creating contact with the legs or the lower trunk (use radar bumpers) in a post stance.

Reading the Defense

When the defender is fronting—playing between the passer and the post player—coaches should have their players use a lob pass over the defender or reverse the ball, pin or seal the defender, and feed the post from the opposite side. Offensive players should use a power move or reverse layup on the lob play. With the defender playing behind, the passer delivers the ball to the head target; then a post player should catch and face using post-facing moves. The post shot is also a possibility in this situation.

The defender positioned on the low side (baseline side) tells the post player to use the post or wheel move or the power move to a jump hook. Similarly, the power move or wheel move is indicated when the defender is positioned on the high side. The guideline for the perimeter passer and the post catcher is that the pass leads to the score.

Reading and reacting for the post player means learning to feel contact, reading the pass, turning to the middle, seeing the whole court, and challenging the defense. Excellent post players with the ball attract two defenders.

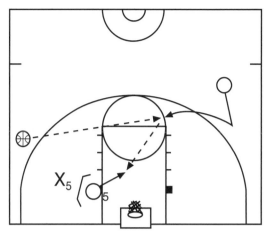

FIGURE 6.7 **Post play: reverse the ball (second side), pin and seal the post defender (use radar bumpers).**

> **CRITICAL CUE:**
> Catch with two hands and chinit in the post.

Post or Inside Moves

Finally, coaches should teach post players to move aggressively and be alert for open teammates. Their objective when using inside moves is to gain a position for a close-in shot or to free a teammate in scoring position for a pass. This happens when the post player attacks and must be guarded by two defenders, which can be achieved best by mastering a few basic, well-executed post moves to score simply.

Post Shot

This move to the middle and into the free-throw lane is a basic tool for the post player and an essential scoring weapon. The move is normally made without dribbling; the footwork and the mechanics of the post shot and the jump hook shot are explained in chapter 4. One advantage of the post shot is that it is a quick move to the middle of the defense and into the high scoring area (free-throw lane). Alternatives are the power move and the jump hook, which are slower and require a dribble.

Power Move

> **CRITICAL CUE:**
> Power move—pivot, seal with a half rear turn, power jump from two feet (bounce and hop), and power layup or jump hook (from two feet).

The power move usually is used to the baseline side when the defender is on the high side (away from the baseline). It may also be used toward the middle when the defender is on the baseline side. The sequence for the baseline power move is to pivot with a half rear turn on the foot closest to the defender and seal off the defensive player with the hips and buttocks. Then the post player takes a one or two-handed power crab dribble between the legs (near the foot closest to the basket), makes a two-footed power jump moving to the basket at the same time, and executes a quick stop with the feet at right angles to the baseline (belly baseline). This dribble sometimes can be eliminated when the post player is in the lane and close to the basket. Finally, the power shot or jump hook shot is used to protect the ball with the body and to score with the shooting hand away from the defense; the backboard is used whenever possible (figure 6.8). This move is fully described in chapter 4 as a strong move from two feet to two feet.

The power move to the middle (figure 6.9) is executed the same way: catch the ball and chinit (the defender on the baseline side), pivot on the baseline foot and use a rear-turn seal, power crab dribble between the legs near the lead foot as a two-footed power jump to the basket and into the free-throw lane is made, and finish with a two-footed power layup or jump hook (may need a shot fake). The most common error is to dribble or drop the ball outside the base as the rear turn or drop step is made—this exposes the ball to defenders in the congested post area. Make the two-handed bounce between the legs and near the front leg as a two-footed hop move is made toward the basket.

Jump Hook

> **CRITICAL CUE:**
> If you catch the ball in shooting range, make a quarter turn and use the jump hook. Point the nonshooting shoulder at the basket.

The jump hook is a two-footed shot, with the hand away from the defender, that is taken in close to the basket. The technique is to chin the ball and move it to the shoulder away from the defender. Then use a power jump (two feet) and use the arm bar to keep the defender from the shot as the ball is taken up over the head and above the defender. The nonshooting shoulder points at the basket. The jump hook can be used with either hand; it is a safe, powerful move that many players prefer to use in heavy traffic or congestion.

FIGURE 6.8 Power move to the baseline: *(a)* catch and chinit, *(b)* half rear turn and seal, *(c)* crab dribble—both hands between the legs (bounce and hop), and *(d)* power shot (facing the baseline).

FIGURE 6.9 **Power move to the middle:** *(a)* catch and chin the ball, *(b)* rear-turn seal, *(c)* two-handed bounce and hop, and *(d)* jump hook, facing the sideline.

Wheel Move (Advanced)

This advanced move, a combination of a power move followed by a post move, is used when the defender begins by playing high-side (or low-side) defense as the power move is made but then anticipates well and cuts off the offensive player who has made a power move. The post player then immediately executes a counter post move (figure 6.10). The sequence is to initiate a power move, then do a quick stop and chin the ball when the defender overreacts, and, finally, carry out a post move as a counter reaction to the defender's position.

FIGURE 6.10 **The wheel move:** *(a)* **the power move to the baseline (cut off by the defender),** *(b)* **post move back to the middle, and** *(c)* **take the post shot.**

Facing Moves

These basic perimeter moves are used when the defender is playing behind the post player, especially with a defensive gap. The offensive player pivots with a front turn or with a rear turn on either foot to face the basket and the defender. The front-turn options are the jump shot, the jump shot with a shot fake, and the crossover post shot (figure 6.11). All live-ball moves may be used in this situation. Other post player options are the rear turn on either pivot foot, followed by a jump shot; the jump shot with a shot fake; or other live-ball moves. This rear-turn move, first popularized by Jack Sikma, formerly of the Seattle Supersonics, tends to clear the defender and to create a gap for the quick jump shot. See figure 6.12.

FIGURE 6.11 A facing move: (a) pivot on either foot, (b) jump shot fake, (c) crossover, and (d) post shot.

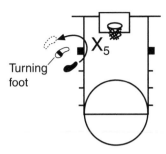

FIGURE 6.12 **Sikma post move: rear turn (right pivot in illustration).**

Passing to the Post

For most post players, the preferred pass into the post is the bounce pass, when passed to the baseline side. The bounce pass is hard for the defender to deflect or steal. However, the air pass is quicker and should be used more often to the middle or on the reverse (second side) pass and certainly on the lob pass (when the defender fronts the low post). On the direct air pass to the post, pass from above the shoulders with an overhead pass and hit the post-hand target away from the defender above the shoulders, or use a one-handed push or flick pass past the defender's ear from the triple-threat position. Perimeter players should be sure they can see the numbers on a post player's jersey before they make the inside pass to ensure that the passing lane is open. The perimeter player passer needs to pass to the hand on the open side (opposite the defender) because the pass should lead to a score. The pass tells the post player which move to make (reading the defender). When the defender plays directly behind the post player, the pass is made to the head of the post player.

TROUBLESHOOTING

Following are some of the common errors, with the coaching response and corrections.

Problem: Post player not consistently creating contact.

Correction: Have players sit into their game, stay in a post stance, and then progressively make contact on pads or managers, dummy defenders, and then live defenders.

Problem: Trouble staying in post stance.

Correction: Have players do more practice with the post player line drill, develop added core strength, keep in stance for progressively longer periods.

Problem: Difficulty staying open.

Correction: Reteach players how to create contact in all situations, use progressive contact drills, and check active feet or footfire to maintain position.

Problem: Inconsistent catching of the ball.

Correction: Increase partner passing and catching with a click (two hands, two eyes), and emphasize possession over position.

Problem: Losing ball (after catch).

Correction: Check capture and chin technique: the fingers up, the elbows up and out, squeeze the ball, use turns to shield the ball and escape defenders.

Problem: Not scoring quickly and simply.

Correction: Work harder before the catch for a deep post position, sit into a lower stance to maintain quickness, practice same scoring moves over and over until they're automatic, read and respond quickly, always assume a miss, score on an angle whenever possible.

COACHING POINTS FOR POST PLAY

- ◻ Want the ball, call for the ball.
- ◻ Teach post players inside moves (one go-to move and one countermove) that they can perform with confidence and, in turn, have the team take the ball inside (*in the paint*) regularly so that players can use these moves. Teams should play from the inside out.
- ◻ Teach players to use the backboard on most inside shots; it is a higher-percentage shot.
- ◻ Consider all players who are competitive and who like contact as potential post players.
- ◻ Have post players keep the hands up inside.
- ◻ Get players in post stance with a two-handed target on or near the post line. Players should always catch the ball with two hands to capture and chin the ball.
- ◻ Emphasize that getting open usually requires contact with radar bumpers (the lower body and thighs) using quick, strong moves.
- ◻ Create contact on offense with radar bumpers to pin and seal the defender in order to get open.
- ◻ Get possession of the ball over position when the pass is made inside.
- ◻ Take defenders in the direction they position themselves.
- ◻ Capture and chin every pass to the post (catch safely).
- ◻ Train post players to read the pass, their contact with the player guarding them, and the position of other defenders. Generally, see and attack the middle and into the free-throw lane.
- ◻ Teach the post shot or the power move and jump hook shot as the basic shot to the middle of the free-throw lane from the chinit position to score simply.
- ◻ Show post players that keeping the body between the defender and the ball during the power move is essential to its effectiveness.
- ◻ Teach players the wheel move as a power move, quick stop, and post move in sequence.
- ◻ In some situations, a post player may catch and face to use perimeter moves, especially in the free-throw line or the high post area or when the defender plays directly behind.

Post Drills

These drills should be developed progressively with no defense, dummy defense in different positions, managers defending with hand-held air dummies for contact, and finally with live defense.

POST WARM-UP DRILL

(Also see chapter 3, Ballhandling.)

Purpose: To teach inside players basic skills while preparing for practice.

Equipment: Basketballs, tennis balls, half-court area, basket.

Procedure: Spend 1 minute per item, select at least six options daily.

- Two-ball dribbling sequences

- Dribbling and juggling
- Tennis ball infield (low and wide, the toes to the outside, sit into the game)
- Imaginary defense slides or moves while talking to the defense
- Moving without the ball on offense (alone or in pairs)
- Rim to rim fast-break sprints
- Crab dribbles with bounce and hop down a line (two-handed ball bounce between the legs near the lead leg followed by a ball chin and two-footed hops down the line)
- Capturing and chinning the ball from an overhead toss or a spin pass to self from the floor
- Round the world jump hooks (left-handed, right-handed) from 4 to 6 feet (1.2 to 1.8 meters) from the basket
- Soft touch or *killer* shots—five spots and five shots (any goal) or with jump hooks
- Mikan series (regular, reverse, power, shot fake and power, freelance)
- Post stance with weight plate in each hand (thumb in hole) as post player moves in half circle from block to block using active feet or footfire

LINE DRILL: POST PLAYER STARTS, TURNS, AND STOPS

Purpose: To teach inside players proper footwork using the fundamental four-line format.

Equipment: Minimum of a half-court floor area.

Procedure: Four lines of players on the baseline at the sideline, outside the free-throw lane (both sides), and on opposite sideline. The movement options are begun with a post stance and a sequence of starts, stops, and turns:

- Post stance into post start (no negative steps)
- Post stance after quick stop at the free-throw line, quick rear turn and return to the baseline (quick stop into post stance)
- Repeat with front turns
- Full-court option—post stance stops at the free-throw line, the half-line, opposite free-throw line, and opposite baseline. Use two quick turns at each location and restart together. Verbalize each move.

Coaching Points

- Post stance and starts
    - Feet wider than shoulders
    - Sit into the game
    - 90-degree elbows, the hands held high
    - Positive step forward
- Stops
    - Quick stop (heel to toe or land lightly)
    - Full-footed stop

- Turns
    - Execute front turns with the right and left turning foot
    - Execute rear turns with the right and left turning foot
    - Lift the heel and pivot on the ball of the turning foot
    - Stay low and level (head)
    - Rip the lead elbow on the rear turn; throw a forearm punch on the front turn

POST PAIR DRILLS

Purpose: To teach and practice basic skills for post players, including post stance, passing and catching, and chinning the basketball.

Equipment: One basketball and player pairs spaced at least 15 to 18 feet (4.6 to 5.5 meters) apart. One player may be positioned in the post.

Procedure: Both players assume a post stance without the ball and perimeter quick stance (triple-threat position) with the ball as they pass and catch and then capture and chin the ball on each pass. The pairs pass and catch repeatedly for 1-minute segments.

Options

- Regular posting and passing and catching in and out.
- Bad pass variation—catcher must give up position to gain possession of the ball by doing a two-handed capture and chin of the ball.
- Floor pass, capture, chin, and pass out. The feeder bowls the ball to the side of the post catcher, who captures, chins, and passes back to the feeder, who bowls the ball to the other side of the post player. The post player should have to step-slide to the right and the left to capture with two hands and chin repeatedly and return the pass to the feeder.
- Back to the feeder or the passer—the post player assumes a post stance, facing away from the passer. The feeder passes to the post player, calls the player's name, and he turns to face the passer and to catch or capture and chin the ball and then to return pass to the feeder.
- The feeder and the rebounder—the post player assumes the post stance as the feeder shoots the ball or tosses the ball in the air near the post player, who performs a 2-and-2, pursuit and capture of the imaginary rebound. Coaches should teach players to pursue the ball, rebound out of their area, and capture and chin the ball with two hands.

Note: Post players should also do general skill drills, such as those in chapters 3 and 4.

Coaching Points

- Post players get in and stay in a post stance.
- Capture and chin the ball every catch.
- Get possession over position.
- Catch every pass.
- Do everything from two feet with two hands.
- Catch the ball with a click (two eyes and two hands).

SPIN PASS POST MOVES

Purpose: To teach players individual offensive post moves.

Equipment: Ball, basket, and optional tossback rebound device.

Procedure: Post players use a two-handed overhead toss and chinit catch, an underhand spin pass to the floor and chinit catch, or pass and rebound from a tossback device to themselves at a desired post location with their backs to the basket. Players execute three to five repetitions of each post move on each side of the free-throw lane. The sequence for inside or low post moves consists of the following elements:

- Post shot—to the middle
- Jump hook shot—around the lane (catch and turn; catch, crab dribble, and shoot)
- Power—to the baseline (power shot on the glass), to the middle (jump hook shot)
- Wheel—to the baseline, to the middle (advanced)
- Face—jump shot, shot fake and jump shot, and crossover post move (front-turn option) or live-ball move (rear-turn option)

Coaching Points

- No defender is used for this drill.
- The coach also may pass to the post to check post stance, post line, footwork, hand target, catching technique, chinning the ball, and post moves.
- Another option is to make three to five consecutive baskets before going to the next move.
- Assume a miss on all shot attempts and rebound until a shot is made.

POST PROGRESSION DRILL

Purpose: To provide players with a self-teaching progressive drill for offensive post moves.

Equipment: Ball, basket, and optional tossback device or method of receiving passes.

Procedure: Post players begin with an underhand spin pass to themselves (or pass and rebound from a tossback) and make post moves in sequence. Five baskets are made for each move in the sequence:

- Power move to baseline—left side, low post
- Jump hook move to middle—left side, low post
- Post move—left side, low post
- Wheel move—left side, middle or low post
- Facing move—left side, low post
- Facing move—high post, left elbow
- Same moves—right side

After players make the fifth basket for each move, two consecutive successful free throws (row five plus two free throws) are required for them to advance to the next move (or repeat the move again).

Options

- Require three to five post move baskets in a row and two or three free throws in a row for advanced players.

- No defense, position defense, air dummy defense, and live defense progression.

Coaching Points

- First do things right, then go toward game speed.

- Assume that all shots are missed; rebound and score on misses.

BIG SPACING AND POST FEEDING DRILL

Purpose: To teach triangle spacing with six players at one basket (post feeding) and big spacing by perimeter players at one basket from four perimeter spots, as shown in figure 6.13a.

Equipment: Ball and basket on the half court with four players at a time (big spacing drill). Two balls and basket on the other half court with two groups of three (post and two perimeter players) on each side, as shown in figure 6.13b.

Procedure

Big spacing: Four perimeter players fill the four perimeter spots on the half court as shown. Players use a regular ball or a weighted ball to swing or reverse the ball around the perimeter as quickly as possible (reversals can be timed).

Coaching Points for Big Spacing

- Players should step and pass, pass with the legs.

- Players cannot space too high or too wide to reverse the ball.

- Players should work the ball around the perimeter.

- Catchers should use a V-cut and shorten the passing lane.

- Passers should pass away from the defenders—using the outside hand target with both hands up (one as a target and one to ward off the defender).

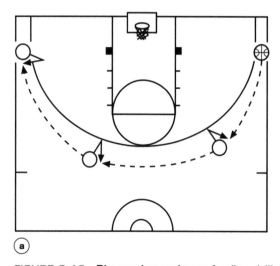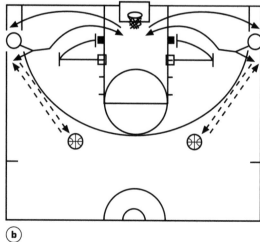

FIGURE 6.13 **Big spacing and post feeding drill:** *(a)* big spacing—perimeter, *(b)* post feeding.

- Coaches should emphasize rip pivots or turns for players to step across the body to protect the pass and increase pass power from the legs. Use two-handed air pass.

- Players should call for every pass (use the passer's name).

Options: Add four defenders; add basket cuts; add dribble drives.

Post feeding: A post player is positioned on each side of the lane. Two perimeter players are spaced at least 15 to 18 feet (4.6 to 5.5 meters) apart, to work with the post player on their side of the floor (six players are working at once). The guard on top passes to the wing on that side, who catches facing the basket or pivots or turns to face the basket and calls out *rim–post–action* (to remind teammates of the priorities with the ball—look for the shot, feed the post, action of pass, or dribble drive). The perimeter wing then passes back to the guard and uses a back screen from the post to cut to the basket. The post player then immediately down screens for the perimeter player and slips or posts up again. On the second catch from the top guard, the wing player feeds the post.

Coaching Points for Post Feeding

- Use an air dummy defender on the post to teach passing away from the defender (pass leads to a score).

- Insist on verbal calls for passes, cuts, screens, and rim–post–action with the ball or on the perimeter.

- Emphasize all passing and catching principles as well as moving and pivoting (turning) concepts.

- Focus on back screen, down screen, and cutter techniques. Post players must always screen and slip to get two scoring options on each screen.

Options: Add defenders later; players can change courts to get work in both drills.

ALL-AMERICAN POST WORKOUT

Purpose: To teach or practice all offensive post moves (for advanced players).

Equipment: Ball, half court, basket.

Procedure: Make all shots in the sequences before going to the next move in this 30-minute workout. Do this daily at game speed with proper and quick repetitions. Work from your favorite side of the lane.

- Four baseline power moves

- Four jump hooks to the middle

- Four turnaround jump shots, pivoting on the baseline side, turning the foot

- Four turnaround jump shots with a shot fake

- Free-throw swish (+2/–2)

    - If player loses (–2), do push-ups or sprints
    - If player wins (+2), shoot a string until a miss; when a miss occurs, the swish keeps the player going

- Four start low, V-cut, and flash to the free-throw line for a jump shot

- Four step out to the short corner for a jump shot on the baseline

- Free-throw swish game
- Four V-cuts and flash to the free-throw line for a shot fake to a jump shot
- Four short corner shot fakes to jump shots on the baseline
- Free-throw swish game
- Four V-cuts and flash to the free-throw line for a shot fake and a drive to a power shot or a dunk in the free-throw lane
- Four short corner shot fakes to a power shot or a dunk
- Free-throw swish game

2-ON-2 FEEDING THE POST DRILL

Purpose: To teach offensive and defensive post play skills, passing to post players, and movement after the pass for a possible return pass.

Equipment: Ball and basket, groups of four players (minimum).

Procedure: Two offensive and two defensive players work on post play from various locations around the free-throw lane. All offensive and defensive principles of post play are applied. Two players are needed as feeders. The first outlet pass or dribble for transition must be made when defenders obtain possession. Have outside offensive players make a V-cut move for a possible return pass when they pass to post players and call the post's name.

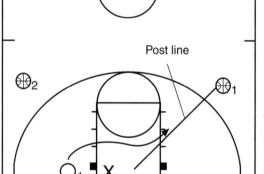

FIGURE 6.14 **2-on-2 feeding the post drill.**

Options

- Two perimeter players undefended, plus one defensive and one offensive post player (rotate after each score). See figure 6.14.
- Two perimeter players and two post players—one offense, one defense. Start the ball on the perimeter at the top of the key. The perimeter player dribbles to either wing and the offensive post player gets open on that side—the post may cut to high post or come outside and screen for a teammate (pick-and-roll or back pick).
- Make-it-take-it 2-on-2.

MIKAN DRILL

This drill, named after George Mikan, the first dominant post player in history, can be used for all players (perimeter and post).

Purpose: To teach players footwork, ballhandling, and layup shooting close to the basket.

Equipment: Ball and basket per player.

Procedure: Alternating layups, shoot with the left hand on the left side and with the right hand on the right side. Players should move the feet quickly and be in a position to shoot as soon as they rebound and chin the ball. Catch and chin the ball with two hands, try to swish each shot, and follow through each time. Never let the ball hit the floor—develop and maintain a rhythm. Go at game speed.

Options

- One minute or three, four, or five in a row

- Regular Mikans

- Reverse layup Mikans

- Power Mikans—jump under the basket on the shot, catch and chin while jumping to the other side; repeat the move going from two feet to two feet

- Power Mikans with shot fake (stay in stance—1-inch [2.5-centimeter] fake); keep the heels down on the shot fake

- Freelance—1-minute consecutive shots or make 10 scores using any move around the basket

5-ON-5 POST PASSING DRILL

Purpose: To teach post players to get open, catch the ball, make post moves, and pass from the post position as they read and react to defenders (especially traps). Teach defensive players to double-team (trap) a post player and rotate to the ball on passes from the post.

Equipment: Ball, half-court space, and 10 players (5 offense, 5 defense).

Procedure: Position three perimeter players and two post players as shown in figure 6.15. In figure 6.15a, the defense allows the first pass (always) and the post player goes 1-on-1 (no traps). In figure 6.15b, a trap is made. After the first pass, all play is live.

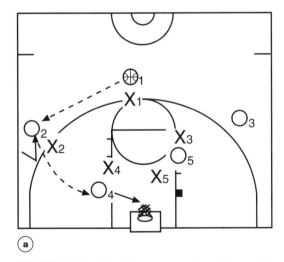
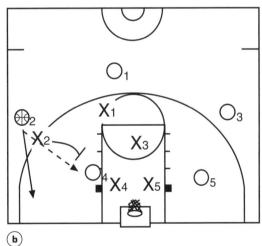

FIGURE 6.15 5-on-5 post passing: after each possession, the defensive team has a quick huddle, decides on a trap, and sprints to defense. In *(a)*, the pass happens with no traps; in *(b)* the defense employs a trap.

POST SCORE THROUGH DEFENSE (OVER AND BACK)

Purpose: To teach post players to capture and chin the ball and score repeatedly from two feet through a defender or blocking pad (getting fouled and scoring).

Equipment: Five basketballs, one defender with a blocking pad and basket.

Procedure: Five players, each with a ball, form a half circle around the basket (five spots) at a 6-foot (1.8-meter) distance from the basket. One defender is in front of the basket, preferably with a blocking pad. One player on offense starts on the baseline, receives a shovel pass or floor pass (good or bad) from the player with the ball, captures and chins ball, and, without dribbling, turns and scores through contact with a two-footed power move. This move is repeated five times (over) and five times returning (back) for 10 consecutive scores through defense. Rotate and repeat.

1-ON-1 POST CUTTHROAT

Purpose: To practice post offense and defense in a 1-on-1 live format. Players play to two or three baskets or for 1 minute.

Equipment: Three perimeter feeders (point, wing, wing), ball, two post players (one offense, one defense), and basket.

Procedure: Offensive and defensive post player in the lane with three or four perimeter players. The ball starts with the defensive post player, who passes it to the perimeter player of choice; live play begins with 1-on-1 post play in the lane. The ball can be passed anywhere on the perimeter before being passed to the offensive post player.

Coaching Points

- Offense—post stance on post line, create contact and seal, players point to where they want the ball on the perimeter, get open and stay open, catch safely, and score simply.

- Defense—avoid contact unless a position or advantage is offered, keep the ball from the post.

chapter 7

Individual Defense

*"My teams are built around tough defense,
stingy shot selection, and being hard-nosed."*

Don "Bear" Haskins, University of Texas at El Paso, Hall of Fame Coach

ndividual defense, a great challenge for both coaches and players, involves developing fundamental skills that depend less on ability than on determination. Defense can become a consistent part of each player's game. Both mental and physical challenges await players developing defensive skills. The effectiveness of this phase of the game especially depends on what is taught, emphasized, evaluated, and *demanded*.

Basic individual defensive skills are needed in all defensive systems: player-to-player, zone, or combination defenses. These essential skills are the following:

- defensive stance and steps;
- on-the-ball, off-the-ball, off-to-on-the-ball, on-to-off-the-ball defense; and
- special situation defense; screens, traps (double-team), and the defensive charge.

Individual defensive skills need to be blended into a consistent defensive system that includes the level of coverage (full-court, three-quarter court, half-court), pressure, lane, sagging style, and assignments (player-to-player, zone, or combination), and the influence of the dribbler. This chapter discusses individual skills that are geared to an aggressive style of play, but coaches can adapt them to other situations or to a specific defensive team philosophy.

Defense is critical to winning, more consistent than offense, and more controllable. Hall of Fame coach Ralph Miller stated that losses are rooted in defensive breakdowns—individual or team defense, defensive rebounding, or turnovers caused by the opponent's defense. Defense also generates fast-break offense, easy baskets, and offensive confidence.

Fundamentals of Defense

Defense is as much mental as physical. Players should be encouraged to be proactive, rather than reactive. Generally, defenders are at a disadvantage. One way to offset this edge is to use the rule that action is usually quicker than reaction. Coaches can emphasize the active elements of defense by the acronym ATTACK.

A—Attitude. The starting point of all defense is the determination to become an aggressive, intelligent defensive player. Players must develop and maintain control of their playing attitude, especially on defense. Coaches cannot coach unless players decide to *play hard* during each defensive possession. Excellent defense requires that players give maximum physical effort.

T—Teamwork. The collective effort of five defensive players is greater than five individual efforts. The synergy of defensive team chemistry can offset the natural advantage of offensive players; play together to survive and thrive with *team* defense.

T—Tools of defense. The four basic physical tools are the mind, the body, the feet, and the eyes. The hands can be a help or a hindrance. When the other tools are used first, especially body position, the hands can be a defensive plus.

A—Anticipation. Players must use good basketball sense and judgment (mind) triggered by vision. See the man and guard the ball—the ball is the only thing that scores. Players should see the ball at all times and use their eyes to anticipate. For example, they should see a careless pass instantly and decide to act quickly. Quickness is based on physical readiness and mental anticipation.

C—Concentration. Players should be alert and ready to play defense at all times. They must assess the situation and be able to take away the opponents' strength. Players must avoid resting, physically or mentally, when playing defense. Communication is an excellent way to aid concentration.

K—Keep in stance. Defensive players must maintain defensive quick stance at all times. They should seldom gamble by making moves that take them out of stance or position, and all players must be constantly ready to take advantage of opponents' mistakes. Keeping in stance is the most important physical readiness concept for defenders. Coaches need to remind players constantly to get in and stay in stance—be ready for the opponent's best move. Coaches and players can use this concept as a subjective measure of defense. Great defensive players and teams can stay in a quick stance during the entire defensive possession.

CRITICAL CUE:
Get in and
stay in stance.

Essentials of Defense

In addition to being proactive defenders, players must know nine essentials of defense: transition, purpose, pressure, position, prevention of penetration, moving, line of the ball, blocking out, and communication.

Transition.   The first task is to anticipate shifting from offense to defense, which requires an organized transition with communication among all five players and includes rebounding balance (assume that every shot will miss and get back on defense or go to the offensive boards). Sprint to protect the defensive basket, pick up the ball, find shooters, and recover to all open offensive players. Players going to defense should sprint toward the defensive end of the floor while seeing the ball (look over the inside shoulder—red-light situation) but may run or slide backward (yellow-light situation) once the offense is contained. Defense starts when a shot is taken on offense and ends with a defensive rebound, steal, caused turnover, or opponent's basket. One useful rule for defenders, when the opponents gain possession of the ball, is to sprint at least three quick steps to defense with vision on the ball, looking over the inside shoulder. See the ball during the whole transition. Transition to the defensive basket should be in straight lines parallel to the sideline, which helps the team cover all outside shooters better.

CRITICAL CUE:
On a shot, go to
defense, or go to
offensive rebound.

Purpose.   The purpose of defense is to prevent easy scores and to gain possession of the ball through rebounds or steals. Defenders must learn to prevent situations leading to easy baskets by opponents (i.e., prevent *all* layups). Make the offense work to get all shots (and only under pressure; i.e., give the opponents one pressured shot). The overall goal of defense is to prevent the opponents from scoring. Since this is impossible, the best defensive purpose is to allow the opponents only one contested shot.

Pressure.   Offensive play has a basic rhythm that can be disrupted by pressure. Defensive play must maintain continuous physical and mental pressure on ball-handlers. Every shot also must be pressured physically and verbally. Bother players who have the ball (live ball or dribbling), swarm the player with a dead ball (used dribble), and be ready to protect the basket and support the defender on the ball when defending off the ball. Pressure *all* shots by making the shooter adjust the shot. The hand should go up through the face area to disrupt the shot. Ball pressure must be combined with off-the-ball position and readiness.

Position.   Coaches should train players to stay in a stance and be in proper court position when on defense. Sprint to the next position as the ball moves on offense. Most fouls occur when defenders are out of position or have not maintained individual defensive stance. Players should get in and stay in a defensive quick stance as they maintain proper defensive position relative to the ball and the basket. Whenever the opponent passes or dribbles the ball, defenders should sprint to help the defender guarding the ball.

Prevention of Penetration.   Offensive players attempt to take the ball toward the basket by passing or dribbling. Defenders must prevent this penetration whenever possible. One defender always pressures the ball while the four other players play zone areas toward the basket to protect it and support the defender playing on the ball. Defenders should prevent middle-of-the-floor penetration toward the goal by offensive players using the dribble or direct air passes to this area when playing on-the-ball defense (especially the power zone shown in figure 7.1). Off-the-ball defense means keeping passes and dribble drives out of the middle of the floor (especially the power zone) by defending zone areas toward the basket area. Defenders should play zone defense and support the defender playing on the ball. Prevent the ball and the offensive player from entering the power zone.

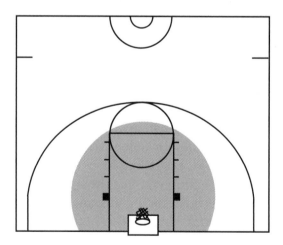

FIGURE 7.1   **Power zone—located 15 to 18 feet (4.6 to 5.5 meters) from the basket.**

CRITICAL CUE:
Defenders move
when the ball moves
(sprint to help).

Moving.   Players must learn to move every time the ball is passed. All five players should adjust their floor positions with every pass. On the ball, after the ballhandler passes the ball, the defender moves instantly toward the ball and the basket—jumping or exploding to the ball. Off the ball, defensive players adjust their positions toward the ball with every pass.

Line of the Ball.   The line of the ball principle states that players should defend their opponent only after they have taken a position ahead of the ball and toward their defensive basket. This position is past the line of the ball, a side-to-side line through the ballhandler's location. In figure 7.2, X_1 and X_2 need to get ahead of the ball at O_1 before getting in proper defensive position to defend the opponent with the ball as well as the other opponents who do not have the ball.

Blocking Out. Each defensive player is responsible for blocking (checking) offensive players from the basket area and gaining the defensive rebound when a shot is taken. Successful coaches recognize that defensive rebounding is an important part of team defense and devote appropriate time to teaching it (see chapter 8).

Communication. Communication is always necessary for group success. All players must react to each other verbally and physically to produce an effective team defense. Essentially, the five players should act as one. Coach Mike Krzyzewski of Duke University says a team is similar to the relation between the fingers and a fist. Fingers alone cannot accomplish nearly what they can do when gathered into a fist. Communication links all five fingers into a fist, just as it links all five players into a defensive team. Especially on defense, players cannot talk too much.

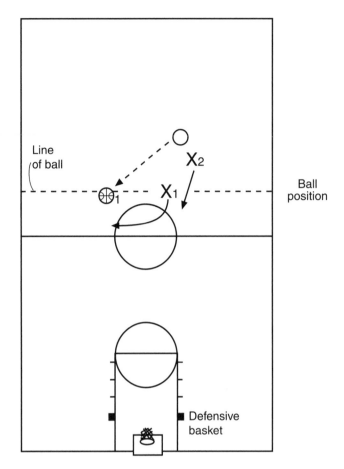

FIGURE 7.2 **Line of the ball.**

On-the-Ball Defense

On-the-ball defense can be considered the spearhead of the defense; all good defense starts by defending the ball. In the defensive location, the concepts of seeing the assigned offensive player and guarding the ball merge and can both be accomplished, but on-the-ball defense is also one of the most challenging defensive tasks, one which requires both technique and determination.

The skills, principles, and defensive concepts in this section are based on the experiences of a lifetime of coaching defensive stance and steps—the footwork needed to be a successful defender when guarding the ballhandler. As players become more skilled ballhandlers as well as bigger and better athletes, the advantage for offensive players increases. Without proper and highly skilled defensive techniques, defending 1-on-1 on-the-ball situations is virtually impossible.

These recommended on-the-ball defensive techniques have evolved to meet the increasing challenges of the modern game and the advantages of offensive players. The concepts have been developed through collective playing and coaching experience, but especially through discussions with Mike Nilson, strength and conditioning coach at Gonzaga University. Mike has incorporated the concepts of balance and quickness into the recommended on-the-ball defensive skills. These recommendations allow all players to become significantly better on-the-ball defenders.

Defending the Live Ball

When guarding a player with a live ball (the player still has the dribble), the defender needs to be in a defensive quick stance with active feet (footfire). Communicate *ball* when the offense catches the ball and then say *ready, ready*. Defenders should be taught to maintain their position between the ballhandler and the basket (ball-defender-basket), as shown in figure 7.3, to prevent dribble penetration as they recognize and take away the ballhandler's strengths (on the preferred or dominant side).

Distracting and disrupting the player with the ball while preventing pass and dribble penetration are also important. Force and encourage slow bounce or lob passes using active feet (patter step) and hands, from a stance with the arms and the legs bent (for quickness and balance). Match the offensive player toes to toes, in a squared up ball-player-basket relationship (don't shade or open the defensive stance and expose the basket). The feet are in a staggered stance, with the inside foot slightly forward and the back foot toed outward slightly. The recommendation is for the back or the butt to be pointed toward the basket to facilitate lateral movement (figure 7.4). This stance is low and wide, with the hips down, the knees spread, and the head lower than the offensive player's head, level with that player's chest. Dropping the back foot too much is an error that results in the defender opening the door for the dribble drive. It is sometimes called *matador defense* because it allows the offensive player easier access to the dribble drive to the side of the dropped foot and causes the defender to become a bullfight matador—waving to the offensive dribble driver as he passes. This foot position also makes it more difficult to move laterally with quickness in order to maintain the ball-player-basket relationship. It also exposes a dribble move to the side of the front foot (figure 7.5) that is difficult to defend. Players should position themselves with their butts to the basket in order to flatten out or

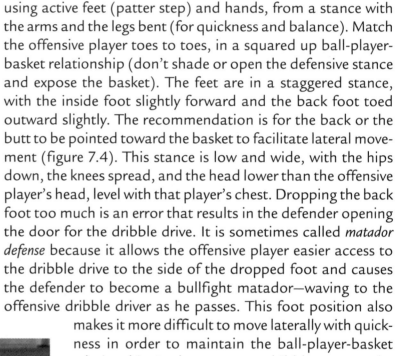

FIGURE 7.3 Ball-defender-basket: the relative relationship of the defender to the basket and the offensive player (with the ball) being guarded.

FIGURE 7.4 Defensive stance with the butt to the basket.

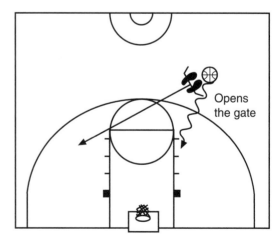

FIGURE 7.5 On-the-ball defense—too much of a staggered stance.

arc the offensive player laterally—to prevent dribble penetration. They seldom need to swing or drop step on a live-ball move if their stance and hands are in the proper position. This position allows the defender to keep the trunk and chest in front of the ballhandler in a ball-defender-basket alignment without grabbing or holding with the hands.

The recommended hand position on the live ball is for the ball-side hand (usually the front hand) above the front foot to mirror the position of the ball. *Mirror* the ball by doing the following:

- Ball overhead—the front hand should be overhead as the arm is extended to deflect the pass as the defender moves closer. This can be done with a quick two-foot hop forward. With the ball overhead, the offensive player reduces the threat of the quick drive or shot (the ball overhead, the hand up, and move closer). Stay in a quick stance, with the front arm extended and vertical and the back hand near the front hand or near the waist in a horizontal arm bar position, ready for contact (figure 7.6*a*).

- Ball in the shooting pocket—the hand in front and over near the ball (if possible), ready to challenge and change a shot attempt and prevent a quick air pass by the ear (figure 7.6*b*).

- Ball low—the hand horizontal and above the ball to prevent a quick shot or bringing the ball up or across the body (high or low rip or circle tight move), as shown in figure 7.6*c*. Playing lower than the offensive player with the ball low is especially important because of the increased threat of the dribble drive. The defender must keep the trunk in

FIGURE 7.6 **Defensive hand positioning—live ball:** *(a)* ball overhead, *(b)* ball in triple-threat position, and *(c)* ball low.

the ball-player-basket position to prevent the driver from lowering the shoulder and getting the head and shoulders by the defender on the dribble drive.

The other hand is flexed at the elbow and is in front of the body, ready to become the disrupter when the ball is moved to the opposite side by the offensive player. This back hand is ready to chase the ball following a pass to this side; get a touch on any pass to that side.

Taking a stand on the ball is the phrase that coaches can use to remind players to get and maintain a ball-player-basket position on ballhandlers as they attempt to distract and disrupt the players with the ball. Be close enough to get a touch on the ball, about an arm's length. This technique applies to defending the live ball and the dribbler.

Note: On an offensive jab step, use a 6-inch (15.2-centimeter) retreat step to that side. This is a power push-step slide to prevent the possible dribble drive.

CRITICAL CUE:
Take a stand on
the ballhandler.

Defending the Dribbler.   Defending a dribbler, the point position, is done with a gap close enough to get a touch on the ball but adjusted to the quickness of both the offensive and the defensive player. On determining the direction of the offensive player using the dribble drive, the defender uses push steps to prevent the drive and maintain or regain the ball-defender-basket position. A slight rear turn is made in the direction of the dribble drive as the defender uses repeated explosive push steps (usually three steps) from the power leg to prevent dribble penetration. A good defensive reminder is that defenders should use their mind, feet, and bodies to stop the dribbler. Anticipate the drive direction (mind), use explosive push steps (lead with the foot in the direction of movement) to maintain the ball-player-basket position, and take contact on the chest or trunk in a legal guarding position to prevent dribble penetration. If the dribbler gets by the defender (head and shoulders past), the defender then turns and sprints to regain the ball-player-basket position (run to recover).

Push-Step Technique.   From a balanced defensive quick stance, players should thrust the lead foot (in the direction of movement) laterally as the head and body weight are shifted in that direction. That foot is toed outward slightly as the same foot position of the quick stance is maintained. Although some coaches prefer pointing the lead foot, keeping the feet parallel is preferable. The power for the push step comes from a forceful push from the power or trail foot. The movement of the lead and trail foot is 6 to 18 inches (15.2 to 45.7 centimeters) laterally as the feet are kept at shoulder width or wider. The trail foot then returns to quick-stance position. Usually, three explosive push steps are sufficient to prevent dribble penetration in one direction. Then, the dribbler is either past the defender (run to recover) or reverses direction on the dribble (the defender must then use three push steps in the opposite direction). Partial rear turns may be needed to maintain proper defensive position prior to the push steps.

The teaching segments for the lateral push-step movement are the following:

* Use a partial rear turn when needed to stay ahead of the dribbler and to maintain the ball-player-basket position (figure 7.7a).

* Explosively push from the trail foot as the lead foot moves laterally 6 to 18 inches (15.2 to 45.7 centimeters) and the head and body weight shifts in the direction of movement (figure 7.7b).

- Focus on lead foot landing with balanced weight distribution (toe and heel hit at once, with 60 percent of the weight on the ball of the foot) while maintaining a parallel stance with the feet (or toes pointed slightly outward).
- The trail foot also moves 6 to 18 inches (15.2 to 45.7 centimeters) as the feet maintain a shoulder-width relationship (figure 7.7c).
- The start and end of the movement are always from and to a balanced quick-stance position (with the feet only slightly toed out).

CRITICAL CUE:
Push step and slide, low and wide, can't get too low, can't get too wide.

Push-step technique is sometimes called *step and slide* motion. A verbal prompt (*push step and slide, low and wide, can't get too low, can't get too wide*) is a good learning reminder.

Three push steps should stop the dribbler; otherwise, the run-to-recover move is needed to regain the ball-defender-basket position. The complete push-step sequence is shown in figure 7.7.

In the point stance, the player's nose is on the ball to get ahead of the dribbler. The near (dig) hand is pointing to the ball, with the elbow bent and the palm up. When step-sliding to the right, the player's near (dig) hand is the left hand. The lead (back) hand is in the "thumb-in-ear" position, the elbow at a right angle, and the forearm acting like a windshield wiper. Moving right, the right hand is the thumb-in-ear or wiper hand, used to take away or prevent the quick air pass by the ear.

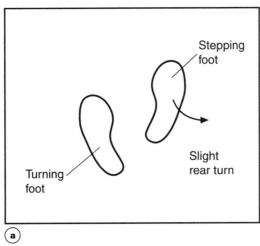

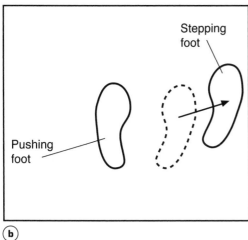
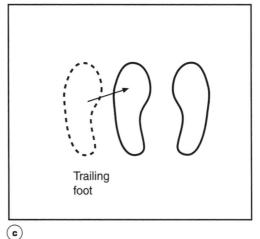

FIGURE 7.7   **Sequence for the push step direction of movement: *(a)* partial rear turn (only when needed), *(b)* push step, and *(c)* return to quick stance.**

Communicate *point, point* when the dribbler puts the ball on the floor. Turn the dribbler in the backcourt, adjust to the ball-defender-basket position in the frontcourt. On a spin dribble, players should jump back away from the dribbler a step to prevent the dribbler from hooking them to go by.

Traditional Method of Defending the Live Ball.   Live-ball defenders must be ready in a defensive quick stance in a ball-player-basket position. The forward foot may be placed opposite the dominant hand of the offensive player. If that player is right-handed, defenders can have the left leg and arm forward to force the offensive player to pass or dribble with the weak hand. Another option is to place the inside foot slightly forward in the ball-player-basket position. Coaches should have players defend with the palm of the lead hand facing the ball (see figure 7.8), allowing them to move easily, flick at, and pressure the ball. This is a more common hand position when players are guarding the live ball.

Players should distract and disrupt with the hands as they keep the inside foot slightly forward. Most coaches prefer to have the inside foot forward, as shown in figure 7.9. In addition, many coaches prefer to point the lead foot during step-slide defensive movement to cut off lateral movement. When a dribbler gets her head and shoulders past, run to recover.

CRITICAL CUE:
Hands on the ball and not on the offensive player.

FIGURE 7.8   Live-ball defense: lead hand palm facing forward, trail hand palm facing up. The right foot is forward against the right-handed offensive player.

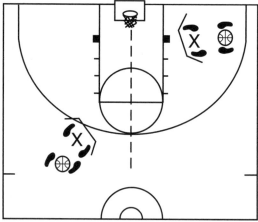

FIGURE 7.9   Foot position—the inside foot forward.

CRITICAL CUE:
Dead ball—
swarm or *sag*.

Defending the Dead Ball

When a ballhandler has used the dribble, the two recommended techniques are *swarming* the ball, tracing the ball with both hands and attacking the player's senses while staying in a stance, as shown in figure 7.10 (pressure option), or dropping back toward the basket while staying in the ball-player-basket relationship to anticipate the next pass and help the team defense (sagging option). The latter can be used especially when the ballhandler is out of shooting range. The pressure option is called the *stick* position (communication *stick, stick*) to alert defensive teammates to deny other passing lanes.

Off-the-Ball Defense

This most challenging and crucial individual defensive skill makes a significant contribution to team defense. Despite a natural tendency for players to relax away from the ball, they must learn the importance of off-the-ball defense. Coaches should teach them that protecting the basket and supporting the defender playing on the ball is as important as attending to the assigned player away from the ball (see

FIGURE 7.10 **Attack the senses on a dead ball.**

the man, but guard the ball). These multiple tasks require greater attention than on-the-ball defense.

The two types of off-the-ball stances are open (pistols) stance, farther from the ball (two passes away), and closed (denial) stance, closer to the ball (one pass away). These stances are shown in figure 7.11: X_2, X_3, and X_5 using a closed stance and X_4 using an open stance to support defender X_1 guarding the ballhandler. The common concept is that off-the-ball defenders are in a position of player guarded-defender-ball.

Several other guidelines can be taught to players about defending away from the ball. The farther the offensive player is from the ball, the farther the defender should be from the assigned opponent, always maintaining a ball-defender-player position. The defender needs to keep a gap (a distance cushion to provide extra reaction time), as shown in figures 7.11 and 7.12. The closer the ball is to the defender, the closer the defender should be to the assigned opponent away from the ball.

What the defender does before the offensive player gets the ball determines what the offensive player can do with the ball. Defenders should keep the ball away from the assigned opponent in favorite spots on the floor. Always take away an opponent's strength on the ball or off the ball.

Player cuts to the ball (ball-defender-player position) in the middle or power zone areas should be prevented. Teach defenders to force offensive players to go around or away from a desired position. If contact must be made, the

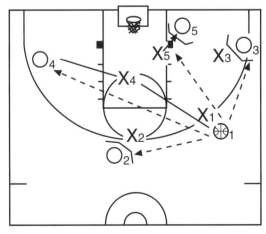

FIGURE 7.11 **Closed stance (X_2, X_3, X_5), open stance (X_4).**

FIGURE 7.12 Open stance—the off-the-ball defender forms the flat triangle and *points pistols* (at responsibilities).

CRITICAL CUE:
Closed (denial) stance—the hand in the lane, the thumb down, the ear in the chest, the body positioned as ball-defender-player being guarded, the foot closest to the ball forward.

defender should beat the offensive player to a desired spot, make contact using an arm bar and a closed stance, force the cutter high, and then reestablish a gap.

Seeing the ball at all times allows players to defend the ballhandler and support the defender playing on the ball more easily. Players should follow the ball visually to anticipate offensive cuts and careless passes. Guard the ball, and see the offensive player being guarded. The ball always scores, not the player.

Players two passes away from the ball should assume an open stance, which allows them to see the ball and their assigned opponents. In this position, one hand points at the ball and the other points at the opponent—*pointing pistols*—forming a flat triangle: ball-defender-player being guarded (figure 7.12).

Defenders near the ball need to develop the skill of denying the pass to the player they are guarding—closed stance. The defender is in a ball-defender-player guarded position. In a closed stance, players should place the back partially to the ball (seeing both the ball over their shoulders and the players they are guarding) while putting the lead foot (the foot closest to the ball) and the lead hand in the passing lane, with the thumb down, the fingers spread, and the palm facing the ball. Put the ear at the level of the chest of the offensive player. Denial pressure can vary from the hand in the passing lane (moderate) to the elbow in the lane and the shoulder or the head in the lane (high).

The back hand near the opponent is the brush hand (the back of the hand feels the opponent, ready for use as the arm bar when the opponent cuts to the ball). Make a fist with the brush hand to prevent grabbing or holding fouls. The defender's vision is *down the gun barrel* of the extended near arm.

In a closed stance (denying the pass to the player guarded), the offensive player needs to V-cut to get open, so the defender must stay in a closed stance and move continually to maintain the desired ball-defender-player guarded position. Also, when overplayed, the player guarded may cut behind the defender in a backdoor move. The proper response to the backdoor cut is to go with and stay in the ball-defender-player guarded closed stance position (snap the head and change the denial hand) until the cutter reaches the lane, then open up and assume the open stance to see the ball. Do not follow the cutter away from the ball. See figure 7.13. The communication on all off-the-ball situations of open or closed stance is *help right, help right* or *help left, help left*. A defender in the key calls *hoop, hoop*.

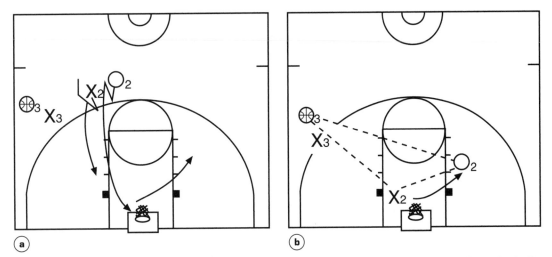

FIGURE 7.13 **Defending the backdoor cut:** *(a)* move with cutter, *(b)* open up away from the ball.

Post Defense

Techniques for players learning to guard an offensive post player in or around the free-throw lane include the ball-defender-player closed stance (with the hand across the passing lane in a ball-defender-offensive player arrangement, figure 7.14*a*) and the fronting stance (see figure 7.14*b*). As a general rule, the ball should be kept out of the power zone (post area) using one of these two stances. In a closed stance, the hand is in the passing lane (ball-defender-player guarded) with the thumb down and the palm facing the ball.

The most common post defense technique is the closed stance, in which players are avoiding contact unless they have a position advantage, keeping a hand in the passing lane, and defending in a position on the side of the defender. This technique is most often used with a high post (free-throw line area) or medium post. This half-front position is a compromise between keeping the ball out of the post area and being ready to check or block out the post player when a perimeter shot is taken. One added position rule is needed: when the offensive post is in the low or medium post position, players should take a position above the post player when the perimeter passer with the ball is above the free-throw line extended and take a closed stance position below or on the baseline side when the ball is below the free-throw line extended (figure 7.15). When the ball changes positions relative to the free-throw line, the defender can choose to go behind the post (easier, but more susceptible to a deep re-post) or in front of the post (more difficult, but prevents post entry passes better) to regain the closed stance with the ball-defender-player guarded position.

When in a fronting stance, the defender should see the ball and stay in defensive stance, with radar bumper contact (the butt front) and the hands up. This allows the defender to anticipate and move for the pass to the post. The fronting stance has

FIGURE 7.14 Post defense: *(a)* closed stance—low side and *(b)* fronting stance.

CRITICAL CUE:
Fronting post—stay in stance with the hands up and butt contact; be ready to move for the pass.

the advantage of keeping the ball from post players better but also the disadvantage of giving the offensive post player a definite edge for rebounding when a perimeter shot is taken.

Offensive post players control defenders by establishing and maintaining contact. Post defenders should avoid contact unless they have an advantage in position, maintaining a safe distance from the ballhandler and continuing to move in order to keep the offensive post player (and the passer) guessing.

The basic fundamentals also apply to defending a post player with the ball; defenders should stay in a defensive quick stance with both hands ready. When an offensive post player receives the ball in the low or medium post area, the defender

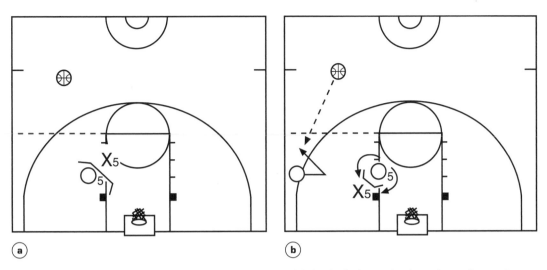

FIGURE 7.15 **Defending the post—closed stance:** *(a)* the ball above the free-throw line and *(b)* the ball below the free-throw line.

should be taught to take a step back and reestablish a ball-defender-basket position to prevent angle baskets. Maintaining distance gives the defender reaction time to defend against an offensive post move, prevents the offensive post player from using contact to control the defender, and allows a teammate time to help from the perimeter.

On-the-Ball to Off-the-Ball Defense

When a player is guarding the ballhandler as a pass is made, a necessary and immediate transition from on-the-ball status (ball-defender-basket position) to off-the-ball status (ball-defender-player guarded position) is achieved by jumping (or exploding) to the ball (primarily) and to the basket (secondarily) to assume a closed or open stance, as shown in figure 7.16. This technique, also called *chasing the ball*, involves attempting to touch the pass with the hand nearest the direction of the pass. Jumping to the ball prevents the passer from using a pass-and-cut move to make a front cut to catch a return pass going toward the basket.

CRITICAL CUE:
On-the-ball defender—
ball moves,
move to the ball
(chase the ball).

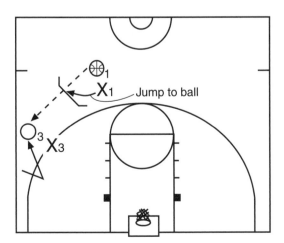
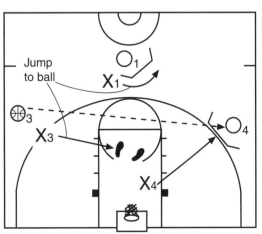

FIGURE 7.16 **Explode (jump) to the ball on every pass or dribble move.**

Off-the-Ball to On-the-Ball Defense

When the opponents have the ball, another defensive transition, called *closing out to the ball*, occurs when players change status from off-the-ball (open stance) to on-the-ball coverage and are in a help defensive position (protecting the basket and supporting the defender on the ball) when the ball is passed to the player being guarded. The correct technique for closing out to the ball is described following and shown in figure 7.17.

- Sprint halfway to the guarded player with the ball (close out short).
- Breakdown into a regular defensive stance using active feet (stutter steps) with both hands above the shoulders and above head level. Approach the ballhandler with caution on the line between the ball and the basket to prevent the drive, but be aggressive and prepared to contest a shot or pass.
- Recommended foot position is with the inside foot up (the belly to the sideline or the baseline).
- Close out in a ball-defender-basket path (prevent the drive).
- Close out short (keep a gap) with the body weight back. Throw the hands up and back to prevent the quick air pass.

The objective on a closeout is to prevent penetration (a dribble or quick air pass past the head) and then pressure the ballhandler, especially on the shot.

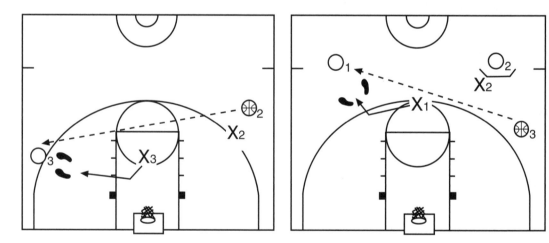

FIGURE 7.17 Closeout—off-the-ball to on-the-ball.

Special Defensive Situations

In addition to the basic skills of on-the-ball and off-the-ball defense, several other tactics can help the team defend against special offensive threats. A situation that occurs mostly on defense but can occur on offense is a loose ball from a bad pass, errant dribble, or any loss of ball control by an offensive player. The best rule for this situation is to get both hands on the ball; if it is in the air, use a two-handed pickup and snap the ball to a quick-stop and chinit position. Capture and chin a

COACHING POINTS FOR DEFENSE

General

- ☐ Get in a stance and stay in a stance.
- ☐ Use the mind, body, feet, and eyes as the first tools of defense.
- ☐ Use the hands only as a secondary defensive weapon.
- ☐ Prevent easy scores; allow no layups and one pressured shot.
- ☐ Keep pressure on the ball.
- ☐ Prevent penetration by the pass or dribble.
- ☐ Move on every pass or dribble.
- ☐ Take away the opponent's strength.
- ☐ Upset offensive rhythm.

On-the-Ball

- ☐ Get low and stay low. Be lower than the offensive player (nose in the chest).
- ☐ Maintain the ball-defender-basket position.
- ☐ Guard players in a live-ball situation: front foot to front foot, hands and feet active, and within touching distance (lead or front hand up).
- ☐ Keep space between yourself and the dribbler (i.e., keep a gap, but get a touch).
- ☐ Guard the dribbler, keep the head and chest in front, jab with the lead hand, and run to recover when necessary.
- ☐ Guard a dead-ball situation: swarm the ballhandler and trace the ball without fouling or sag away from the ballhandler.
- ☐ Jump (explode) to the ball when a pass is made (chase the ball). Always move toward the ball on every pass or dribble—sprint to help.

Off-the-Ball

- ☐ Close out to the ball when it is passed to an assigned offensive player; sprint, breakdown, and prevent the drive (always close out short—prevent the drive). Close out on the driving line to the basket.
- ☐ Maintain the ball-defender-basket position.
- ☐ Get in an open (*pistols*) stance far from the ball or a closed (the hand across and the thumb down) stance close to the ball.
- ☐ Keep the ball from offensive post players unless they are no offensive threat.
- ☐ Be able to help and make the decision to bluff or switch on screens, penetrations, or closeouts.

loose ball (a two-handed skill). If the ball is on the floor, dive on the loose ball with both hands. Rules require players to pass to an open teammate before getting up from the floor with the ball.

CRITICAL CUE: Capture and chin a loose ball; never dribble a loose ball.

Help and Decide

On clearouts or any penetration situation, the off-the-ball defenders make critical decisions: help and rotate (protect the basket and cover the penetrating dribble) and decide (to switch defensive assignments, trap with the defender on the ball, or bluff to buy recovery time for the teammate guarding the dribbler). Communication is the key—be ready to help and communicate the decision. Two options are shown in figure 7.18. The critical help situation in this case, called *help on the help* by X_1 in figure 7.18*a*, occurs when X_3 helps on dribble penetration of O_2 outside the free-throw lane.

Defenders should use the help-and-decide defensive technique to combat the offensive tactic of a dribble penetration, which clears out one side of the court for the ballhandler to dribble drive to beat the defender. The off-the-ball defender should be ready to help and decide to help or switch if the defender on the ball is beaten or when the assigned player vacates the area.

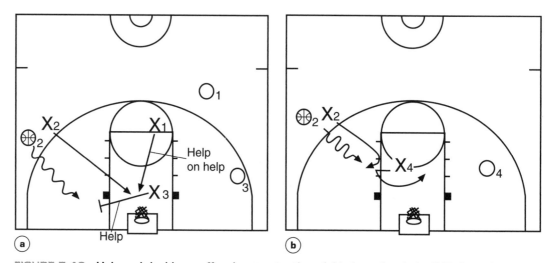

FIGURE 7.18 **Help and decide on offensive penetration:** *(a)* **help and switch,** *(b)* **help and recover.**

Screens

When an offensive player screens or shields a defender to assist a teammate in getting an open shot, special tactics must be used, including avoiding screens whenever possible—defenders should be in motion when offensive players approach them to set a screen. Screens generally can be defeated by fighting through (going over or under) the screen, in which case a teammate may help out the screened defender by using a show-and-go move (figure 7.19); by switching assigned opponents, especially when a defender is unable to get through the screen (figure 7.20); or by trapping the dribbler on a screen. The defender guarding the screener switches forward, calls the switch, and contains the ballhandler.

On screens away from the ball, players should avoid or slide through these screens, usually on the ball side. Be a moving target; don't be screened. Players should stay sideways and use their arms as shock absorbers to prevent the screener from getting to their bodies. The player guarding the screener should jump to the ball, stay ball side, and help a teammate through the screen. Give help when needed.

Traps

Coaches also may want to develop defensive techniques to handle an exceptional offensive player or to function as a surprise tactic. Trapping occurs when two defenders double-team an offensive ballhandler (2-on-1) in certain court areas or on ball screens. Coaches should emphasize that both players must stop the ball-

FIGURE 7.19 **Fighting through screens:** *(a)* go over the top, *(b)* helper *shows* to help, *(c)* teammate recovers when the offensive player leaves.

handler from escaping the trap by being in good defensive basic position, keeping the feet active, positioning themselves knee-to-knee, and keeping the inside hands up to prevent a quick air pass. The objective is to force a lob or bounce pass, and players should learn not to reach for the ball or commit a foul. All other off-the-ball teammates should close off the nearest passing lanes to prevent any passes from the trap into their zones (play a three-player zone). The best places to set traps are in the corners of the court (figure 7.21). An example of a frontcourt trap is also shown. The trap is made in a frontcourt corner, and the other defenders deny the near passing lanes and force the offense to play on half of the court.

CRITICAL CUE:
Defensive traps—the feet active, the inside hand up, contain without fouling.

FIGURE 7.20 **Switch screen:** *(a)* helper (on right) steps up to switch on the ballhandler; *(b)* the helper calls the switch and a teammate exchanges the assigned players to defend.

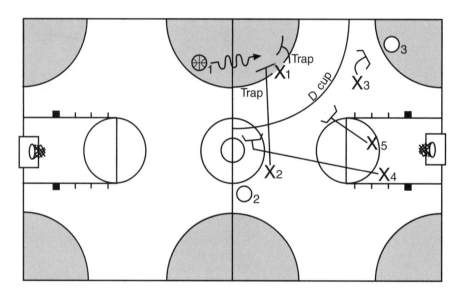

FIGURE 7.21 **Optimal trapping locations.**

Defensive Charge

The defensive charge—one of the fundamental defensive plays in basketball—is used when a defender has beaten an offensive cutter to a desired position on the floor and is in a legal guarding position. This charge must be taught properly not only for its great potential as a team play (it can prevent an opponent's three-point play and result in two free throws for the defender), but also because it involves a contact skill that must be developed progressively to avoid injury. The rules that apply to this situation are that the defender is entitled to any spot on the floor that is taken in a legal guarding position; the dribbler needs no room, but the defender must be in a legal position before the offensive player's head and shoulders pass the defender's body; away from the ball, the offensive cutter must be given the chance to change direction (never more than two steps); the defender must always be in a legal guarding position before a player becomes airborne; and defenders can move their feet and protect their bodies.

Players should be taught these techniques for taking the charge:

1. Get in and stay in a good defensive basic stance and keep the feet active (foot patter) to adjust position. The defender must be knocked down from the legal position, but not flop on contact.

2. Take the blow in the chest area.

3. Resist giving up an established position, but keep most of the weight on the heels (must be knocked down).

4. Keep the arms out of the action and use them for protection as in screen setting technique—protect vital areas (different areas for men and women).

5. Fall properly—with the arms up and in front, the buttocks should hit the floor first, followed by the lower and upper back as the palms slap the floor. Keep the head in a curled chin tuck position (see figure 7.22).

FIGURE 7.22 Defensive charge—falling properly: *(a)* The defender must be knocked down (position for protecting the vital parts with the arms—women cross the chest, men cover groin area); *(b)* landing—rear end first, back roll, the head curl or tuck; *(c)* scramble to regain basic position.

6. Assume that the officials will not call an offensive foul and scramble up to regain basic position.

7. Know when to take the charge. Disrupt the offensive player's movement, but pick a situation in which the offensive player has poor body control and is not alert.

Pressuring the Shot

A special skill is needed when defending the player with the ball and a set or jump shot is taken. The general rule is to pressure every shot as follows:

- Stay in the stance and have the ball-side hand up when the ball is in the shooting pocket (triple-threat position)—don't leave the feet until the shooter does.
- Use the lead hand to force the shooter to alter the shot—don't try to block it; make the shooter change the shot. The lead hand goes up and past the face on the shot.
- Keep the lead hand up in a vertical position with the wrist back (don't slap down and cause a foul).
- Apply verbal pressure also (shout, make noise, scream, call names). Yell *shot* to alert teammates of a rebound situation (help them see and hear the shot).

TROUBLESHOOTING

Common defensive errors and coaching responses:

Problem: Players do not get in and stay in a stance.
Correction: Review or reteach stance and gradually increase the time spent in defensive stance—increase emphasis and reminders. During team play, develop team consequences when a player comes out of a stance.

Problem: Lack of motivation to play defense.
Correction: Reason with players; provide concrete reasons for the necessity of effective defense. Emphasize and demand high levels of defense.

Problem: Slow reaction to ball movement.
Correction: Emphasize sprinting to the next assignment.

Problem: Not talking on defense.
Correction: Emphasize communication; during drills, require talking on every ball movement (incentives and consequences) and recognize the defensive communicator of the day.

Problem: Fear of taking defensive charges, diving on floor for loose balls.
Correction: Do sequential, progressive teaching and physical practicing of the skill to ensure safety and provide experience. Recognize great team plays (incentives).

Problem: Not playing hard on defense.
Correction: Convince players that getting coached depends on their best effort; establish playing hard as a tradition; substitute in competitive practice and game situations.

Problem: Lack of defensive confidence.
Correction: Provide success situations in practice, demand effectiveness and execution that produce success, and define success in terms of proper technique and effort instead of the ultimate result (makes or misses).

Defensive Drills

Insist on execution first, but demand intensity on defense. Players must learn to play hard individually in order to develop a cohesive team defense.

STANCE AND STEPS PROGRESSION

Purpose: To provide a sequential method of developing defensive stance and power push-step (step-slide) technique.

Equipment: Floor space for movement (half court).

Procedure: Players are spaced facing the coach and perform the sequences on command or at their own pace. Five repetitions of each move are recommended.

1. One-foot balance, defensive stance, with the chest up, the butt muscles on stretch, the trunk slightly forward (alternate hops with the right and the left foot).

2. Lateral jumps (one foot to one foot—right to left and left to right); side jumps from a one-foot stance to a one-foot stance on the opposite foot.

3. Lateral jumps with recovery steps (place the other foot down to gain balance in the push-step slide).

4. Consecutive lateral jumps with recovery steps—three repetitions in one direction (left and right).

5. Lateral seamless push steps—three repetitions in each direction.

6. Piggyback seamless push steps (three right, three left, three left, three right).

7. Free-throw lateral lane slides—push steps from outside the lane to the opposite side and return (right to left, left to right).

8. Baseline closeouts and lateral push steps (three right, three left). Four lines or line drill with one offensive player 15 to 18 feet (4.6 to 5.5 meters) from the baseline defensive players.

   - Pass to offender (O), defender (D) closeout
   - O goes two dribbles right, D closes out and defends with push steps
   - O two dribbles left, D closes out and defends with push steps
   - O two dribbles right, reverse to two left, D closes out and defends
   - O two dribbles left, reverse to two right, D closes out and defends
   - O two dribbles right or left, D closes out and defends
   - O two dribbles right or left, then one spin dribble reverse, D closes out and defends

Coaching Points

- Stay in defensive quick stance.
- Emphasize quickness with balance.
- Take a stand on the ball—maintain the ball-defender-basket relationship.
- Use explosive push steps.
- Step and slide, low and wide.
- Defend with the mind, the feet, and the body (in balance).
- Do it properly first and then quickly.

MOVING STANCE AND STEPS

Purpose: To develop individual defensive stance and steps.

Equipment: One ball for coach, half court (minimum).

Procedure: All players are spaced about the court, facing the coach with a clear view. They assume a basic defensive stance at the coach's signal (*palm down*) and respond to the coach's signals and commands with continuous defensive stance and step moves. The coach uses the ball for most signals. The direction moves used are shown in figure 7.23.

Signals and Meaning Movement

Palm down for live ball	Basic stance; active feet
Ball in stomach or back dribble	Slide forward
Ball in right front or dribble drive right	Angle slide right
Ball in left front or dribble drive left	Angle slide left
Finger point left to right or side dribble	Push step
Ball in triple-threat position, then toss ball on the floor or loose ball	Close out and dive on the floor for loose ball
Ball overhead or dead ball	Stay in stance or the hands around the ball
Shoot the ball in place or shot	Defenders call shot; block out and rebound imaginary ball

Note: This drill can be done with three steps and active feet for any step-slide signals and then later continuously until the next signal is given.

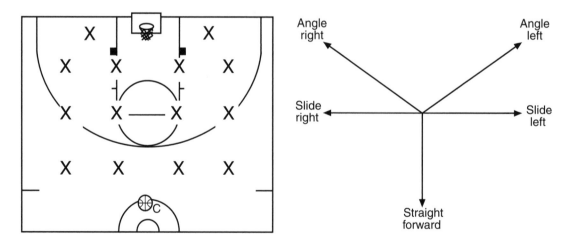

FIGURE 7.23 **Moving stance and steps—direction of movement.**

LINE DRILL: INDIVIDUAL DEFENSE

Purpose: To develop individual defensive skills in a progressive manner.

Equipment: Ball for every two players (at least four balls or one per line).

Procedure: Players form four lines on the baseline. Players execute an offensive or defensive zigzag (zigzag in pairs). The first player in each line assumes a defensive stance with the next player in an offensive stance. The offensive player zigzags down the floor while the defender maintains defensive distance and a ball-defender-basket position. Players switch positions on the return trip.

Options: These moves should be done in this sequence as a learning progression.

- Offensive zigzag—90-degree change of direction without the ball and then with the ball (dribbling).

- Defensive zigzag—(three push steps) or using 45-degree backward defensive slides (the lead hand with the palm up, flicking at an imaginary ball, the trail hand near the shoulder or the thumb in the air). On change of direction, players lead with the elbow as they rear turn and continue slides at a 90-degree change of direction—going baseline to baseline using swing steps and push-step sliding technique.

- Defensive zigzag—90-degree change of direction with running steps (simulates getting beaten by the dribbler). The move always starts and ends with push-step sliding steps; slide diagonally left (dribbler gets past), sprint to reestablish position, break down and slide again; change direction and repeat (slide, run, slide). Continue baseline to baseline.

- Offensive-defensive zigzag—offensive and defensive pairs. The offensive dribbler first coaches the zigzag defender while zigzag moving and carrying the ball under the armpit to simulate the dribble. Start with three push-step slides and then continuously zigzag. Then the offensive player dribbles down the floor (using pull-back crossover, regular dribble crossover, spin dribble, or behind-the-back dribble moves)—the focus is still to make the defender perfect.

- Offensive-defensive zigzag in pairs—live offense and defense in two alleys down the court.

- 1-on-1 full court—live offense and defense to score; defender slides, runs when needed, turns the dribbler in the backcourt, pushes to the weak hand or the sideline in the frontcourt, maintains ball-defender-basket relationship, prevents layups. Mix all player pairs.

ON-THE-BALL AND OFF-THE-BALL DRILL: 2-ON-2

Purpose: To teach defenders to adjust quickly to on-the-ball and off-the-ball positions while defending penetration (help and decide situations).

Equipment: Two lines of players at wing positions, one ball, and a half court.

Procedure: The coach starts with the ball in the middle (both defenders in a closed stance) and then dribbles to one side as the defenders adjust to positions of closed and open stance. The coach may pass and offensive players go live or penetrate at any time. The drill rotation is from offense to defense to the back of the opposite line (figure 7.24).

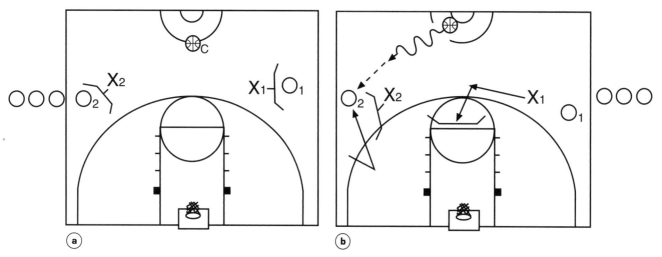

FIGURE 7.24 On-the-ball, off-the-ball 2-on-2: *(a)* starting positions and *(b)* the coach dribbles and passes.

CLOSEOUT DRILL

Purpose: To develop the individual defensive skill of closing out on an off-the-ball offensive player who has just received a pass.

Equipment: One ball and basket per group; ideally one ball and basket for every two players.

Procedure: When practicing the closeout technique, the defensive player starts under the basket with a ball (figure 7.25). The offensive player is in basic position, facing the basket within a range of 15 to 18 feet (4.6 to 5.5 meters). The defender passes the ball to the offensive player with a crisp air pass and closes out to defend. The coach can select a pass, preferably a nonpreferred hand pass. The rule is to first prevent the drive by breaking down in the stance halfway to the ballhandler (the feet active, the inside foot forward, both hands up with the palms facing the ball). Then pressure the ball and shooter, and block out when a shot is taken. From that point, live competition between offense and defense ends when a basket is made or the defense gains possession of the ball. The dribbler is limited to two dribbles.

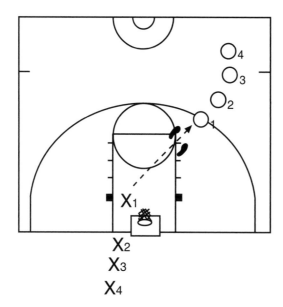

FIGURE 7.25 **Closeout.**

Options

- Closeout—shot only

- Closeout—shot fake, drive only (right, left)

- Closeout—live offense (rotate lines each time)

- Closeout—live offense and defense (rotate)

- Closeout—live, make-it-take-it (defense must stop offense to rotate)

CLOSEOUT DRILLS: 1-ON-1, 2-ON-2, 3-ON-3, 4-ON-4

Purpose: To practice all outside moves by perimeter players.

Equipment: One ball and one basket per group.

Procedure: Form a line of players under each basket off the court. The first player steps under the basket with the ball and is the defender. A line of offensive players is placed 15 to 18 feet (4.6 to 5.5 meters) away, facing the basket (corner, wing, or point position). The defender makes a crisp air pass with the nonpreferred hand (with the feet on the floor) to the first player in the offensive line and then closes out to defend that player. The drill begins as soon as the pass is made for both offense and defense. The perimeter offensive player should catch the ball with the feet in the air facing the basket, read and react to the defender's actions, and apply fundamentals to shoot or make an outside move.

Players may rotate to the back of the opposite line each time, play make-it-take-it, or any arrangement of their choice. The drill may be run as a 3-on-3 option (figure 7.26) that then becomes a teamwork competition with on-the-ball and off-the-ball play.

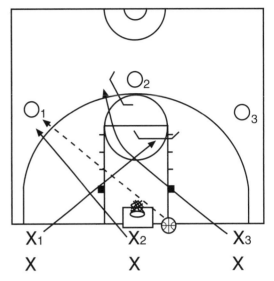

FIGURE 7.26 **3-on-3 closeout—coach passes, closeout defenders cannot cover players in their line, must communicate.**

DEFENSIVE SLIDE DRILL: MOVING STANCE AND STEPS

Purpose: To develop individual defensive steps.

Equipment: Full-court boundary lines.

Procedure: All players begin the drill in the court corner and use defensive steps as described. They follow the path noted in figure 7.27. Players should allow the preceding player to reach the adjacent free-throw line before starting. The drill includes the following 10 movements:

1. Forward slide
2. Slide left
3. Close out to baseline
4. Slide right
5. Angle slide, run, slide
6. Slide right
7. Close out to the half-court line
8. Face belly to the sideline with an angle left side
9. Face belly to the sideline or the baseline with an angle right side
10. Close out to the free-throw line

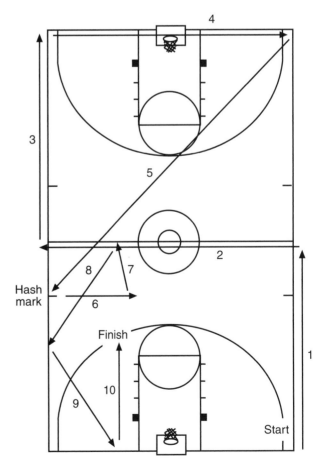

FIGURE 7.27 **Moving stance and steps, may be started from right or left side.**

Players repeat the circuit starting from the left side of the court. They complete one circuit starting at each corner of one end line. Coaches may want to record the time to complete the circuit after using the drill several times and after emphasizing proper technique.

HALF-COURT DRILLS: 2-ON-2, 3-ON-3, 4-ON-4

Purpose: To develop individual defensive skills in a team setting.

Equipment: One ball, half court.

Procedure: Three (or four) offensive and three (or four) defensive players play a half-court game centered around different offensive moves and situations to be played by the defender. Start with different sets and situations. The coach may rotate after one defensive stop (successful team defense) or set challenging group goals such as two or three consecutive defensive stops.

Options

- Screens (on-the-ball and off-the-ball)
- Post play
- Penetration
- Closeouts
- Traps
- Charges

HALF COURT PLUS TRANSITION: 4-ON-4

Purpose: To develop individual defensive skills in a team setting and make the transition from defense to offense after defensive rebounding.

Equipment: One ball, full court.

Procedure: Begin play as 4-on-4 half court, defending against any offensive situation desired. When defenders successfully gain the ball on a steal or a defensive rebound (a defensive stop), they may fast break to score at the other end of the court. Four new defenders then take positions, and the successful defenders now come to the original half court as offensive players.

Rebounding

"Offense sells tickets, defense wins games, rebounding wins championships."

Pat Summitt, University of Tennessee Lady Volunteers (Seven-Time National Champions)

CRITICAL CUE:
Defensive rebound—
regain the ball;
offensive rebound—
get the ball.

In basketball, rebounding may be defined as gaining possession of the ball after a missed shot. Players need to learn both offensive and defensive rebounding skills. The objective of offensive rebounding is to maintain possession of the ball after the team attempts a shot, while defensive rebounders attempt to gain possession of the ball after the offensive team has attempted a shot. Rebounding is a major part of the game at all levels. It may even have a greater influence on a game played by younger players because of the higher percentage of missed shots at the beginning level.

Rebounding Tools

Rebounding requires determination and discipline. Although height and jumping ability are advantages, the keys to rebounding are determination and technique. Statistics on the leading rebounders in professional and college basketball are not merely a list of the tallest players or the ones with the highest vertical jump. Most rebounding, even in college and professional basketball, is done below the rim. The positioning and the ability of players to be quick to the ball (horizontal movement), not leaping ability (vertical jumping), may be the most essential skills for rebounding at both professional and school levels. Rebounding requires more than physical tools; considerable effort, determination, and proper execution of skills are necessary.

Joan Crawford was a 5-foot, 11-inch (1.8-meter) center who was an AAU star in the 1950s and 1960s as she led her team and the competition in rebounding. She took her USA team to the 1957 World Championship and was inducted into the Naismith Hall of Fame in 1997. Denise Curry, at 6 feet, 1 inch (1.9 meters), also a 1997 Hall of Fame inductee, holds the UCLA rebounding record, was the 1981 USA Player of the Year, a Gold Medal Olympian, and was named "French Player of the Decade" for the 1980s. Dennis Rodman came from a small NAIA school in Oklahoma and led the NBA in rebounding for many years. He is only 6 feet, 8 inches (2 meters) tall, which is short for an NBA frontcourt rebounder.

CRITICAL CUE:
Rebounding
depends on skill,
position, effort, and
determination.

Without question, certain physical attributes are advantageous to rebounders. Players who are tall, have long arms, large hips, and well-developed leg and upper-body musculature have an advantage over other players.

Vertical jumping ability is an asset for a rebounder. Coaches should ensure that all players learn rebounding skills, not just jumping skills, although players should develop jumping ability to their full potential. Coaches can use strength programs and other devices to enhance players' vertical jumps in practices. In addition to helping them jump their highest, coaches must make sure that they are jumping correctly. Proper jumping technique involves bending the knees, jumping from both feet, and using the thrust of both arms to reach full extension (2-and-2 rebounding). Teaching players to jump in this manner not only develops their leaping abilities to the maximum but also helps them maintain their balance in contact jumping situations and reduces the number of over-the-back fouls when rebounding.

Motivating Players to Rebound

The first step in teaching rebounding is to convince players that it is a relevant and important skill to learn and perform in game situations. Explain that the entire team—not just those who are tallest, play post positions, or have exceptional jumping ability—must master rebounding skills. Every player can become a good rebounder. If coaches bypass this initial step, they will probably be disappointed by the rebounding performance of certain players during the season, especially the smaller players.

Reasons for Rebounding

Give players solid reasons why rebounding is such an important skill to develop. They must come to see rebounding in terms of its importance in getting and maintaining control of the ball and its key role in team offensive and defensive production. Rebounding as the final phase of defense is also a critical part of team defense. Rebounding at both ends of the floor can have a significant positive effect on offensive and defensive efficiency.

Ball Possession.   Rare is the player who does not like to shoot the basketball. But players can't shoot if they don't have the ball. Rebounding is the primary way of gaining or maintaining possession of the ball.

At the offensive end of the court, offensive rebounds to maintain possession frequently lead to quick and easy baskets. An offensive rebound is like causing an opponent's turnover—it takes the ball away from the other team. At the defensive end, rebounding gains possession, the final part of defense. Complete the defense with a defensive rebound.

Fast Break.   The ability of a team to begin a fast break depends entirely on defensive rebounding and turnovers by opponents, which is why teams with a well-developed fast break develop effective defensive rebounding. Whether a team's offensive style is fast or slow, the basic strategy should emphasize getting the ball up the court quickly to prevent opponents from sending their whole team to the basket for an offensive rebound on a shot attempt instead of keeping some players back to defend against the fast break.

Players usually like to fast break, so it should be easy to motivate them to concentrate on rebounding: no rebounds, no fast break. Defensive rebounds equal more fast-break chances.

The fast-breaking Boston Celtics of the 1960s were at their best when triggered by a defensive rebound and outlet from Bill Russell, one of the best college and professional rebounders in history.

Winning.   Perhaps the strongest evidence of the importance of rebounding is the high correlation of successful rebounding with winning basketball games. One U.S. study examining rebounding and winning over a 10-year period found that, 80 percent of the time, teams that out-rebounded their opponents won. National leaders in team rebounding in the United States win more of their games and list rebounding as the third most important factor related to winning. Teams that lead the nation in fewest turnovers (the second most important factor) plus field-goal and free-throw accuracy (the most important factor) win more games. This statistic suggests that teams who gain possession of the ball only after their opponents score, at best, trade basket for basket with them. The effective rebound allows a team to pull ahead.

Work Ethic.   Rebounding is a blue-collar skill that depends mostly on hard work. It is the mark of players and teams who get down in the trenches to do the physical dirty work required of rebounding. Players should develop the tradition of rebounding (for themselves and their team) because it enhances a hard work core value.

Reinforcing the Motivation

Coaches can convince players to rebound if players understand that it is essential for ball possession as well as for the fast break and that it is important (the third most important factor) to winning.

Praise and encourage players who give maximum effort in rebounding, and single out individual players for particular rebounding accomplishments (e.g., most rebounds in a half, most defensive rebounds for the game, best blockout, most consistent rebounder). Make sure that they know how much their coach and teammates value rebounding as a team skill and that their efforts to perform well in rebounding will be rewarded.

After all players feel responsible for rebounding and understand why they must rebound, then explain and demonstrate the fundamental rebounding skills.

Rebounding Rules

Four concepts (the big bullets of the boards) apply to offensive and defensive rebounding and are critical for any player or team to be successful in rebounding:

1. **Assume** that each shot is missed and do the assigned job.
2. **Keep hands up** when in rebounding areas, on offense or defense.
3. **Use 2-and-2** rebounding—when going for any rebound (offense or defense), rebound from two feet with two hands. Go up tall and small, and come down big and wide.
4. **Capture and chin the ball** on all rebounds; use two hands to capture the ball and chin it to protect the ball. Chin it—two hands, the fingers point up, the ball under the chin or from shoulder to shoulder (the power position), the elbows out and up (big and wide).

Assume is the prompt used to remind players and coaches to assume that every shot will be missed. When that becomes a habit, players are conditioned to focus on carrying out their rebound assignment on every shot attempt. Even on an uncontested layup by a teammate, players should always assume a miss—then they will develop the habit of rebounding consistently.

The verbal prompt *hands up* is a reminder of this essential skill needed in rebounding, especially when players are blocking out on defense or near the offensive rebounding basket. The arm position is shown in many of the figures in this chapter. Players should start in quick stance, ready to jump (the legs bent, sit into the stance), with the hands up and ready to rebound the ball (the upper arms horizontal and level with the shoulders, the forearms vertical and slightly forward). The rationale for teaching players the hands-up arm position is the following:

- Keeps players ready for a quick rebound (hits the rim and bounces directly to the player with no time to respond).

- Allows players to prevent the opponent from rebounding (just get close, with the hands up). This prevents the opponent from getting his hands up to rebound the ball.

- Makes a difference when players are blocking out on defense. The hands-up technique prevents the defensive rebounder from using the illegal method of hands down to feel and hold the offensive rebounder (see figure 8.1).

FIGURE 8.1 **Hands-up rebounding:** *(a)* hands up (offense and defense), *(b)* improper defensive blockout (hands down).

The term *2-and-2 rebounding* refers to the important skill of rebounding from two feet with two hands. Hall of Fame coach Jim Brandenburg popularized this concept. Because rebounding is a contact skill, players should use a quick stance (sit into the game), with the feet shoulder width before and after jumping into the air for a rebound. Likewise, the effective rebounder needs to capture the ball securely with both hands, preferably at the peak of the jump.

The teaching technique for 2-and-2 rebounding is as follows:

- Get into a rebounding ready position (quick stance, the hands up).
- Execute the 2-and-2 rebound (go up tall and small and come down big and wide) (see figure 8.2).
- Capture and chin. Grab the ball with two hands and rip it to a position under the chin or into the power position and against the chest. The fingers should be pointed up, not out, the elbows should be out and up, and the ball should be forcefully squeezed under the chin.
- Protect the ball (chin the basketball). This technique is shown in figure 8.2*b*.

FIGURE 8.2   **2-and-2 rebounding:** *(a)* go up tall and small, *(b)* come down big and wide, capture and chin the ball.

All players need to learn the "big bullet" principles that are essential to successful rebounding: assume, hands up, 2-and-2, capture and chin.

Defensive Rebounding

The suggested rebounding technique requires that players gain the inside position on an opponent, block out the opponent, and then get the rebound. Getting a position between the basket or the ball and the opponent enhances the defense's positional advantage to secure the rebound bouncing from the rim or the backboard. Although rebounding seems to consist of three distinct phases, these occur as quickly as if they were a single action. The rebounding technique is commonly referred to as *blocking out*, but it is sometimes also called *boxing out* or *checking* an opponent.

All players should understand the following fundamental rebounding principles associated with blocking out.

- See or hear the shot (teammate guarding the shooter calls *shot*).
- Assume that the shot will be missed.
- Locate the opponent.
- Go to the opponent and block out.
- Go to the ball.
- Get and keep the ball.
- Move the ball out or down the court.

See or Hear the Shot

Players must be aware of when and where a shot is taken. Whether they are guarding an opponent on defense or attempting to get open on offense, they should know where the ball is at all times. Coaches should emphasize to players the need to position themselves so that they can see both their assigned player and the ball on defense and use their peripheral vision while moving to get open on offense. Players who are blind to the ball usually have other problems with fundamental skills, such as positioning and movement, that should be corrected.

Once players see a shot being taken, they call out *shot* to alert teammates (who may have momentarily lost sight of the ball) that they should get in position to rebound (hear the shot). The defender guarding the shooter has the primary responsibility for making the defensive call. However, none of these verbal alarms are as effective as a player's own observation of the shot being released.

Assume That the Shot Will Miss

Every shot attempt means a potential rebound. Players must learn to assume that every shot will be a miss and to go to their rebound assignment. When players develop this habit, they will be conditioned to do their assigned rebound tasks every time a shot is taken, regardless of the outcome.

Find the Opponent

Almost without exception, young players fall into the habit of watching the flight of the ball when shots are in the air—the most common rebounding mistake. This can prevent them from being able to gain an advantage in rebounding position. Once the ball is in the air, their first reaction should be to locate the opponent they are responsible for blocking out or the opposing player nearest to them (visual contact before physical contact).

This does not mean that players should not be aware of the direction and distance of the shot, but they must avoid becoming spectators when the ball is in the air. Coaches should train players to be active rebounders by teaching them to locate an opponent while maintaining a sense of the direction and timing of the shot. Move the feet; rebound with the feet.

To determine whether players are only watching the shot in flight, use a simple rebounding drill in which the opposing player holds up a given number of fingers after the shot is released by another player. After rebounding the ball, the player guarding the offensive player should be able to report the number of fingers the opponent held up. If not, the player probably was focusing too much on the ball in the air and not enough on the opponent.

Go to the Opponent and Block Out

Now the player has set the stage for the next step—the actual blocking out of the opponent. Players may not have difficulty with the first three steps, but blocking out is challenging for almost all players, especially for beginners.

The purpose of boxing or blocking out is to gain a positional inside advantage over an opponent for a rebound. Normally, a player is more likely to rebound a missed shot

FIGURE 8.3 **Inside (right) and outside (left) positions.**

if positioned closer to the basket than the opponent. This is called *inside* position because the player is between the basket and the opponent (opponent-rebounder-basket). However, it is best to get that inside position away from the basket and congestion (form a deep pocket).

Occasionally—when an opponent is far underneath the basket and a shot is taken from a long distance, for example—outside position (the opponent between the player and the basket) is preferable. But the inside position is generally the desired position for a player while blocking out an opponent. Figure 8.3 illustrates the difference between inside and outside positions.

Before actually blocking out, a player must go to where the offensive opponent was previously located, as shown in figure 8.4 (visual contact, then physical contact). The player should move quickly and not allow the opponent to gain a positional advantage. Coaches should teach players to use pivots and turns to help them gain inside position for the blockout.

When blocking out an opponent, a player must be in a stance similar to a quick stance with the following modifications. The feet should be parallel and shoulder-width apart; the arms should be raised, with the upper arms parallel to the floor and bent at the elbows; and the hands should be palms up and forward. Figure 8.4 shows the standard blockout position.

The box or blockout is the phase of the rebounding sequence in which players usually make contact with an opponent. Contact is normally initiated by the player with the inside position. Because players must turn to the basket and be in quick

FIGURE 8.4 **Go to the offensive player to block out. Make contact with the hands up.**

stance to rebound the ball (having already located the designated opponent after the shot was released), they can no longer see the opponent being blocked out. Players must use another sense, the sense of touch, to keep track of the opponent's location. The buttocks, back, upper arms, and elbows are used most often for this purpose. Sit into the game and make contact using radar bumpers and active feet. Feel with the radar bumpers, not the hands. Keep the hands up.

Figures 8.5 and 8.6 illustrate the preferred action technique for beginning and intermediate players—go to the opponent, use a front turn to step into an opponent's path (right foot to right foot or vice versa) followed by a rear turn to make contact and take away the opponent's momentum and remaining path. Be proactive—go to the opponent. An advanced technique that can be used by elite players is called *blast and box*, which is shown in figure 8.7—the defender blasts the offensive player with a forearm shiver *(a)* and then slides into a regular blockout *(b)* before pursuing the ball or rebounding (board the ball). In this method, the defender locates and meets the opponent with a forearm shiver blast to take away momentum to the basket. This is followed by a front turn move to slide into a box or blockout position. Go to the opponent, blast and box, then board (pursue the ball).

Figure 8.8 illustrates why it is so important that players make contact with the opponent. In figure 8.8a, no contact was made, and as a result, the opponent has a clear lane to the basket and an advantage for the rebound. The player in figure 8.8b, however, established contact and prevented the opponent from gaining an inside position for the rebound. Turns and pivots are not always viable options for defensive rebounders, so it is important for coaches to emphasize that the key concern in defensive rebounding is not so much the technique used to block out the opponent but whether or not the opponent is effectively blocked out.

Against an exceptional offensive rebounder, players might use a face-block technique: face the player and use a two-forearm shiver technique to get and maintain contact. This move prevents that defensive rebounder from pursuing and capturing the ball—teammates must do so.

Despite widely held perceptions, basketball is a contact sport. Coaches know that some players are better prepared than others for the physical side of rebounding. In drills and games, they should match up the players according to size, strength, and readiness for contact.

Go to the Ball

The old saying that certain players have a nose for the ball may be true. Some rebounders seem to be in the right place for a rebound on every missed shot. These

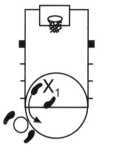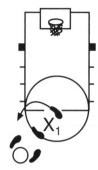

a. Front turn   b. Rear turn

FIGURE 8.5 **Front turn and rear turn blockout.**

FIGURE 8.6 **Rear turn completion of blockout with contact.**

CRITICAL CUE:
Defensive rebounding —go to the opponent and make contact with a front-turn or rear-turn move.

FIGURE 8.7 **Blast and box, then board:** *(a)* forearm shiver blast, *(b)* radar bumper blockout.

FIGURE 8.8 **Blockout contact:** *(a)* contact not made, *(b)* contact made.

apparently instinctive rebounders have probably studied where shots taken from various places on the court are likely to go when they are off the mark and then they hustle and actively pursue the ball.

Coaches can help players develop a rebounding instinct by pointing out the rebounding distribution diagrammed in figure 8.9. Shots taken from the side of the court are much more likely (70 to 75 percent) to rebound to the opposite side. Players should learn to take a position on the opposite side of the basket from where the shot was taken (the weak-side or help-side position). Get at least two rebounders to the weak side on all shots from the side of the court. However, players should be taught that shots taken from the middle of the court more often tend to rebound to an area in the middle of the lane. Also, make sure players know that shots taken from close range rebound closer to the basket than shots launched from long distances. Finally, players should be aware that some rims tend to make the ball rebound farther away from the basket, whereas others seem to cushion the impact of shots and produce much shorter rebounds. Have players test the bounce of the rims during warm-up.

Three-point field-goal shots rebound a longer distance, shots from in front (the top of the key) rebound near the free-throw line, and shots from the side generally rebound outside the free-throw lane on the opposite side of the court.

Hustle is another explanation for the success of some players in getting to the ball. Players who are good rebounders take the approach that every free ball is theirs, telling opponents, "I want the ball more than you do." Coaches can instill this mentality in players by giving praise and other rewards for coming up with the most rebounds, loose balls, and steals (sometimes called *garbage plays*).

Timing and jumping ability are two helpful attributes for rebounding. However, all the spring in the world means nothing if a player does not know when or how to use it. There are several useful drills for helping players get a feel for when they should leave the floor for a rebound. One especially effective drill is to have players repeatedly toss the ball off the backboard and attempt to grab the rebound at the maximum height of the jump each time. See "Rebounding Drills" for additional drill ideas. Instill the concept of angle jumping to the ball and rebounding out of the area (to the side)—pursue and board the ball (see figure 8.10).

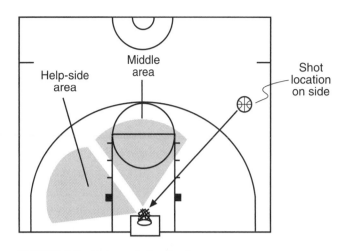

FIGURE 8.9 **Rebound distribution areas.**

FIGURE 8.10 **Angle jump to the ball.**

Get and Keep the Ball

Too often, players make perfect rebounding plays only to lose possession because of poor ball protection. When teaching rebounding, coaches should emphasize that all players' efforts to gain possession of the ball are for naught if they fail to protect it afterward.

Jim Brandenberg, former Montana and Wyoming Hall of Fame coach, popularized the concept of rebounding from two feet with two hands (2-and-2 rebounding). Using this strong, balanced technique of two-foot jumping and two-handed grabbing for rebounding reduces the chances of the ball slipping out of the players' hands or of an opponent dislodging it from their grip. Coaches can help players develop this skill by insisting that they go after every rebound in this manner. Young players should keep their eyes open and focused on the ball as they capture the rebound.

Occasionally, the ball may come off the rim in an area where the player is unable to grasp it with both hands. Players should then gain control using only one hand (block and tuck with two hands) or tap the ball to a teammate.

Maintaining possession of the rebound once it is captured is frequently more difficult than it might seem. Opposing players try to knock the ball from the rebounder's hands. Often they trap the rebounder with two or even three players, making it nearly impossible for the player to pass or dribble the ball. Players need to learn to handle such situations.

When players rebound the ball in the vicinity of an opponent or opponents, their first move should be to bring the ball in under the chin with the elbows out and a hand (with the fingers pointing up) on each side of the ball, squeezing it tightly (see figure 8.11)—chinning the ball. The best position is directly under the chin, but the ball may be moved from shoulder to shoulder anywhere in the power position to protect the ball away from defenders. The teaching points are the following: the fingers up (to prevent dangling the ball and exposing it away from the body), the elbows out and up; players should squeeze the ball and make themselves big. Tell

FIGURE 8.11 Chinit—the elbows out, the fingers up: *(a)* side view and *(b)* front view.

players to chinit on rebounds and whenever handling the ball in a congested area in order to capture and retain control of the ball. Tell players not to swing the elbows around to ward off an opponent because this can constitute a violation or foul. They may take up space to clear their area with elbows out (make themselves big). A rebounder chinning the ball can always use a pivot or turn to move away from pressure (danger) to protect and shield the ball. Players should keep the head up and look for teammates breaking downcourt or to an open spot in the backcourt.

When a rebounder gains possession of the ball after a missed shot, a single opponent (usually one that the rebounder has blocked out) is often nearby and attempts to steal the ball or pressure the rebounder. Coaches should teach players to pivot away from the opponent, as shown in figure 8.12. The player should have an open passing lane to a teammate or be able to dribble without having the ball stolen. Caution your players not to put the ball on the floor immediately after rebounding a shot in traffic, which presents an opportunity for an opponent to steal or deflect the ball.

When rebounders find themselves surrounded by two or more opponents, they should not panic. If they are trained to remain calm, to keep the ball in the protective power or chinit position, and to look over the entire court, options present themselves. One escape move coaches can teach players is the step-through technique shown in figure 8.13. This can be followed by a two-dribble push to advance the ball up the floor. Big players can then quick stop, chin the ball, and look for a pass to an open teammate. Perimeter players can continue dribbling up the floor. This technique

FIGURE 8.12 **Pivot away from pressure.**

FIGURE 8.13 **The step-through move (outlet pass or two-dribble push).**

can be used when the defenders trapping the player leave an opening large enough for the player to slither through. Sometimes an overhead pass fake causes defenders to leave their feet and creates an opening for the offensive player to step or dribble through. Players should not force their way through the defensive players, which may result in a charging foul.

Another option for a rebounder surrounded by opponents is to throw a pass over them. Even smaller players can use this approach if they make the proper fakes prior to the pass. If the rebounder is being trapped by two or more opponents, a teammate should be open or able to break open to receive a pass. Also, one of the defenders can reach in and foul the rebounder. Tell players to keep their composure when they are trapped by opponents after a rebound and wait for one of these options to open up. Fake a pass to make a pass is a rule for these situations, advocated by Morgan Wootten of DeMatha High School.

Move the Ball

CRITICAL CUE:
Use outlet pass or two-dribble push to start fast break.

Once possession is assured, the player with the defensive rebound must choose one of the options: pass to an open teammate up the floor, use a two-dribble push to clear the ball, or wait for a ballhandling perimeter player to come for the ball. Whatever action the player takes should begin with the head up and the ball in a protected power position.

Passing the Ball. The preferred method for moving the ball after a defensive rebound is the outlet pass. No opponent can outrun a sharp pass down the court. Emphasize that this pass is the first option players should look for after a defensive rebound whether the game strategy calls for a fast break or simply moving the ball quickly.

Several types of passes are used to get the ball to a teammate breaking down the court. The long air pass (also called a baseball or one-handed pass) is used when a teammate is open at the other end of the court. The two-handed overhead pass is used when a teammate is around the midcourt area and opponents are in the line of the pass. The two-handed chest pass is used to get the ball to a teammate who has broken open within 10 to 30 feet (3 to 9.1 meters) to the side or to the middle of the court. Because traffic is often less on the sides of the court than the middle, teach players to look first for open teammates in this area on the rebound side of the court before looking to the middle.

Successful passing is the responsibility of both the passer and the catcher, so coaches should teach players to get open after a teammate has claimed a defensive rebound. If the opportunity to beat an opponent down the court is available, a player should take advantage of it. Guards should be instructed to move quickly to a spot where the rebounder can get the ball to them. A particularly good spot for guards to position themselves for outlet passes after a rebound is the rebound side of the court—between the opponent's free-throw line and the half-court line—with their backs to the sideline to allow the outlet catcher to see the whole floor (especially defenders).

Good basketball teams retain possession of the ball after defensive rebounds. Coaches must emphasize that the transition from defense to offense can lead to a successful offensive possession or a return to defense, depending on how players handle the ball.

Dribbling the Ball.   Certain players should not be put in the position of dribbling the ball from one end of the court to the other. However, it has recently become more common for coaches to allow players on their teams to take a rebounded ball the length of the court using the dribble. As bigger and better players develop the ability to rebound and dribble, the benefits of this full-court maneuver have become apparent.

One major advantage of having a defensive rebounder dribble the ball to the other end of the court is that it eliminates the possibility of passing errors. There can be no errant pass if there is no pass. In addition, the rebounder or dribbler can quickly assume the middle position on the fast break without having to wait for a teammate to get open. Players must be able to respond to this situation. Have teammates practice spreading out and filling the passing lanes as they run down the court.

Having defensive rebounders dribble the ball usually creates a numerical advantage over the opposition. Because one or more opponents are often slow to react in making the transition from offense to defense, a defensive rebounder or dribbler can get down the court ahead of them. If players are trained to recognize the situation quickly and hurry down the court, the team can frequently have a 5-on-4 or even 5-on-3 advantage.

In general, almost all big players can be taught to rebound, pivot and face up the court, use one or two dribbles (two-dribble push) to clear the ball, use a quick stop, chin the ball, and look for a clear pass to a ballhandling teammate.

Offensive Rebounding

A coach must decide on a rebound philosophy, especially on offense. Generally, all players should have the same assignments and rules for defensive rebounding. On offense, coaches decide which offensive players should be assigned to go to the boards (go to a gap) as offensive rebounders and which players, on the shot, should transition back to defense. Most teams have three players rebound and have two players get back on defense (one as full safety and one to stop the advance of the ball). For a more aggressive approach, a team could have four players rebound and have one safety getting back on defense.

Offensive rebounding is especially difficult in a successful ball-defender-basket defense because players have the advantage for getting the inside position. However, offensive players can gain an edge by knowing when and where a shot is going to be taken. Coaches should emphasize the need for players to anticipate shots by teammates, as well as to react to their own shots; otherwise, players have difficulty being successful against good defensive rebounders. Getting around a rebounder in proper position for blocking out is not always possible. Players should not go over the defensive rebounder's back when attempting to get an offensive rebound because this can lead to being charged with a foul.

The primary position objectives (in order of importance) for an offensive rebounder are the following: Players should go to a gap and not a back, get an inside position and block out the defender, get at least even with the defender by going to one side and around to the basket (go to a gap, as in figure 8.14), make contact with and nudge the inside defender under the basket—pin inside by chesting with the hands up (figure 8.15), and tap to self or teammate only to keep the ball alive when they can't get both hands on the ball.

CRITICAL CUE:
Offensive rebounding—
go to a gap,
not a back.

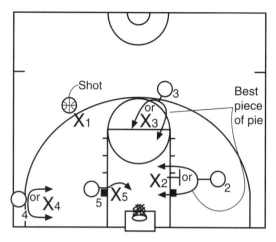

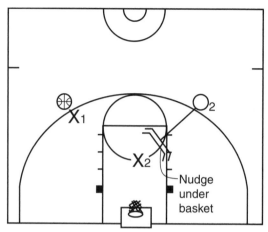

FIGURE 8.14 "O" boards—go to a gap: go to a gap, best piece of pie (help side, baseline).

FIGURE 8.15 "O" boards—block in (when defense is too close to the basket).

The techniques for going to a gap are the V-cut, or swim, move (primary) and the rear-turn roll. On the shot, the offensive rebounder selects the best gap by the defender (depending on position and percentages) and makes a V-cut to the gap. When blocked out, the offensive rebounder executes a tap with the outside hand or arm, followed by a forceful, quick overhead swim stroke with the near hand or arm to get at least even with the defender in the hands-up position (figure 8.16). Another move to get by or even with a defender is the rear-turn roll, which is best used against a physically aggressive defender who actively blocks out. The offensive player meets the contact with the forward leg in the direction of the desired gap. Using that foot to make contact and as the turning foot, the offensive rebounder

FIGURE 8.16 *(a)* V-cut and tap with the outside hand or arm, and *(b)* swim by with the near hand or arm.

FIGURE 8.17 **Rear-turn roll for offensive rebounding: (a) meet block-out contact with turning foot, (b) 180-degree rear turn to get outside, and (c) 180-degree front turn into the gap.**

makes a 180-degree rear turn to get the stepping foot outside the defender's foot in the desired gap. Then, using that stepping foot as the new turning foot, the rebounder uses a 180-degree front turn to get by the defender at the gap in a hands-up position (figure 8.17).

Offensive rebounding is important because it gives the offensive team another opportunity to score. This new life for the offensive team also discourages the defensive players, who have lost a chance to gain possession of the basketball. Many options are available to the offensive rebounder.

Shooting After Rebounding

When a player gets an offensive rebound, the first option is to shoot the ball. Players should first look to shoot, but, if this is not possible, then they should pass to a teammate (passing outside for a three-point field-goal attempt is a good option) before finally exercising the option of dribbling (action over reaction). Coaches should emphasize that this is a very good time to take advantage of the defense. Because the defensive opponent is unable to prevent the offensive player from getting in position for the rebound, the defensive player may also be in a poor position to defend against a shot. An offensive rebounder can take shots without dribbling or shots after dribbling.

Tips. If players are skilled and big enough, they should tip the ball back at the basket. Tipping is actually a misleading term for a leaping player shooting a rebounded ball before returning to the floor. Tips that involve slapping at the ball with one hand are usually unsuccessful. Coaches can teach players to catch the ball with the elbows locked and to shoot it with both hands if possible (tip with two hands).

Tipping the ball is the most efficient way of taking advantage of the defensive players' being out of position. By not bringing the ball down from the jump, offensive rebounders take away the defenders' opportunity to recover and give them almost no chance to block the tip attempt. Make sure players are physically mature and skilled enough before suggesting the tip as a rebounding option. The tip is too difficult for beginning players.

Shots Without Dribbling.   Encourage players to go up with the shot after a rebound without putting the ball on the floor. Dribbling takes time and allows the defense to recover. It also exposes the ball to the defense, making it more likely that a defender will steal or deflect the ball. If players have learned the correct rebound jumping technique, they should land with the ball ready to go back up for the shot. They can shoot the ball from an overhead position (explode to score from the forehead) or chinit position, but they should always keep the ball up.

Often players develop the bad habit of dribbling the ball right after they get it from a pass or a rebound. Coaches should make a point of noting instances when players do not put the ball on the floor after rebounding and praise them for this.

A good time to help players develop the habit of going back up with a shot after a rebound is during individual shooting practices. Tell them that, on every missed shot, they should hustle for the rebound, get their balance, and, with the shoulders square to the basket, go back up with another shot (keep the ball overhead and explode to the basket; chin the ball and explode; or chin the ball, do a shot fake, and explode). Players should continue to shoot and rebound until they make the basket and then start over from a new spot on the court. Shooting without dribbling after an offensive rebound can become an automatic response.

Shots After Dribbling.   Although it should be avoided whenever possible, it is occasionally acceptable for a player who has grabbed an offensive rebound to dribble before shooting. One obvious example is when a player grabs a rebound far away from the basket and has an open lane to the goal. Because this situation presents an easy scoring opportunity, players should dribble the ball in for the layup (attack the basket) when the path to the basket is clear. Another option is dribbling out of the lane to clear the ball from a congested area.

Passing After Rebounding

The player who has captured an offensive rebound also can pass the basketball to a teammate. The pass is the second option (after shooting) that players should look for after getting an offensive rebound. When they turn to the basket to look for the open shot after the rebound, they also should locate any open teammates to whom they could pass the ball for an easy shot, especially for a three-point shot. Coaches can encourage players to take advantage of the defensive players' having to recover after the rebound, either by taking a shot or by passing to a teammate (usually outside) who has a good shot. Coach John Wooden believes that a good option is a pass out of the collapsed defense resulting from an offensive rebound for a trey.

Sometimes an offensive team chooses to reset the offense, either to run a play or to take more time off the clock. Then the option to shoot has the lowest priority for the offensive rebounder, and passing and dribbling become the more preferred options.

COACHING POINTS FOR REBOUNDING

- Rebounding is the responsibility of all of the players on the team.
- Ball possession, the fast break, and winning are all closely associated with good rebounding.
- Assuming that a shot will be missed is the most important principle of rebounding.
- The 2-and-2 rebounds are effective; rebound from two feet with two hands.
- The hands should be kept up when players are blocking out or near the basket.
- The best rebounding technique emphasizes blocking out the opposing player.
- The blocking-out technique includes the following:
  - Being aware of when a shot is taken and assuming that it will be a miss.
  - Finding, going to, and blocking out an opponent (blast and box) while paying attention to the direction and distance of the shot.
  - Going to (pursuing) and capturing the ball and getting it into the protected position under the chin (capture and chin the ball).
- Chinit is the most important technique of rebounding.
- Offensive rebounders—assume a miss, go to a gap with the hands up.
- 2-and-2 offensive rebounders should look to shoot, pass, or dribble—in that order.
- Defensive rebounding—blast, box, and board.
- Defensive rebounders should either pass, dribble, or hold the ball, depending on their skills and the situation.

Dribbling After Rebounding

In most situations, the offensive rebounder should dribble only if a shot or a pass is impossible. Dribbling usually only affords the defensive players an opportunity to recover and possibly steal the ball. Because the offensive rebounder is often surrounded by defenders, the chances of a turnover are even greater. Coaches should continually advise players to look first for a shot and then for a passing opportunity before dribbling when they get an offensive rebound.

CRITICAL CUE:
Get the offensive rebound, then score, pass, or dribble (in that order).

Rebounding Assessment

Coaches should keep rebounding statistics for each player and for the team as a whole. Offensive and defensive rebounds should be recorded separately to help identify players who have success or difficulty rebounding at a particular end of the court. This information may reveal a problem with a player's offensive or defensive rebounding technique or indicate that a player is not hustling enough at one end of the court. Individual rebounding statistics are one of the many pieces of information that coaches can use in evaluating the contribution of each player, particularly those positioned nearest the basket.

An excellent team goal is 60 percent of all rebounds, 30 percent of offensive rebounding situations, and 80 percent of defensive rebounding situations. Percentage goals are generally better than rebound numbers because they are valid for all styles of play (slow or fast).

Assessment of individual rebounding can be carried out as a percentage; compare the number of times a player did the assigned job with the total number of rebounding situations. A player with an offensive rebound efficiency of 70 percent might have done the job 14 times in 20 situations (shot attempts while on offense), thus requiring a coach or program assistant to define and evaluate all 20 possessions and to decide on pass or fail. For example, on a shot attempt, did the offensive rebounder go to a gap (V-cut or swim move or rear-turn roll or nudge under the basket), make a 2-and-2 attempt to capture the rebound, and (if captured) chin the ball? If a player is a designated safety on the shot attempt, did the player sprint back to half court before the shot hit the rim and prevent the layup and organize the defense?

Individual defensive assessment is more challenging. Each player is graded on each attempt. For example, when an assigned offensive player is inside the three-point arc, did the defender blast, box, and board; have the hands up on the blockout and near the basket; and actively pursue, capture, and chin the ball with a 2-and-2 rebound move? A percentage of rebound defensive efficiency is obtained by dividing successful rebound attempts by the total shot attempts. A goal of 80 percent for offensive and defensive rebound efficiency is a reasonable but challenging target. If players do their rebounding job 80 percent of the time, the team will be successful. This efficiency does not require getting the rebound, although it enhances a team's chances.

Rebound percentages can be tracked in practice or in games. One evaluator can directly rate two players at a time, in practice or games. In practice, any competition situation involving offense and defense is charted (1-on-1, 2-on-2, and up to 5-on-5). The two players selected should be anonymous during each practice and the results should be totaled, announced, and posted after each practice. For games, video analysis allows a coach, given enough time, to assess each player on each possession to determine a percentage of offensive rebound efficiency, a percentage of defensive rebound efficiency, and a percentage of total rebound efficiency. Assessment should be performed at least every fifth game to ensure realistic feedback in order to change behavior and enhance learning. The totals for all individual players can be used to obtain a team percentage of rebound efficiency: offense, defense, and total.

Rebounding Drills

An important part of rebounding is aggressiveness and making legal contact with opponents. Players should be given drills that progressively develop the trait of aggressiveness.

LINE DRILL: 2-AND-2, CAPTURE AND CHIN REBOUND ADDITION

Purpose: To teach 2-and-2 and capture and chinit rebound techniques.

Equipment: Half court, one basketball per line.

Procedure: Start without the ball first—using the 2-and-2 rebound technique, get an imaginary rebound at the free-throw line, the half-line, the opposite free-throw line, and the baseline. Then the first player in each line has a basketball and creates her own rebound with a two-handed or underhand overhead toss, uses 2-and-2 rebound tech-

TROUBLESHOOTING

Some common rebounding errors are identified, and possible remedies are given. Coaches should provide appropriate feedback in order to change player behavior and enhance learning.

Problem: Lack of motivation to rebound.

Correction: Review importance and rationale for rebounding and sell players on correct technique, effort, and rebound success.

Problem: Errors in rebounding based on the fabulous four principles (big bullets).

Correction:

- Assume—evaluate to ensure that each shot attempt causes each player to know, understand, and attempt to carry out rebound responsibility.

- Hands up—practice and correct or reinforce this position until it becomes automatic.

- 2-and-2—penalize players for loss of the ball on one-foot or one-handed rebounding (unless they are tipping to self or to a teammate).

- Capture and chin—remind and reinforce, penalize for loss of possession of the ball as a last resort.

Problem: The player loses or cannot capture the ball.

Correction: Check 2-and-2 technique. Stand under the basket to see if they are capturing the ball with a click (using both hands, with both eyes open and focused on the ball). Beginners often close their eyes during contact rebounding.

Problem: Small rebounding pocket on defense.

Correction: Defenders are not going to the assigned player to block out (blast or make contact) first. Often, this problem is caused by defenders who follow the flight of the ball on a shot attempt (ball watchers or rebound spectators). Coaches should teach them to see the defender first (visual contact after a shot attempt). Locate the assigned offensive player visually (see the player) and then physically (block the player). Visual contact comes before physical contact.

Problem: Hands down.

Correction: Feel or hold the defender when defensive rebounding. Caution players that it is illegal to hold when blocking out and impossible to capture the quick rebound in a hands-down position. Players should keep the hands up for the quick rebound, make contact with radar bumpers, and use active feet to maintain contact until pursuing the ball. Get the elbows level with the shoulders.

Problem: Rebounders who only rebound overhead or near the basket.

Correction: Focus on angle jumping at less than vertical angles out of the area, 2-and-2 technique for capturing with balance and protection. The only rebounds under the basket are made shots.

Problem: Dangling the ball or putting the ball overhead and away from the power or chinit position.

Correction: Losing the ball usually occurs by players not capturing and chinning the ball. Have players attack rebounders; slap from under, pressure, reach over, or bat the dangling ball.

nique, captures and chins the ball, and then uses a PPF rear turn to pass to the next person in line, who repeats.

The learning progression is the following:

- Imaginary 2-and-2 rebound.

- Toss directly overhead.

- Toss to right, left, or in front (force rebounders to use 2-and-2 technique to rebound out of their area, i.e., angle jump to left, right, or forward to capture and chin the ball). A variation is to use a coach at the top of the key as the tosser in each line for the first two progressions.

- Toss overhead in pairs—the second person can contest the rebound and pressure the rebounder to check the chinit position. The rebounder must pivot away from pressure and execute an outlet pass back to the next person in line.

- Practice two-dribble push upcourt. Rebounder can do 2-and-2 rebound, capture and chin the ball, pivot from pressure, and practice the two-dribble push toward the half court. On completion with a quick stop, the rebounder can pivot and execute an outlet pass back to the next person on the baseline.

LINE DRILL: DEFENSIVE REBOUND ADDITION

Purpose: To teach the techniques of defensive rebounding through simulation.

Equipment: Half court (minimum).

Procedure: The drill is organized in four lines on the baseline. The coach gives the verbal command *shot*. The first player in each line sprints on the court 6 to 15 feet (1.8 to 4.6 meters) from the basket in defensive closeout position and then uses the blast, box, and board technique. Each player simulates the blockout, captures the imaginary rebound, chins the ball, and makes an outlet pass. Then the next four players sprint onto the floor in basic position or quick stance for defense.

Variations

"D" Boards Help-Side Box: The first four players sprint onto the floor in an offensive basic stance near the free-throw line extended, and the next four assume a proper defensive basic position to support the defender (pointing pistols at the imaginary ball and the player being guarded) while facing a sideline. On the command *shot*, all four defenders carry out defensive rebound assignments, and all must make contact at the free-throw line. No ball is needed for this variation.

"D" Boards With a Ball (Blocking the Shooter): The four defensive players on the baseline each have a ball in triple-threat position. They pass to the offensive player at the free-throw line and then close out from off-the-ball to on-the-ball position (prevent the drive, contest the shot). The offensive player is the buddy coach, who checks the defensive rebound technique of the partner while catching the ball with feet in the air and ready to shoot, executing a shot fake, and then shooting a short shot (12 to 15 feet [3.6 to 4.6 meters] out and without using a basket) and focusing on shooting up, not out while holding the follow-through until the ball hits the floor. The shooter coaches the buddy, who becomes the next shooter and then goes to the back of the line. Many "D" board repetitions can be practiced in a short time using this variation.

LINE DRILL: OFFENSIVE REBOUND ADDITION

Purpose: To teach players the techniques of offensive rebounding: getting past the defender to block out, getting to a gap (getting at least even with the defender), and making contact to move the defender closer to the basket (when the defender doesn't move away from the basket to block out).

Equipment: Half court.

Procedure: The players are organized in four lines on the baseline, with the first four players at the free-throw line level, facing away from the baseline, in a quick-stance and hands-up position. For a more realistic perspective, place the lines at the half-line and the first four players at the top of the key level, facing the baseline. The coach controls the drill with the following commands:

- Swim move by right or left, and block out with the hands up.
- Swim move by right or left, and go to a gap.
- Go to a gap, with the hands up, and return to the baseline.

The first player in the line learns the feeling of the hands-up, ready-to-rebound position, moves to the back of the line as the second person practices offensive rebounding technique and then becomes the first in line (the hands up, ready to rebound). The drill is performed without a ball and is controlled by the coach. Many repetitions of basic offensive rebounding technique can be done in a short time.

The same procedure can be carried out to practice the rear-turn roll variation. The offensive player approaches the defender from behind, places one foot or knee in the middle of the defender (split legs), and performs a rear turn and then a front turn to get to the gap and by the defender.

REBOUND AND OUTLET DRILL

Purpose: To teach players the skill of taking a defensive rebound off the backboard and making an outlet pass (or dribble).

Equipment: One ball per basket (the drill can be run simultaneously with two lines, one on each side of the basket).

Procedure: This is a defensive rebounding and passing drill. Have the receiver call the passer's name while breaking to get open.

The first player X$_1$ passes to X$_4$, gets open for a return pass received with a quick stop in the free-throw lane, and tosses the ball underhand above the rectangle level to simulate a defensive rebound (figure 8.18). Player X$_1$ angle jumps to the ball, captures the ball with two hands, brings the ball to the forehead, makes a front turn on the right pivot foot, makes an outlet pass to X$_4$, and takes the place of X$_4$. Player X$_4$ passes to

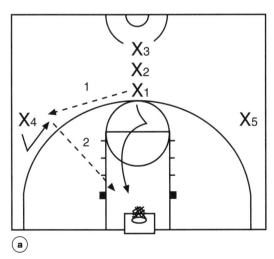
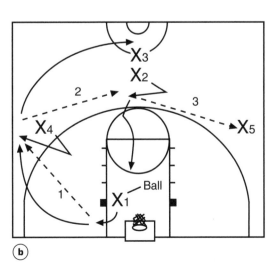

FIGURE 8.18 **Rebound and outlet drill for defensive rebounding:** *(a)* start and *(b)* continuation.

X$_2$ and then goes to the back of the line. The sequence is repeated on the other side with players X$_2$, X$_5$, and X$_3$.

Variation: The outlet lines can be placed at the half court, and the "D" rebounders can use the two-dribble push, quick stop, and pass to outlet the ball.

REBOUND NUMBER

Purpose: To practice seeing the opponent and the ball when a shot is taken.

Equipment: Ball and basket.

Procedure: Divide players into pairs, with two or three pairs per basket. Put two players on offense and two on defense; one offensive–defensive pair on each side of the lane, halfway between the baseline and the free-throw line. A coach is positioned at each of the free-throw lines with a ball. The defensive player on each side of the lane in basic position guards the offensive player. The offensive players begin to move to get open. The coach can pass to them if they get free. Otherwise, the coach takes a shot and each offensive player immediately raises a hand and holds up a certain number of fingers as they rebound. The defensive players try to block out the offensive players and get the rebound. If one of the defensive players gets the rebound and both defenders correctly name the number of fingers their offensive opponent held up, the offensive players move to play defense during the next repetition of the drill.

CLOSEOUT AND BLOCKOUT DRILL

Purpose: To simulate team competition in a controlled 1-on-1, 2-on-2, or 3-on-3 rebounding situation that includes on-the-ball and off-the-ball blockouts.

Equipment: Ball, basket, and half court.

Procedure: One, two, or three offensive players at 15 to 18 feet (4.6 to 5.5 meters) from the basket and the corresponding number of defensive players under the basket with a ball start the drill. The drill is played as a competitive make-it-take-it exercise that is restarted only when a basket is made. In defensive rebound situations, the defense must clear the ball above the top of the key area before changing to offense. The coach may require the three defenders to stay on defense whenever an assignment is missed.

LINE DRILL: FULL-COURT OFFENSIVE BOARDS WITHOUT THE BALL

Purpose: To teach players the offensive rebounding skills by simulation.

Equipment: Half court (minimum).

Procedure: The first four players make a get-ahead-or-get-even move from basic position, move to the free-throw line area, jump quickly, simulate capturing the ball, land in the chinit position, and use a designated scoring move. They repeat this process at the half-court line, the opposite free-throw line, and the opposite baseline. The return is made when all groups of four reach the end line. Offensive spacing (15 to 18 feet [4.6 to 5.5 meters]) should be kept with the player immediately ahead.

ADVANCED FIGURE-EIGHT REBOUND DRILL

Purpose: To teach players to control the rebound.

Equipment: One ball per basket.

Procedure: In groups of three players at a basket, the middle player starts the drill with a pass off the backboard (above the rectangle) to the next player. The object is continuous, controlled two-handed tipping or chinit rebounding by the group for a given number of repetitions, with players tipping or rebounding and then going behind.

Most players need to rebound the ball with a two-footed and two-handed rebound and chinit move and then go back up with an offensive scoring move designated by the coach (overhead, power shot, or shot fake and power shot). Rebounders should keep the feet at right angles to the baseline (point the toes at the baseline) and shoot the ball above the rectangle so that it rebounds from the backboard to the next rebounder.

GARBAGE DRILL

Purpose: To teach players to score on the offensive rebound.

Equipment: Two balls per basket.

Procedure: Two lines of players at the free-throw line area face the basket with a ball in each line. The first player passes the ball to the backboard with a two-handed underhand toss and rebounds the ball and then uses a designated scoring move. After scoring (and only after scoring), the player passes the ball to the next player in line and goes to the end of the opposite line. Each player assumes a miss and continues until the basket is made. The scoring moves should be the following:

- two-handed tip and score;
- overhead (keep the ball on the forehead—two hands), quick jump to score;
- chinit and score;
- chinit, fake (lift the ball head high and keep the legs locked), then score; and
- chinit, pass to an outlet player for a trey.

A final competition phase of the garbage drill can be added to teach aggressiveness and scoring in the lane. The coach has one ball at the free-throw line and works with two players at a time, one from each line. The coach usually shoots the ball and players rebound until one captures the ball and scores. The players should use a two-handed rebound or two-handed pickup and chinit on a loose ball. The player with the ball must score in the lane without dribbling while the other player defends. There are no out-of-bounds areas, and the ballhandler may use the coach for a release pass (which is returned if a quick move to get open is used).

NBA (NO BABIES ALLOWED) OR SURVIVAL REBOUNDING

Purpose: To teach aggressiveness to the players.

Equipment: One ball per basket.

Procedure: Groups of four to eight players are at each basket, with three players in the game at one time. If six to eight players are used, extra players should be shooting free

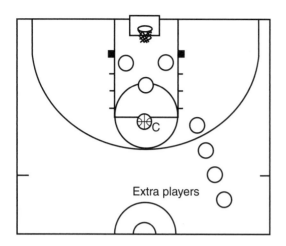

Extra players

FIGURE 8.19 **No babies allowed (NBA) rebounding.**

throws until they are rotated into the game. A coach or manager is positioned at each basket to shoot the ball (intentionally missing) and acts as a passing outlet for the rebounder. See figure 8.19. The rules of competition are as follows:

- Play starts with a missed shot.

- All three players attempt to get the rebound.

- The player who obtains the rebound is on offense, and the other two players become defenders. Rebounders use scoring moves; all shots must be taken in the free-throw lane without dribbling.

- The rebounder may outlet to the coach and get open for a return pass in the lane.

- There is no out-of-bounds boundary for play.

- Three scored baskets allows a player to rotate out (other players retain their totals). When starting, the best variation is one scored basket to move out of the drill and into the line feeding players into the drill.

- Significant fouls are the only ones called by the coach. A player may lose a score by fouling or by not playing defense.

INDIVIDUAL REBOUNDING

Purpose: To have players practice rebounding skills on their own.

Equipment: Ball, basket, and tossback rebounding device (or a partner).

Procedure: Carry out rebound options at game speed using two-footed and two-handed rebounding technique.

Options

- Toss the ball against the backboard or above the rim with a two-handed underhand toss to create a rebound—an angle jump to capture the ball and make an offensive scoring move (overhead; chin and score; chin, shot fake, and score). Assume a miss.

- Toss the ball to create a defensive rebound—make a quick outlet pass to the tossback or the partner or use a two-dribble push to clear the ball.

- Advanced—players jump as high and as quickly as they can; they pop the ball with two hands against the backboard on each jump.

- Place the ball on the free-throw lane block—grab it with two hands, explode to the backboard, and score from 2 feet (.6 meter) without gathering—capture, chin, explode to basket. Place the ball on the opposite block and repeat.

- Super rebounds—start outside the lane and pass the ball off the backboard to the other side of the lane. Take one step, jump over to get the rebound, and land outside the lane on the other side. Repeat five times and finish with a power move score.

REBOUND PROGRESSION: 3-ON-0, 3-ON-3

Purpose: To provide a three-player rebound format to review and practice rebounding skills as a team and as part of a practice or a game warm-up.

Equipment: Ball, basket, half court, and three air dummies (if available).

Procedure: Half of the team performs the drill near the basket while the other half stretches or performs other skill work. There are two sections with the drill:

1. In the offense (3-on-0) team rebounding, the coach controls and shoots the ball to create the rebound. Variations include the following:

    – Regular 3-on-0 at any three positions (on shot, low post player rebounds to the middle or the weak side, two to the weak side).

    – Tip up (to keep alive) and tip out.

    – Out-of-bounds save—the coach bounces the ball toward the out-of-bounds area—must be a *saver* and a *savee* (a teammate not pursuing the ball) verbally communicating (*ball* and *help*).

    – 3-on-3 with air dummies or dummy defenders—offensive players must go to a gap and rebound.

    – No Babies Allowed—the player who gets the rebound tries to score and the other two players harass. All three offensive rebounders assume a miss, rebound until a score, and then sprint toward the half-line (to the top of the key) with vision of the ball and the basket over the inside shoulder.

2. The defense (3-on-3) team rebounding uses three air dummies or dummy offensive players to block out. The coach shoots and three defenders blast, pursue, and outlet the ball to the coach or execute a two-dribble push outlet and then pass to the coach. Follow the BOPCRO sequence: **B**lock **o**ut or blast, **p**ursue and **c**hin the ball, **r**ebound, and **o**utlet.

CUTTHROAT REBOUNDING: 3-ON-3, 4-ON-4

Purpose: To simulate game-like offensive and defensive rebounding in a continuous, coach-controlled drill.

Equipment: Ball, basket, half court, with three groups of players (three or four) separately identified (e.g., red, white, and blue).

Procedure: Begin with a group on offense, a group on defense, and a group behind the baseline underneath the basket. The coach has the ball and is underneath the basket behind the baseline to start and control the drill. Two outlet receivers are positioned near the sideline rear half court.

The rotation is as follows: As a shot is missed, both offensive and defensive groups rebound. When the defensive group gets the ball, the players use the BOPCRO sequence to the outlet and move to offense (the baseline group comes in on defense). When the offensive group gets a rebound, the players stay on offense (after a score, they transition to half court and stay on offense). The baseline group again comes in on defense. The ball is always returned to the coach to continue the drill. The drill may be continued for a period of time. Winners can be determined by the most defensive rebounds, offensive rebounds, or points scored. The coach can emphasize any of these options.

WAR REBOUNDING

Purpose: To emphasize aggressive defensive or offensive rebounding in a 5-on-5 situation.

Equipment: Ball, basket, half court.

Procedure: This is a live drill started by the coach shooting the ball (and missing most of the time). It is played on live, made, or missed shots, without regard to out-of-bounds lines, in order to get players to capture, secure, and chin the ball in all circumstances. The usual scoring scheme is 1 point for a defensive rebound, 2 points for a score, and 3 points for an offensive rebound. Coaches can emphasize offense or defense by giving points to that phase only and allowing a team to stay in the scoring mode when players score (e.g., defensive rebound score, stay on defense). The drill may start with many variations:

- Closeouts—defenders start on the baseline, pass to an offensive player, pass to the coach for the shot
- Skip pass, then shot
- Secondary fast-break set, swing the ball, then shot
- From zone defense
- Any special offensive set or situation, then shot

This drill can be done for a time period or to a given score.

Team Offense

"Basketball is a game of finesse and reason, especially on offense."

Phil Jackson, former Coach of the Chicago Bulls and Los Angeles Lakers,
used a concept from a Lakota Indian war chant—"Don't overpower, outsmart the opponent."

Coaches should instill in players the confidence to go all out—to have fun, to learn and improve, and to take chances and make mistakes, especially on offense. By preparing players to handle all situations and improving their basketball IQ, coaches can strengthen their confidence that they can be successful.

The following areas should be covered to prepare the team for all situations: general offensive principles, responsibilities of players at each offensive position, offensive team tactics, and special situations for team offense.

General Offensive Principles

CRITICAL CUE:
Team offense must have high-percentage shots, transition, balance, movement, and execution.

Unless coaches are familiar with the offensive strengths and weaknesses of team members, they should select a basic offense that can be adapted to a variety of players and that is flexible enough to allow team members to use their individual strengths. The coach's basic philosophy should be stable and evolve slowly, but the offensive and defensive style of play should change to fit the players.

Offense depends heavily on proper spacing and timing; all five players should be spread out on the court area, moving and cutting together at the right time. Any offense should have court balance; that is, it should produce high-percentage shots with assigned offensive rebounders and assigned players for defense when a shot is taken. Balance also refers to maintaining proper court spacing—about 15 to 18 feet (4.6 to 5.5 meters)—between offensive teammates. Finally, offensive balance also consists of offensive rebounding and concern for defense when a shot is taken. Making the quick transition from offense to defense (and vice versa) is called developing the transition game—going to offensive rebound or back to defense quickly. Balanced scoring from several players is always better than dependence on a scoring star in a team game.

A good offense includes player movement as well as ball movement and may, with more experienced players, include screening. Scoring should come from the inside (close to the basket) as well as the outside (on the perimeter of the defense). Develop the offense from the inside out; establish an inside game and a complementary outside game, preventing the defense from concentrating on one area or one player. The execution of any system is much more important than the system itself. What a team does is not as critical as how well the players do it.

Player Positions and Responsibilities

Each player on a basketball team has a position to play that is related to role, ability, and skill. The three basic positions are guard, forward, and center (or post) (figure 9.1). Some coaches use other names, such as point, wing, and inside player.

The center is usually the tallest player, with forwards next, and guards being the smallest. Centers and forwards tend to be the best rebounders, whereas guards are often the best ballhandlers. Guards also tend to play outside more than forwards and centers. No matter what term is used, all perimeter players and all inside players should learn the basic skills so they can be interchangeable in selected situations.

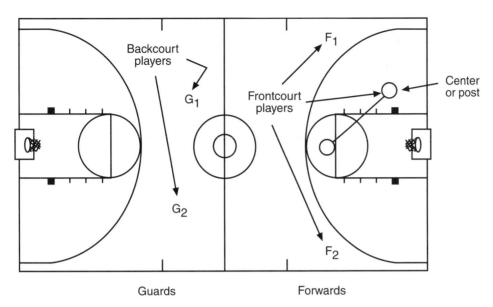

FIGURE 9.1 **Player positions.**

Guards. Guards grouped together are usually called the team's backcourt. This grouping can be broken down further into point guards (normally the best ballhandler and often the player who directs the team on the floor) and shooting guards (also called *big guards* or *off guards*). Because of their dribbling ability, point guards can often create a scoring chance for a teammate (such as the shooting guard) by penetrating and passing, that is, by driving past defenders to the basket and passing to an open or unguarded teammate (penetrate and pitch or drive and dish). Point guards are called *playmakers* because they direct teammates and create scoring opportunities. The point guard is usually among the best ballhandlers on the team and should also be a leader who can become the coach on the floor. Choose shooting guards from among the best shooters, scorers, and ballhandlers on the team.

Forwards. Forwards are sometimes called *corner* players because their normal offensive position is in the corner of the frontcourt. Most teams play a small forward and a big forward (sometimes called the power forward or strong forward). The small forward is more of a swing player who can play guard or forward and who plays facing the basket, where good ballhandling and outside shooting are essential. The big forward is often a strong rebounder who swings from outside to inside (back to the basket). Small forwards should be able to play as combination guard–forwards, handle the ball well, play outside on the perimeter, and rebound. Big forwards must be combination forward–centers.

Center or Post Player. Choose players for the center position from among the biggest players, those who relish playing inside, near the basket, where contact and congestion are readily accepted. The center is usually the biggest player, who plays inside around the free-throw lane in the high post (near the foul line) or in the low post (close to the basket) and outside the free-throw or three-second lane with the back to the basket. The center and two forwards are collectively known as the frontcourt.

Offensive Team Tactics

Develop team tactics to prepare the team to face all basic defensive situations, including the following:

- a transition game as an organized way to go from defense to offense (primary fast break—to keep the defense honest and put immediate pressure on the defense and secondary fast break for when the defense is back but not fully organized),
- a press offense to be used against defensive presses, from half court to full court,
- a player-to-player set offense for situations in which opponents guard the players individually,
- a zone set offense to be used against zone or area defenses,
- a set offense that can be used against combination defenses (zone and player-to-player),
- a delay or control offense to use when time and score dictate controlling the game and maintaining ball possession for longer periods before a shot and forcing the opponents to defend a larger court area,
- a transition game from offense to defense (providing offensive rebounders while preventing the opponent's easy scores and fast breaks), and
- special situation plays: jump ball, out-of-bounds, free throws.

Primary Fast Break: Transition From Defense to Offense

A team can set up a good shot by running the fast break when the team that gains possession of the ball brings it up the court before the opponents can get into a good defensive position. This outnumbered fast-break situation is called a *primary* fast break. The fast break, which usually develops after a rebound, steal, or possibly after a made basket, is the fastest way to make the transition from defense to offense. As soon as the defense gains control of the ball, it uses the outlet pass or dribble to start the break—passing being the first option and dribbling the last when moving the ball up the court. Then the other teammates attempt to beat the defenders up the court while staying spread out. Players should run at top speed under control when executing a fast break up the court. One player should stay a few steps behind the action in a defensive safety role for balance.

CRITICAL CUE:
Three-lane fast break: the ball in the middle, the side lanes wide, and a banana cut to the basket (at the top of the key) or drift to the corner for three.

A typical three-lane fast-break pattern is shown in figure 9.2. A team needs a three-lane fast break (the ball in the middle) when the players outnumber the opponents, 3-on-2. In a 3-on-1 situation, the offense should convert to a two-lane fast break (2-on-1 plus a trailer), as shown in figure 9.3. In a two-lane fast break, the offensive players should split the floor (stay at least as wide as the free-throw lane) to make the defender commit. The best ballhandler should handle the ball at the completion—*go to the glass unless forced to pass*. The dribbler always needs to offset the middle to the side of the lane, preferably dribbling with the outside hand. Advanced players can dribble with the inside hand (easier to push a bounce pass by the defender) and shoot the reverse layback shot if the defender doesn't take the dribbler.

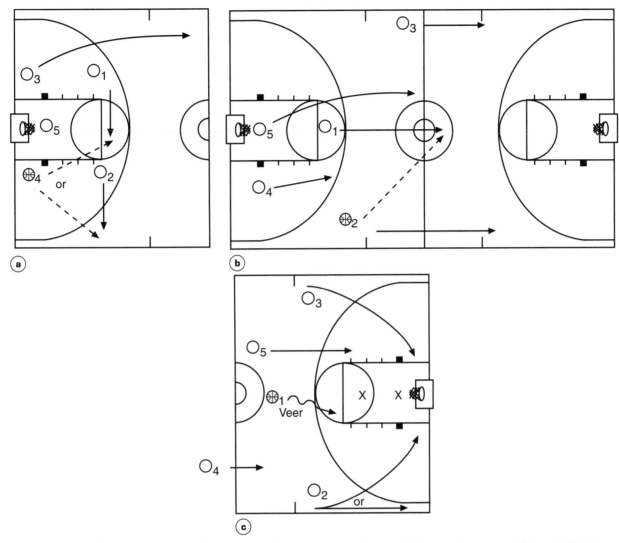

FIGURE 9.2 Primary fast breaks: *(a)* starting after defensive rebound, *(b)* spreading out and filling the lanes, and *(c)* completion of three-lane fast break.

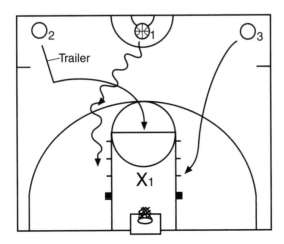

FIGURE 9.3 Primary two-lane fast break.

Secondary Fast Break: Transition From Defense to Offense

If a primary fast break (outnumbering the defense 3-on-2, 3-on-1, or 2-on-1) is not available, teams should develop a secondary fast break. This move keeps pressure on the defense by taking the ball up the side to the baseline (flattens or collapses the defense), posting a player inside, and reversing the ball to the second side before flowing into the set offense. A secondary fast break is shown in figure 9.4.

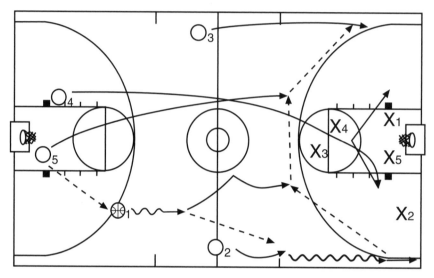

FIGURE 9.4 Secondary fast break (4 out, 1 in).

Press Offense

Fundamentals such as spacing, cutting, meeting the pass, catching and facing the basket, passing first, and dribbling last are more important than any specific press offense.

If the defense is defending on a full-court (all over the court) basis, coaches need a press offense to help the team get the ball in bounds safely. Players should get the ball in bounds before the defense gets set (i.e., use the transition fast break to beat a pressing defense before it is set). Designate a frontcourt player to take the ball out after all made baskets and quickly inbound the ball to a guard, as shown in figure 9.5a. The inbound pass catcher should stay out of the corners and not get too close to the sideline (prime trapping areas).

Against any zone press, coaches should teach players to attack the defense in the backcourt or frontcourt by having a sideline pass outlet, two middle pass outlets (short and long), and a safety valve pass outlet slightly behind the ballhandler, as shown in figures 9.5b and 9.6. Emphasize to players the need to use good passing and catching fundamentals and remind them to move to get open and to keep their poise. Pressing defenses take chances. Players should be prepared to take advantage of those overcommitments.

Generally, players need to attack a pressing defense. Be aggressive and look to score layups by getting the ball up the side or to the middle of the pressing defense.

As a last resort, the offense can use the safety valve to reverse the ball and attack on the second side, as shown in figure 9.7. In extreme emergencies, with the ballhandler in a trap or double-team, the nearest teammate (usually the safety valve)

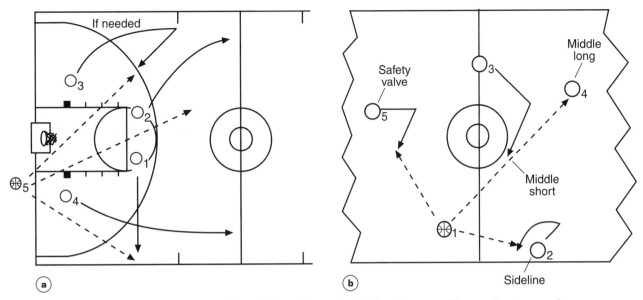

FIGURE 9.5   Press offense—get the ball in quickly: *(a)* get the ball in; *(b)* press offense when trapped.

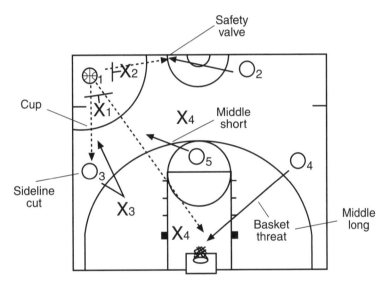

FIGURE 9.6   Beat the trap: form the three-player cup (O₃, O₅, O₂) with a basket threat.

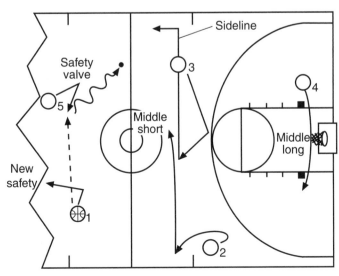

FIGURE 9.7   Press offense—reverse the ball and attack.

can come to the ball directly behind the trap (usually not defended) for a pass. The ballhandler can use a rear turn to protect the ball and make the pass. The safety valve player should attack the press immediately.

Set Offense

If the defense is set and waiting after the primary and secondary fast breaks, a set offense should be used to get a good shot. The team should get into a basic starting formation and then use the fundamental skill moves with and without the ball to create scoring opportunities. This basic set or formation may take a variety of starting positions. Coaches should select a preferred starting formation that fits personnel and favored tactics.

The 2-2-1 Give-and-Go Offense. The first team play in basketball was the two-man play called *give-and-go* or *pass-and-cut*. This play is the basis of this offense, a two-person play in which the passer passes to a catcher and cuts to the basket for a possible return pass as the foundation play. This play is started from a four out–one-in, two-guard and two-forward set, as shown in figure 9.8 (which also shows possible give-and-go, or pass-and-cut, options). It can be initiated by any two players at any time. Basic rules of the offense are the following:

1. The court middle is the cutting highway. Cutters must cut through the middle after a pass, go toward the basket, and clear the middle in two seconds. This cut controls the defense.

2. Players should read and react to defenders: pass and cut against the sag (soft) defense, cut in front of defenders when possible, and backdoor on defensive overplay.

3. Cutters can post up briefly, but then must clear the middle area.

4. Players should make a catching spot available to the passer, space themselves 15 to 18 feet (4.6 to 5.5 meters) away, and meet the pass.

5. Against zone defenses, cut through the middle of defensive gaps or holes. Drive into gaps after a catch.

6. Offense is player generated (much freedom) and rule based. The penetrating cut is the key.

7. The post player is stationed on the low post near the block; responsibilities are to rebound the weak side and be ready for the strong-side 2-on-1 dumpdown on cut or pass penetration. The post player may post up when the ball is on that side and flash post for a layup only occasionally when the defender is not alert.

8. Some optional moves also can be used by verbal call:
   - Perimeter screen on the ball
   - Perimeter pass and screen off the ball
   - Perimeter drive on clearout on one side of the floor
   - Flash post by cutters (two-second rule)

9. On traps or double-team, players should pass to the middle cutter in a hole or to another player coming to the ball (emergency).

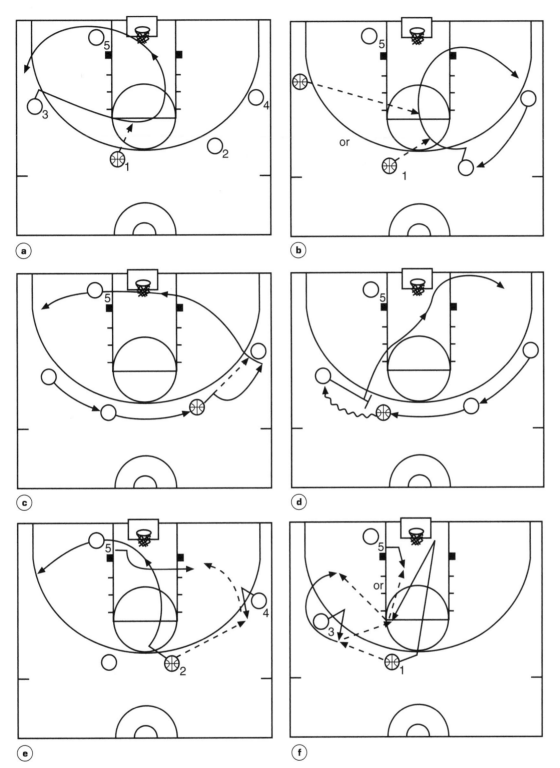

FIGURE 9.8 Pass-and-cut offensive variations: *(a)* go—forward cut, *(b)* go—guard cut, *(c)* go—guard around, *(d)* guard ball pick, *(e)* guard to forward pass-and-cut or post flash, *(f)* guard to forward pass-and-cut to post up.

10. Offense can be run from full court, three-quarter court, or half court. The movement of the ball and the cutters is more important than the formation or the set. Coaches should watch player spacing. Players should cut with a purpose; they may go on the same side or on the opposite side on the middle clear.

11. Offense teaching progression:
    - 2-on-0, 2-on-2 (guard, forward)
    - 3-on-0, 3-on-3, 3-on-3 with the weak-side post
    - 5-on-5 half court, full court

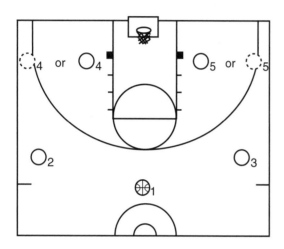

FIGURE 9.9 **A 1-2-2 double low-post set (may also be open post).**

The 1-2-2 Give-and-Go. Another offense for beginning players is the 1-2-2 give-and-go offense, which can be used effectively against player-to-player defenses. The give-and-go offense is a simple team offense that uses passing, catching, basic moves without the ball, and individual moves with the ball. The 1-2-2 double low-post or open-post set is a one-guard, open-post formation that allows any player to V-cut into the post area and keeps the middle open for individual offensive moves plus give-and-go options (figure 9.9). The give-and-go offense from the 1-2-2 open-post formation can also be used against zone or combination (zone and player-to-player) defenses by depending less on cutting and emphasizing more individual moves from stationary spots.

The rules for this offense are the following:

1. The give-and-go from the point to wing pass is a pass and go-to-the-basket move after a V-cut is made by O_3. Cutting players who don't receive the return pass should balance the floor opposite the first pass (figure 9.10a). The give-and-go from the wing position to the corner position is shown in figure 9.10b. Notice how floor balance is regained.

2. If a wing player is overplayed or denied the pass by a defender, players should use a backdoor cut to the basket and replace on the same side (figure 9.10c). A corner player who is overplayed should make a backdoor cut and come back to the same side (figure 9.10d).

3. A wing or forward may V-cut into the post area (high or low). Players who make ball cuts and don't receive the ball within 2 seconds should return to the same starting position (figure 9.10e).

4. When a shot is taken, the point guard (O_1) should go to defense near the half-court line, and the other four players should go to offensive rebounding positions. This rule applies to all offensive situations: The offensive team should always have defensive balance and make a quick transition to defense. Coaches may prefer to have two players change to defense as fullbacks when a shot is taken.

The 1-4. The 1-4 double high-post set is a formation that requires a good point guard. It is difficult to press, there are four possible entry passes, and the offense needs two inside players (figure 9.11).

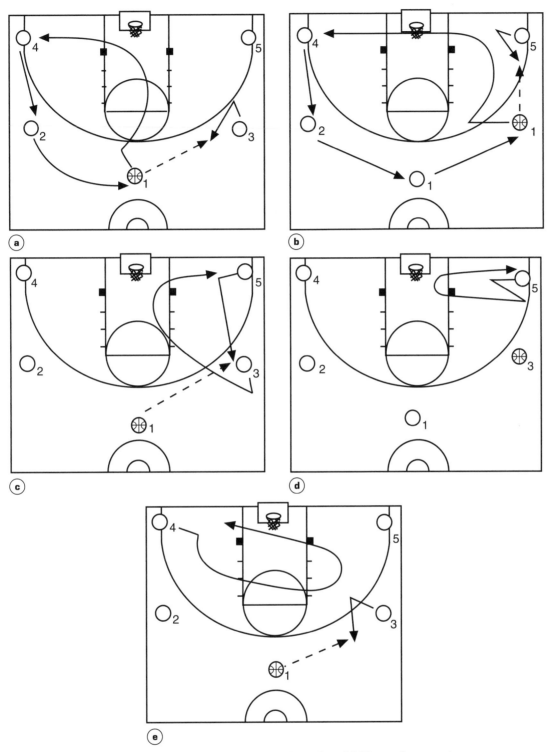

FIGURE 9.10 1-2-2 offense: *(a)* Give-and-go from the point. *(b)* Give-and-go on wing-to-corner pass. *(c)* Backdoor cut by the wing. *(d)* Backdoor cut by the corner. *(e)* V-cut to the post area and go back.

The 1-3-1. The 1-3-1 high-to-low post set has a point guard in front; it positions forwards for individual moves and requires two inside players (the high-post player must be able to face the basket). See figure 9.12.

The 1-2-2 Stack. Coaches might consider using a 1-2-2 stack formation, which calls for a point guard in front, one open side for individual moves, and a stack on the other side. This set may be used with one player (O_4) cutting to any position, while the other stack player acts as a screener and then takes up a single-post position (O_5). The stack allows a variety of cuts by player O_4, as shown in figure 9.13.

The 2-2-1 or 2-3 Set.   The final possibility for an offensive formation is the traditional 2-2-1 or 2-3 set (figure 9.14). This is a two-guard front with a single post (high or low). The sides and corners of the court are open for forward moves. The 2-3 formation is more vulnerable to pressing defenses.

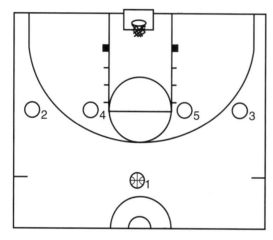

FIGURE 9.11   **A 1-4 set or formation (point O_1, two wings O_2 and O_3, and two posts O_4 and O_5), sometimes called a double high post.**

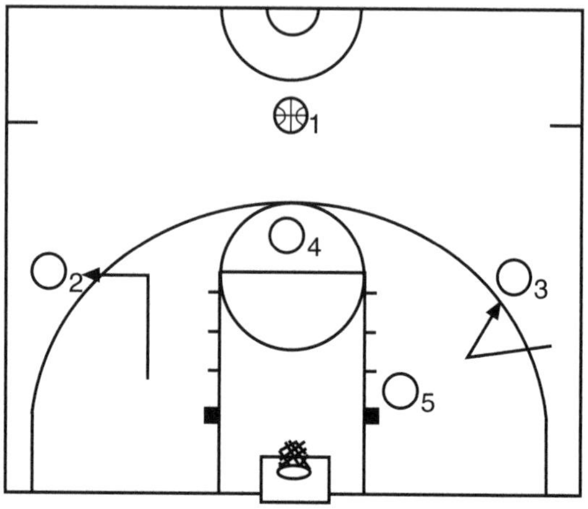

FIGURE 9.12   **A 1-3-1 high-to-low post set.**

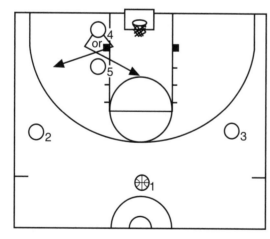

FIGURE 9.13   **A stack set with a one-player front.**

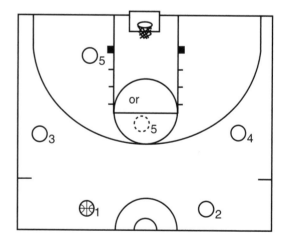

FIGURE 9.14   **A 2-2-1 or 2-3 set (high or low post).**

Zone Offense

Against a zone defense, coaches can opt for the modified, recommended give-and-go offense or may select another formation. In any case, teach players to use the following rules:

• Perimeter players align in the gaps on the perimeter and step up into shooting range (figure 9.15).

- Attack the defense, but be patient. Look for opportunities for dribble or pass penetration inside the zone after passing around the perimeter.
- Watch floor spacing between other offensive players. This spreads the defense and makes it difficult to cover offensive players.
- Cut through zone—test the zone by moving players and relocating, as shown in figure 9.16.
- Screen the zone—beat a zone defense by screening inside or outside on the zone, as shown in figure 9.17.

Coaches should encourage player and ball movement. Because most zone defenses are ball oriented, ball fakes are effective. Players should put the ball overhead in order for the defenders to see the ball and react to a fake (pass or shot). Fake a pass to make a pass. Players should only place the ball overhead after catching and pitting it in triple-threat position.

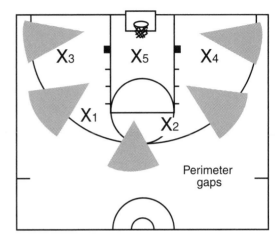

FIGURE 9.15 **Against zone defense, align in the gaps.**

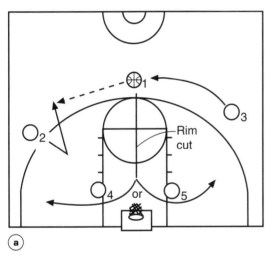

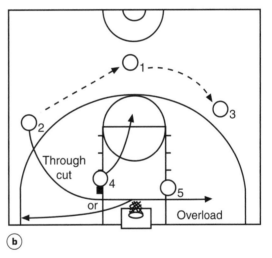

FIGURE 9.16 *(a)* **Point cuts through the zone.** *(b)* **Wing cuts through the zone.**

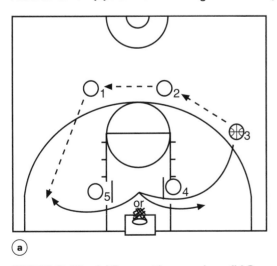

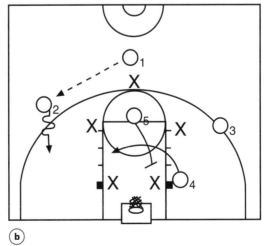

FIGURE 9.17 *(a)* **Screen the zone low.** *(b)* **Screen the zone inside.**

Offense Against Combination Defenses

When combination player-to-player and zone defenses are used (triangle-and-2, box-and-1, or diamond-and-1), the team needs an organized approach to attack them. The regular player-to-player offense can be used or the zone offense—coaches need to choose an offense that has player movement, ball movement, and screening action. Analyze the defense and use the offense (play or set) that exploits that defense. For example, the set shown previously in figure 9.17a could be used with the offensive player guarded one-on-one defensively being the baseline runner using the screens.

When the team has a lead late in the game, coaches may decide to have players spread out on the court and use the whole frontcourt to make the defense cover a larger area. This is called a *delay* game (or *control* game), and usually only close-to-the-basket shots are taken. In these situations, running a normal offense may be best, with stricter rules on shot selection, or making a certain number of passes before a shot is taken (unless the shot is a layup). This offense can be used with or without a shot clock.

When a shot rule is applied until 8 to 10 seconds remain, the ballhandler looks for dribble penetration and other players start individual moves to set up a good shot. Time and score dictate when the team should control the ball and use the clock (delay-game tactics). The most common formation for this offense is shown in figure 9.18, where four offensive players are placed in the four corners and the best dribbler or ballhandler is out front in the middle of the court. Player O_1, usually the point guard or playmaker, constantly looks for chances to penetrate and pass. All offensive players should read and react to the defense and wait for their defender to make an error they can capitalize on. Coaches should be sure to have good free-throw shooters playing when using the control game, because defenders may foul more, out of frustration or by design.

Stay on the attack; don't get passive and lose momentum. Players can decoy the defense by appearing to delay but always looking for chances to score. If they don't want to shoot, they can run a normal offense and act as though they are attacking.

With 8 to 10 seconds left, a special play may be used (figure 9.19). The options are O_1 using the pick, O_2 or O_3 moving for the penetrate and pitch three-point field-goal attempt, O_4 using the backpick by O_5, and O_5 stepping out after the screen.

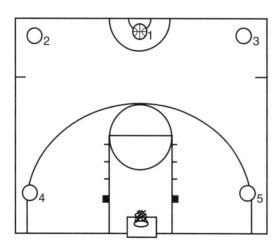

FIGURE 9.18 **Four-corner offense-delay or control game.**

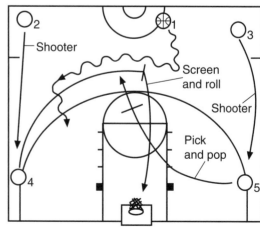

FIGURE 9.19 **Last-second score.**

Special Situations for Team Offense

Team offense should be prepared to face a variety of special situations: out-of-bounds plays, free throws, jump balls, and last-second scoring plays. The purpose is to prepare a team for any game situation.

Bringing the Ball Inbounds. Every team must have a plan for bringing the ball into play underneath its own basket and on the sidelines. Examples of formations and plays, shown in figures 9.20 and 9.21, can be used against any defense. Most important, a team needs to be able to inbound the ball safely against all defensive tactics.

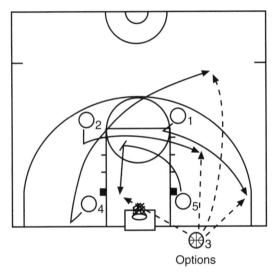

Options

FIGURE 9.20 Under out-of-bounds play. O_5 and O_2 run a pick-and-roll play.

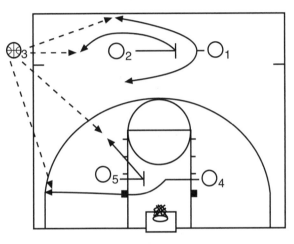

FIGURE 9.21 Side out-of-bounds play. O_2 screens for O_1, O_5 screens for O_4, and O_3 has four passing options.

Free Throws. Free-throw situations also must be planned carefully. On an offensive free throw, the two best rebounders should occupy the second-lane spaces and attempt to gain an offensive rebound in the middle of the lane or to the baseline side of the defender. Player O_3 is stationed in a position to be alert for any long rebound or loose ball that might be tipped out, and O_1 and O_3 have safety (fullback) responsibilities on defense and must not let any opponent get behind them for a long pass reception (figure 9.22). For a defensive free-throw situation, player X_1 must be alert for a loose ball or long rebound. Player X_2 blocks out or checks the shooter by getting between the shooter and the basket. Players X_4 and X_5 check the opponents on their side of the lane (second-lane space) while player X_3 rebounds in the middle area (figure 9.23). When a defensive rebound is captured, all team members make a transition to the fast break.

Jump Balls. Special plays should be developed for jump-ball situations to start games and overtime periods. The smaller, quicker players defend the basket. No matter what the formation is, the ball should be tipped to an open spot (where two teammates are next to each other without an opponent in between). See figure 9.24.

Last-Second Shots. The last-second shot, diagrammed in figure 9.25, may be used in the delay game or in any situation where a move to the basket is made with 8 to 10 seconds remaining, depending on the level of play (younger players need more time), allowing time for a good shot opportunity, a possible offensive rebound, and a second shot, but not enough time for the opponent to get a good shot at the other end of the court.

No matter what offensive situation, formation, play, or system is chosen, execution is the key—it is not what players do but how well they do it. Practice these special situations using the clock.

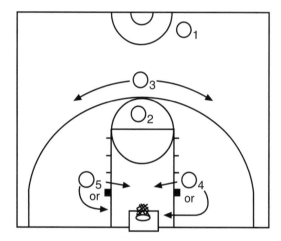

FIGURE 9.22 **Offensive free throw.** O_2 is shooting, O_4 and O_5 occupy the second-lane spaces on each side, O_3 is at the top of the circle (the key), and O_1 is defensive safety.

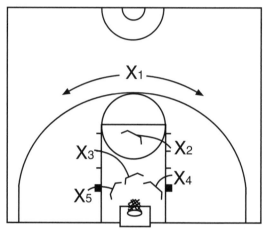

FIGURE 9.23 **Defensive free throw.** Four defenders block out or check their opponents on the free-throw lane.

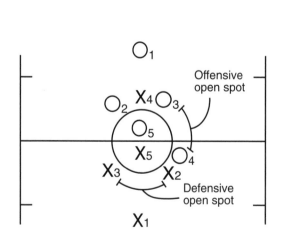

FIGURE 9.24 **Jump ball.**

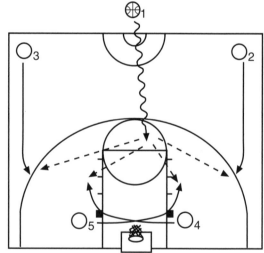

FIGURE 9.25 **Last-second shot.** O_4 and O_5 cross under the basket while O_2 and O_3 slide into scoring position and are ready to shoot. O_1 has four passing options.

Defensive Transition: Offense to Defense

An organized plan is needed to execute offense properly. Players should make a transition to defense *quickly,* without being outnumbered on the fast break, in order to set the defense. One method is for the coach to create transition roles for all of the offensive players:

• Fullback—the designated safety, usually the point guard, who is responsible for preventing easy scores (no layups). As any shot by teammates is taken, the fullback sprints to the half-court center circle and retreats, running backward to the basket, and directs the defense from there (figure 9.26). When the fullback shoots, another player makes the call and switches assignments. On an offensive fast break, the last player down the floor becomes the fullback and never crosses the half-court line until a score is made or the secondary fast break begins.

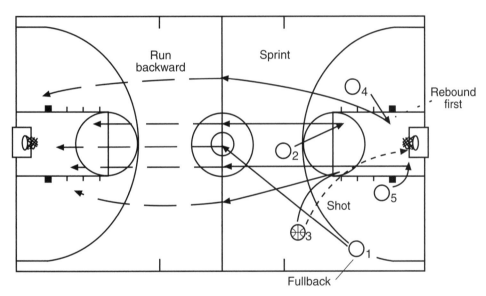

FIGURE 9.26 **Defensive transition.**

• Tailbacks—all other players, when the shot is taken, are responsible for going to the offensive boards (assume a miss) until the opponents get the ball or a basket is made. When that happens, all four players sprint to half-court, seeing the ball over their inside shoulder while running backward to their defensive assignment (i.e., they get their *tails* back on defense) if they are not outnumbered. Most teams use three tailbacks with the fourth player (usually the shooter) used as a rebounder at the free-throw line or a long rebounder, who then transitions to defense early and becomes a halfback who is responsible for stopping the ball coming up the court.

Variations of the plan can be developed for special situations (e.g., to pressure the rebounder, to stop the ball coming up the floor, etc.).

COACHING POINTS FOR TEAM OFFENSE

- ◻ Be quick, but don't hurry—focus first on execution and timing, later on speed.
- ◻ Maintain balance in all areas:
  - – Individual—physical and emotional.
  - – Offensive and defensive.
  - – Offensive rebounding and defensive coverage (on all shot attempts).
  - – Floor spacing—spread out and move the ball.
  - – Inside and outside scoring.
  - – Passing and scoring.
- ◻ Strive for spacing and timing.
- ◻ Teach intelligent teamwork on offense.
- ◻ Teach players to put the team first and individual plays second.
- ◻ Encourage players to play fearlessly—to make mistakes, but to learn from them.
- ◻ Develop individual play within the team context.
- ◻ Have the ball and the players move on offense. Players should move with a purpose.
- ◻ Be patient with team offense. Play must be coordinated with player movements; as a result, learning progress is slower than with team defense.

CHECKLIST FOR TEAM OFFENSE

- ◻ General principles developed
- ◻ Positions and responsibilities defined
- ◻ Offensive fundamental skills
- ◻ Body control
- ◻ Ballhandling
- ◻ Shooting
- ◻ Perimeter play
- ◻ Post play
- ◻ Rebounding
- ◻ Press offense
- ◻ Transition to offense (primary, secondary fast break)
- ◻ Player-to-player set offense
- ◻ Zone set offense
- ◻ Combination set offense
- ◻ Delay (control) offense
- ◻ Special situations: jump balls, offensive free throws, out-of-bounds plays
- ◻ Transition to defense

TROUBLESHOOTING

Most offensive errors occur because of improper sequential and progressive development. It is critical to go slowly and carefully with no defenders, then 5-on-0 at game speed to get spacing and timing. Only then can defenders be added to simulate game conditions; first use a dummy, then live in all variations of defense so offensive players learn to read and respond properly to all defensive situations.

Drills for Team Offense

Team offense should first be executed slowly and correctly. Then moves are carried out at game speed to develop team coordination and timing. An emphasis on proper spacing is needed unless players are screening or cutting to the basket.

SKELETON OFFENSE DRILL: 5-ON-0

Purpose: To teach movements and assignments for basic team offensive formation.

Equipment: One ball, five players, and half court.

Procedure: Five players at a time take the court to practice team offensive formations, plays, or movements, and individual assignments within the team offense. The offense should be initiated from all situations: backcourt, frontcourt, out-of-bounds, and free throws. Offensive play should be completed with a score each time (rebound each shot), and transition should be made to half-court. This drill includes five offensive players at a time and no defenders.

Options

- Half court offense—all sets
- Half court to full court (defense to offense)—after made or missed baskets; press offense; secondary fast break; set offense
- Half-court defense to full-court offensive options to defensive transition

On all offensive shots, assume a miss and make a transition (always rebound until the basket is made). Players should always make a transition to half-court on all drills whether a shot is made or missed.

TEAM OFFENSE-DEFENSE DRILL: 5-ON-5

Purpose: To teach team offense and defense in a progressive manner that culminates in 5-on-5 competition.

Equipment: Ball, basket, and half court or full court.

Procedure: Five defenders and five offensive players practice team play. They should practice all offensive situations in order to prevent surprises at game time. The progression is to have defenders play dummy position defense and then no-hands defense (players may grasp the jersey in front), before going to game-like offense and defense with no restrictions and different defensive tactics.

Play should continue until the offense transitions to the other end of the floor (i.e., go from half court to full court).

Options

- Half court only
- Half-court make-it-take-it, full-court transition on misses
- Half court to full court (defense to offense transition—press offense, fast break, set offenses)
- Full court—stop for corrections, shooting drill breaks (field goal, free throw)

BLITZ FAST-BREAK DRILL

Purpose: To teach the fundamentals of two-lane and three-lane fast-break offensive and defensive plays.

Equipment: One ball, 10 to 16 players divided into two teams, and a full-court space.

Procedure: The two teams are aligned as shown in figure 9.27, with opposing teams at half court. One team is selected to start on defense at one end of the court; the other team starts on offense at half court.

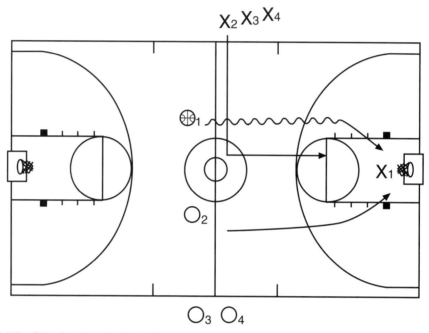

FIGURE 9.27 **Blitz fast break: 2-on-1.**

The drill begins when player O_1 crosses the half-line with the ball for a 2-on-1 fast-break situation; player X_2 is allowed to help X_1 in the outnumbered situation after touching the center circle. The defender X_1 should bluff, anticipate, and delay the offensive duo in the two-lane fast break until X_2 can recover to help—talk and get both players covered if they don't complete the break.

When the basket is made or missed, X_1 or X_2 captures the ball and advances the ball in a two-lane fast break toward the other basket. As soon as the X team gains possession of the ball, the next O player, O_3, touches the center circle and becomes the defensive safety (figure 9.28). When X_2 crosses the half-line with the ball, O_4 can sprint to defense after touching the center circle. The drill usually continues to nine baskets. Score can be kept on the scoreboard. Coaches should officiate.

The other blitz fast-break option is the three-lane fast break, 3-on-2, with at least twelve players to form the two teams. The alignment is shown in figure 9.29. The two defenders usually align in tandem with the inside player forward (X_4) and the outside player (X_1) covering the basket and taking the first pass on a closeout.

The other defender sprints to help as soon as the middle ballhandler crosses the half-court line. Then dribbler O_1 veer dribbles to one side after reading the back defender X_1 and passes to the open teammate. When defenders on the X team get the ball, they form a three-lane fast break to the other end, with the ball in the middle. As soon as the

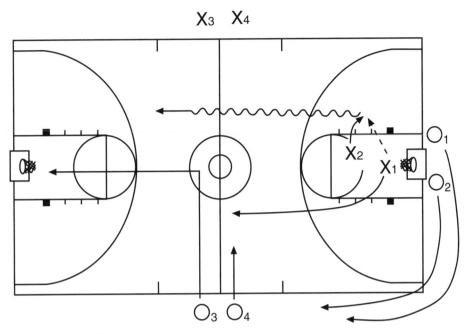

FIGURE 9.28 **2-on-1 blitz fast break, part two.**

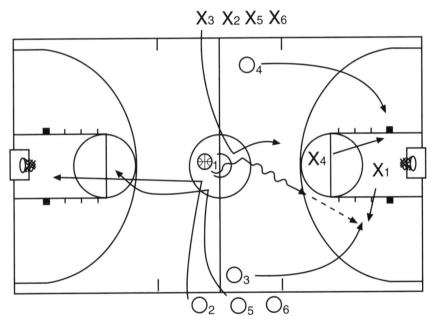

FIGURE 9.29 **3-on-2 blitz fast break.**

X team gains the ball, the next two O players, O_2 and O_5, sprint to defense after touching the center circle. The drill runs continuously until one team reaches 10 baskets.

Options

- 2-on-1 blitz.
- 3-on-2 blitz.
- Start sideline players at the top of the key; have the defender touch the top of the key circle before going to the other end.

TRANSITION FAST-BREAK DRILL

Purpose: To teach transition basketball from a structural start and unpredictable finish.

Equipment: Ball, two opposing teams, and a full court.

Procedure: Figure 9.30 shows the start at one end of the floor. The coach begins by passing to any offensive player (O_4 in this case) and calls numbers or names for one or two defenders. When a name is called, that player touches the baseline before going to defense, thus creating an outnumbered fast-break situation. The defensive team sprints back and talks to protect the basket, stop the ball, and cover all offensive players quickly. The offensive team attacks, reads the defense, and runs the primary or secondary fast break. Play continues for one, two, or three transitions before starting over.

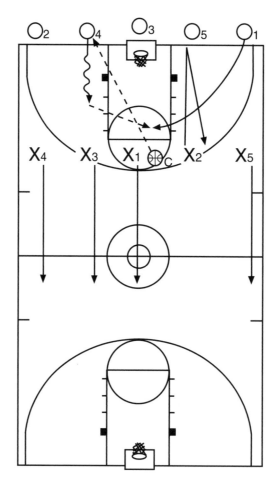

FIGURE 9.30 Team transition fast-break drill.

chapter 10

Team Defense

"Team defense and ballhandling are the cornerstones of successful teams."

Henry "Hank" Iba, Oklahoma State, Olympic Coach, Hall of Fame Coach

Coaches should build the team on a solid foundation. Defense, one of the most concrete and unchanging elements of the game, can be the most consistent phase of team play and should be the heart of a team's strength. A team that prevents its opponents from getting good shots is tough to beat.

In addition, because younger players have limited individual and team offensive skills, team defense can be an even more dominant aspect for beginners. Convince players that defense is the key to building a foundation for team play. Beginners have trouble understanding the relation between defense and preventing opponents from scoring and winning games and need to be convinced that defense and preventing a score by opponents are as important as scoring points for their own team.

Defense tends to be reactive rather than proactive—a defender usually reacts to the moves of an offensive player. Players must learn to be aggressive and initiate action on defense; teach players to act—not react—when playing defense. With determination and practice, a team can develop effective defensive play that is more proactive.

Team defenses are based on individual defensive fundamental skills. Motivate players to develop pride in their ability to play defense. Any team can be made better by developing a sound team defense.

A basic precept of team defense is to prepare players for action and to prevent problems. For example, a player in quick stance can often anticipate moves by offensive players before they are made and then take those moves away. Teach players to be ready for anything, which means being prepared to defend against an opponent's best offensive moves. This preparation makes the defender mentally and physically ready for secondary offensive moves by an opponent. Players should get in a defensive quick stance and stay in that stance—a measure of team defense.

One main objective of any defense should be to make the other teams do things that they do not want to do. Offense depends on confidence and rhythm, which players can disrupt on defense. Take away the opponents' strengths—make them learn how to play differently during games. This forces offenses to perform secondary moves and options instead of moves that are their strengths—which is especially difficult to do during games. Make them play to their weaknesses by taking away their strengths. Defense is a game of give and take; if players take something away, they will likely give up something in return. This applies to strengths and weaknesses as well as each defensive level and category of defense.

Communication is the glue that holds team defense together. For effective defense, teams need to develop and implement excellent communication skills—verbal and nonverbal, talking and listening. In the team sport of basketball, players cannot communicate too much, and coaches cannot emphasize communication too much.

Team defense also depends on the effectiveness of team offense (ballhandling and taking good shots). Efficient offense tends to energize and complement team defense, as well as take the pressure from the defense and make it more proactive.

CRITICAL CUE:
Prevent easy scores (allow only one contested shot).

CRITICAL CUE:
Take away the offensive player's best move or strength.

CRITICAL CUE:
Can't talk too much on defense.

Defensive Court Levels

The many varieties and styles of defense can be played at various levels of the court (figure 10.1). Coaches can instruct players to begin defending the opposing team at any point on the court.

The full-court team defense is a pressing defense in which defenders guard or pick up opponents as soon as possible all over the court. In a three-quarter-court

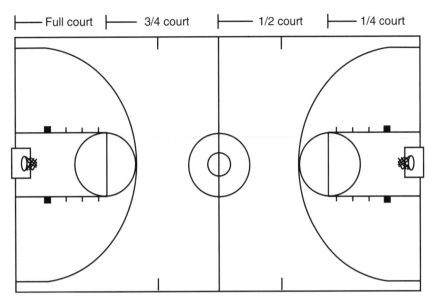

FIGURE 10.1 **Levels of defense—defending and protecting the basket on the right.**

defense, defenders usually allow the first inbounds pass and then pick up offensive players near the free-throw line or the top of the offensive circle. The most common pickup point is at midcourt, where the opponents are first guarded at the half-court line. Half-court player-to-player team defense is recommended for most players of elementary to junior high school age. Coaches can also activate team defense at the top of the defensive key. This quarter-court defensive level is used if the other team has greater individual talent. It is the foundation level. As teams get better at defense or have better talent, the level of defense can be increased.

A team defensive level set at full court or three-quarter court puts more pressure on opponents but forces an increase in court coverage. This level takes away the free movement of opponents in the backcourt but gives the opponent the possible advantage of beating the pressure and getting an easy score from an outnumbered situation.

Defensive Categories

Team defenses fall into three general categories: player-to-player, in which each defender is assigned to a specific offensive player to guard or defend against; zone, in which each player is assigned a specific area of responsibility depending on the position of the ball and the offensive players; and combination, having elements of both player-to-player and zone defenses. All defenses can be started at different levels and with various amounts of pressure (proactive pressing rather than reactive sagging defense).

Player-to-Player Defense

Coaches should emphasize player-to-player as the basic defense for all players. The player-to-player defensive approach is valuable because the techniques can be applied in all defenses; it should be the primary, and probably the only, defense used for elementary to junior high school levels of play.

CRITICAL CUE:
Use only player-to-player defense for young players through eighth grade (ages 13 to 14). No pressing defenses until players are in junior high school (at the earliest).

Elementary, middle, and junior high school teams often use defenses and pressing tactics to take advantage of lower skill levels in perimeter shooting and ballhandling. This approach hinders the long-range development of young players and should be discouraged. Players at these age levels should focus on fun and fundamentals, with everyone getting a chance to play in every game in order to use strengths and work on weaknesses.

If players in this age group learn the basics of player-to-player defense, they can adapt to other defenses later. Player-to-player defense is also the most challenging and most personally rewarding type of defense. No defender can hide: The offense is likely to score an easy basket after any defensive lapse, with personal accountability specifically ensured. As a result, player-to-player defense promotes individual responsibility to the team. The basic principles of the defense are explained in chapter 7.

Zone Defense

Zone defense assigns each player defensive responsibility for a certain area or zone, rather than for an individual offensive player, and it focuses more on the ball. Zone defense usually changes as the ball moves and is designed to protect a limited area of the court. Zone defenses are often weaker in the gaps or seams between defenders and on the outside, but they can be modified to disguise those weaknesses.

Zone defenses can be designed to give and to take away; sagging zones give up more outside shots but take away the inside. Lane or pressure zones take away outside shots but may be vulnerable inside.

Zones can also be changed to lane defenses that are designed to intercept passes, trapping defenses (two players double-teaming one offensive player with the ball), or sagging defenses where the inside area near the basket is heavily protected.

The 2-3 Zone. The most commonly used zone defense is the 2-3 zone. Figure 10.2a shows the basic coverage areas of this defense; figure 10.2b shows the weak areas. Coaches can use this defense when playing a team with a good post player or when they need to ensure good corner coverage. Figure 10.3 shows that the players shift with the ball in various positions.

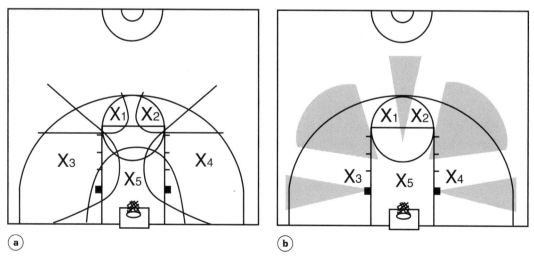

FIGURE 10.2 The 2-3 zone defense: *(a)* coverage and *(b)* weakness areas.

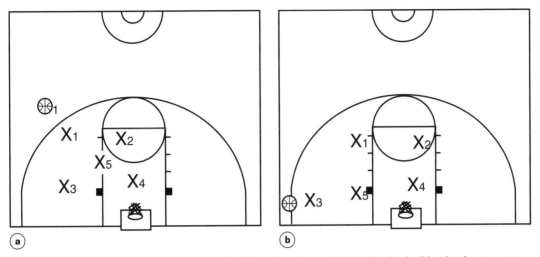

FIGURE 10.3 The 2-3 zone *(a)* with the ball on the wing and *(b)* with the ball in the frontcourt corner.

The 1-3-1 Zone. The 1-3-1 zone defense is also commonly used to cover the high post and wing area: It is strong in the center, the wings, and the point. The coverage and gaps are shown in figure10.4. The shifts of the 1-3-1 zone are shown in figure 10.5, with the ball in the corner and on the wing, respectively. Most zones revert to a 2-3 formation with the ball in the corner.

The 1-2-2 Zone. The 1-2-2 zone defense has good coverage on the perimeter but is vulnerable inside. Its coverage and weakness areas are indicated in figure 10.6. The movement and shifts of this 1-2-2 zone (figure 10.7) are similar to those for the 1-3-1 zone.

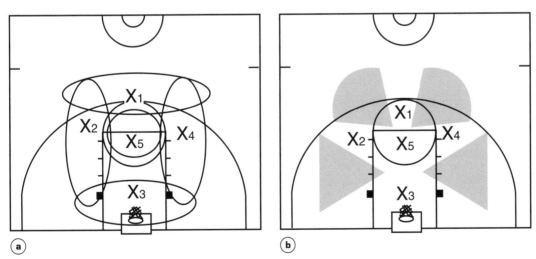

FIGURE 10.4 The 1-3-1 zone defense: *(a)* coverage and *(b)* weakness areas.

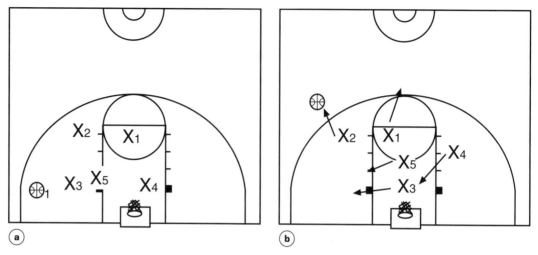

FIGURE 10.5 The 1-3-1 zone *(a)* with the ball in the corner and *(b)* with the ball on the wing.

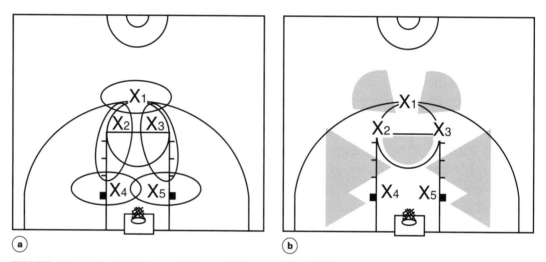

FIGURE 10.6 The 1-2-2 zone defense: *(a)* coverage and *(b)* weakness areas.

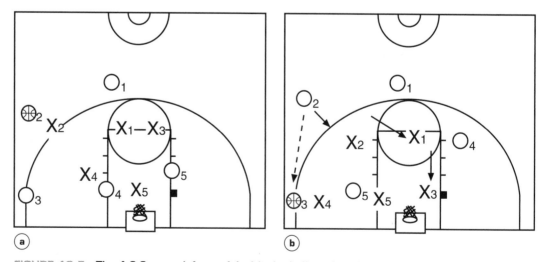

FIGURE 10.7 The 1-2-2 zone defense *(a)* with the ball on the wing and *(b)* with the ball in the corner.

Combination Defense

Combination defenses may take several forms. Generally, they are used to take away an opponent's strength and confuse offenses. For example, a triangle-and-2 defense might be used against a team with only two good scorers; a box-and-1 could be used against an opponent with one key player or ballhandler who is high scoring.

Triangle-and-2. Two defenders are assigned player-to-player on selected opponents while three defenders play a triangular zone, as shown in figure 10.8. To use this defense effectively, coaches must decide on the extent of floor coverage and shifts for the triangle zone defenders. They must also decide how they want the two player-to-player defenders to play (tight, loose, ball denial, etc.). This defense takes away the effectiveness of two offensive players (usually perimeter players) but is vulnerable in other outside shooting areas.

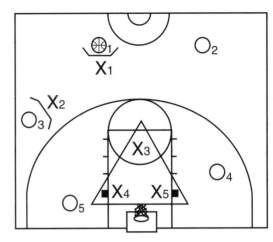

FIGURE 10.8 The triangle-and-2 combination defense (X_1 and X_2 player-to-player).

Box-and-1 or Diamond-and-1. One defender is player-to-player while the other four play a zone defense near the basket. This works well against a team with one outstanding scorer or ballhandler. Two forms of this defense are shown in figure 10.9. Coaches should assign the opposing player who is the best scorer, ballhandler, or team leader to the best player-to-player defender. Determine who is the key player for the other team. Then determine how to take away that player's strength.

This defense takes away the effectiveness of one player, with four zone players used to help and protect the basket, but it can also be vulnerable to outside shooting.

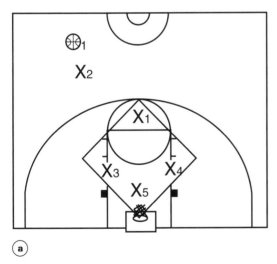 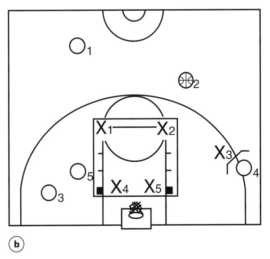

FIGURE 10.9 *(a)* The diamond-and-1 combination defense. *(b)* The box-and-1 combination defense.

Pressing Defenses

Player-to-player pressure defenses can be played at any level: half court, three-quarter court, or full court. All basic principles apply, but helping situations are much more challenging as the defense expands to full court. A premium is placed on individual defenders' stopping and pressuring the ballhandler because of the greater floor area to cover. This type of pressure defense was first developed in the 1940s in men's college basketball and has become commonplace today, especially on teams with greater athletic talent.

Zone pressure defenses can be played at all levels. Probably the most famous instance of a full-court zone press was popularized in the unprecedented success experienced at UCLA under John Wooden. The staple of his first national collegiate championship team was the full-court 2-2-1 zone press, as shown in figure 10.10. Zone presses tend to speed up game tempo, whereas player-to-player pressure defenses may slow the tempo.

This press is usually used as a containing press, keeping the ball out of the middle, that sets at least one sideline trap before half court (figure 10.11). Player X_1 covers the middle, X_5 covers the sideline, and X_3 protects the basket on this trapping sequence.

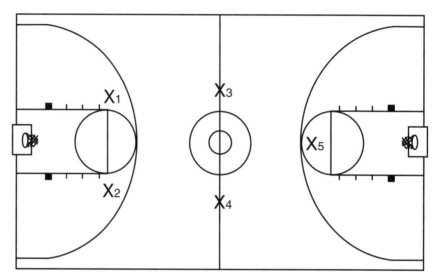

FIGURE 10.10 **2-2-1 zone press.**

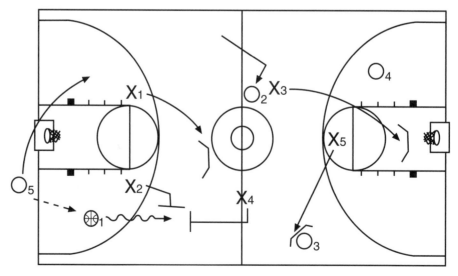

FIGURE 10.11 **2-2-1 zone trap.**

Coaches need to make decisions about when to trap (usually when the dribble comes to the defense and near the half-court line), how to rotate, whether to use continuous trapping, when to drop back to the regular half-court defense, and what type of defense to transition into on the half court. With player-to-player defense, one method is to retreat to the basic defense after one trap: protect the basket, stop the ball, and pick up all open players (in that order). Communication is a key in that transition.

A half-court zone press is exemplified by the 1-3-1 defense used by the Kentucky team, coached by Joe B. Hall, that won a national championship in 1978. The basic set is an extended 1-3-1, shown in figure 10.12.

The perimeter players X_3, X_4, and X_2 play in the passing lanes and force the offense to pass over the top (slower passes). The ball is forced into the corners and trapped, as shown in figure 10.13.

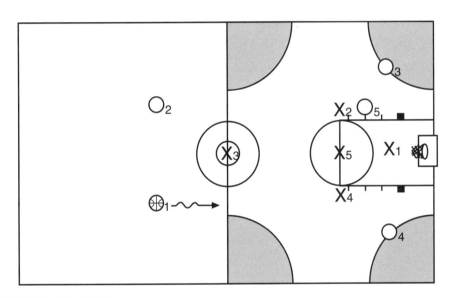

FIGURE 10.12   **1-3-1 half-court zone press.**

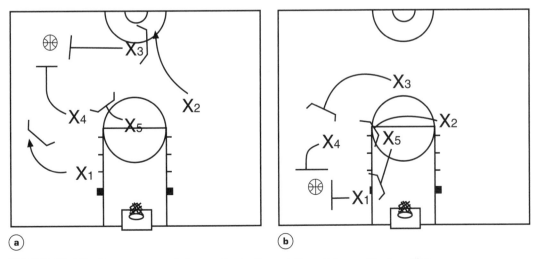

FIGURE 10.13   **Corner traps:** *(a)* **near the half-court line,** *(b)* **near the baseline.**

COACHING POINTS FOR TEAM DEFENSE

- Select one defense as the primary team defense. The half-court player-to-player defense is recommended for young players through junior high school level.
- Make attitude and motivation major concerns when developing team defensive play.
- Focus on practicing against all offenses. Prevent surprises for the defense during games by preparing the team fully in practice for all game situations.
- Place equal emphasis on offense and defense, but spend more time on offense (requires ballhandling and shooting).
- Require defenders to play hard—all five players must move with every pass or dribble.
- Begin with an effective transition from offense to defense.
- End with the defensive rebound, steal, or opponent's turnover.
- Require communication—verbal and nonverbal, talking and listening.

CHECKLIST FOR TEAM DEFENSE

- General principles developed
- Defensive fundamental skills
- Stance and steps
- Defense on-the-ball (live ball, dribble, dead ball)
- Defense off-the-ball (closed or open)
- Defense closeouts (off-the-ball to on-the-ball)
- On-the-ball to off-the-ball defense (jump or explode to the ball)
- Special situations for defense
  - Post defense
  - Help and decide (bluff, switch, trap)
  - On-the-ball screens
  - Off-the-ball screens
  - Double screens
  - Defensive charge
  - Pressure the shot
  - Loose ball
- Defensive rebounding
- Team defense
- Player-to-player
- Zone
- Combination
- Levels of defense
- Zone press
- Out-of-bounds, under
- Out-of-bounds, side
- Defensive free throws
- Transition to offense

TROUBLESHOOTING

The biggest challenge on defense is to get players to play as hard as possible at this end of the floor. Especially on defense, coaches cannot coach well unless players play extremely hard with maximum effort. Convince players that they can't be successful without an all-out effort. Part of that effort is to give maximum mental effort, which requires high levels of communication for defensive effectiveness. Be your best on defense, both physically and mentally. The "mad dog in a meathouse" approach does work on defense. Playing as hard as you can and as long as you can is a good defensive rule to follow.

Drills for Team Defense

Defense needs to be learned for all situations and built up from individual play (1-on-1) progressively to team play (5-on-5). See chapter 7 for individual defensive drills as the foundation for developing team defense.

- Moving stance and steps
- Line drill—individual defense, especially 1-on-1 (live ball, dribble, passer, dead ball)
- Closeouts—1-on-1, 2-on-2, 3-on-3, 4-on-4
- On-the-ball to off-the-ball 2-on-2
- Defensive step slide—moving stance and steps

HALF-COURT 3-ON-3, 4-ON-4 (SHELL DRILL)

Purpose: To break down all situations of two-person and three-person offensive play and to learn to defend them in a team situation.

Equipment: Ball, half court, 8 to 12 players.

Procedure: Each practice can emphasize a selected offensive situation to defend. Prepare the team for all situations (no game surprises). Set up a drill rotation; offense to defense to off-court.

Options

- On-the-ball screens
- Off-the-ball screens
- Double screens
- Use of traps
- Two out, two in (perimeter, post)
- Four outside players, flash post on the cut
- Give-and-go moves

- Dribble penetration focus
- Post play (single, double)
- Three out, one in
- Three in, one out
- One-guard front or two-guard front

HALF-COURT TO FULL-COURT DRILLS: 3-ON-3, 4-ON-4, 5-ON-5

Purpose: To practice basic half-court defense and transition to offense; to practice basic half-court offense and transition to defense.

Equipment: Ball, full court, and at least two groups of players.

Procedure: Set up selected offensive situations to defend and then transition to offense on missed shots; work on selected offensive situations and then carry out an effective defensive transition on made or missed baskets.

Options

- 3-on-3
- 4-on-4
- 5-on-5 team offense and defense

FULL-COURT DRILLS: 3-ON-3, 5-ON-5

Purpose: To teach all phases of defense progressively—3-on-3 breakdowns and 5-on-5 with full teams.

Equipment: Ball, full court, and at least two groups of players.

Procedure: For 3-on-3 full court, players or groups should change after no more than three circuits of full court up and back. The ball must be dribbled over half court, and no breakaway lob passes are allowed in an early progression.

Variation: Play full-court 3-on-3 games to two baskets using the following rules:

- Offense calls fouls (count as a score)
- No lob passes over half court (breakaway)
- No dribble on offense (pass and cut, pass and pick away from the ball)
- New team ready to come in, winner stays

This drill is one of the best, most taxing offensive and defensive drills that can be used. Players must play full-court offense and defense while executing all fundamental skills.

Drill Finder

Drill	Level	Specific focus	Warm-up component	Conditioning component	On DVD	Page
Basic Body Control						
Quick-Stance Check	Basic	Basic stance				17
Quick-Stance Mirror	Basic	Basic stance				17
Mass Quick Moves Drill	Intermediate	Basic stance	✓	✓	✓	17
Line Drill: Quick Starts, Steps, Turns, and Stops	Basic	Starting, turning, and stopping	✓		✓	19
Line Drill: Quick Jumps	Basic	Jumping skills for rebounding and shooting	✓	✓		20
Line Drill: Rebound Jumping and Turns	Basic	Jumping skills for rebounding	✓	✓		21
Line Drill: Quick Stance, Starts, Steps, Jumps, Turns, and Stops	Basic	Body-control movements	✓			21
Line Drill: Starts, Stops, and Turns	Intermediate, advanced	Quick stance, quick starts, quick stops, quick turns, and passing and catching skills	✓		✓	21
Advanced Body Control						
Line Drill: Move Without the Ball	Basic	Basic moves without the ball	✓			35
V-Cut Drill	Basic	Basic moves without the ball in 2-on-0 and 2-on-2 situations			✓	36
Pick-and-Roll Drill	Intermediate, advanced	Screening and cutting options for on-the-ball screens				37
3-on-0 Motion	Advanced	Scoring options on screens away from the ball; two-ball shooting				37
3-on-3 Motion Screen Drill	Advanced	Screening and cutting options for off-the-ball screens				38
Ballhandling						
Ballhandling Drills	Basic	Controlling the ball; becoming familiar with the ball	✓			62
Line Drill: Passing and Catching	Basic	Passing and catching techniques; all basic passes	✓			63
Two-Player Passing and Catching Drill	Basic	Passing and catching using a push pass with either hand after a dribble			✓	64
2-on-1 Keepaway Passing Drill	Intermediate	Passing and catching between partners who must pass by a defender		✓		64
Moving Pairs Passing	Basic	Partner passing and catching skills while moving and against a defender	✓		✓	65
Wall Passing	Basic	Individual ballhandling skills of passing and catching	✓			66
Line Drill: Stance, Starts, and Skill Breakdown	Basic	Selected footwork skills from a quick stance and a quick start	✓			66
Line Drill: Starts, Stops, and Turns	Intermediate	Combining dribbling, starting, stopping, passing, catching, and turning skills	✓		✓	66

Drill	Level	Specific focus	Warm-up component	Conditioning component	On DVD	Page
Ballhandling *(continued)*						
Mass Dribbling	Basic	Basic ballhandling skills of dribbling	✓		✓	66
Full-Court Dribbling	Basic	Ballhandling skills of dribbling		✓		67
Wall Dribbling	Intermediate, advanced	Ballhandling skills				68
Ballhandling Basics	Basic	Basic dribbling, passing, and catching skills	✓		✓	69
Shooting						
Line Drill: Shooting Addition	Basic	Shooting in a simulated game situation			✓	99
Layup Progression Shooting	Intermediate	Proper and quick execution of game-type layups	✓		✓	101
Field-Goal Progression	Basic, intermediate, advanced	Improved shooting through feedback	✓		✓	102
Soft Touch or Killer Shooting	Basic, intermediate, advanced	Shooting mechanics and confidence building	✓		✓	104
Groove It Shooting Drill	Intermediate	Evaluating shooting effectiveness and range				105
Pairs or In-and-Out Shooting	Intermediate, advanced	Shooting in a 2-on-0 game simulation; all shooting situations		✓	✓	105
Make-It-Take-It Row Shooting	Basic, intermediate, advanced	Self-testing shooting skills		✓		106
Individual Drill for Grooving the Shot	Basic	Mechanics of shooting hand and balance hand; increasing shot range				107
Field-Goal Correction Drill	Basic	Troubleshooting				107
Free-Throw Progression	Basic, intermediate, advanced	Free-throw shooting fundamentals	✓		✓	108
Foul-Shot Golf	Basic	Free-throw shooting				109
Knockout Shooting	Intermediate, advanced	Shooting in a competitive situation				109
Row Plus Free-Throw Shooting	Intermediate, advanced	Competitive shooting				110
Footwork and Field Goals (or Free Throws)	Intermediate, advanced	Competitive shooting				110
Mental Practice Drill for Field-Goal and Free-Throw Shooting	Intermediate, advanced	Building shooting confidence through automatic verbal prompts, shooting rituals, and self-evaluation				111
Outside Offensive Moves: Playing the Perimeter						
Warm-Up for Perimeter Players	Basic	Warm-up for fundamental skills	✓			127
Line Drill: Live-Ball, Dead-Ball, and Completion Moves Addition	Basic	Live-ball and dead-ball moves; review of dribble moves	✓			127
Outside Moves Using a Spin Pass	Basic	Outside moves	✓	✓	✓	128
Closeout: 1-on-1, 2-on-2, 3-on-3, 4-on-4	Basic, intermediate, advanced	All outside moves			✓	129
1-on-1 Drill	Basic, intermediate, advanced	1-on-1 competition for perimeter players		✓		129

Drill	Level	Specific focus	Warm-up component	Conditioning component	On DVD	Page
Outside Offensive Moves: Playing the Perimeter *(continued)*						
Partner Penetrate and Pitch Drill	Basic, intermediate	Live-ball moves; passing to teammate for score at completion of dribble drive			✓	130
Timed Layups	Basic	Ballhandling and layup shooting		✓	✓	131
Perimeter Game	Intermediate, advanced	All perimeter moves with the ball		✓		131
Inside Offensive Moves: Playing the Post						
Post Warm-Up Drill	Basic	Basic post skills	✓		✓	146
Line Drill: Post Player Starts, Turns, and Stops	Basic	Proper footwork	✓			147
Post Pair Drills	Basic	Post stance, passing and catching, and chinning the ball	✓			148
Spin Pass Post Moves	Basic	Individual offensive post moves	✓		✓	149
Post Progression Drill	Basic, intermediate, advanced	Offensive post moves	✓			149
Big Spacing and Post Feeding Drill	Intermediate, advanced	Triangle spacing; big spacing			✓	150
All-American Post Workout	Advanced	All offensive post moves	✓	✓		151
2-on-2 Feeding the Post Drill	Intermediate, advanced	Offensive and defensive post play skills; passing to post players; movement after the pass for a return pass				152
Mikan Drill	Basic, intermediate, advanced	Footwork; ballhandling; layup shooting close to the basket	✓	✓		152
5-on-5 Post Passing Drill	Advanced	Post players: getting open, catching, post moves, passing from the post position while reading and reacting to defenders; Defensive players: double-teaming post players, rotating to the ball on passes from the post				153
Post Score Through Defense (Over and Back)	Intermediate, advanced	Capture and chin the ball		✓		153
1-on-1 Post Cutthroat	Basic, intermediate, advanced	Post offense and defense in 1-on-1 live format		✓		154
Individual Defense						
Stance and Steps Progression	Basic	Defensive stance and power push-step (step-slide) technique	✓		✓	177
Moving Stance and Steps	Basic	Individual defensive stance and steps	✓	✓		178
Line Drill: Individual Defense	Basic	Individual defensive skills		✓	✓	179
On-the-Ball and Off-the-Ball Drill: 2-on-2	Basic	Quick adjustment to on-the-ball and off-the-ball positions while defending penetration (help and decide situations)			✓	179
Closeout Drill	Basic	Closing out on off-the-ball offensive player	✓			180
Closeout Drills: 1-on-1, 2-on-2, 3-on-3, 4-on-4	Intermediate, advanced	All outside moves of perimeter players		✓	✓	181
Defensive Slide Drill: Moving Stance and Steps	Basic	Individual defensive steps				181

Drill	Level	Specific focus	Warm-up component	Conditioning component	On DVD	Page
Individual Defense (continued)						
Half-Court Drills: 2-on-2, 3-on-3, 4-on-4	Intermediate, advanced	Individual defensive skills		✓		182
Half Court Plus Transition: 4-on-4	Intermediate, advanced	Individual defensive skills; transition from defense to offense after defensive rebounding		✓		182
Rebounding						
Line Drill: 2-and-2, Capture and Chin Rebound Addition	Basic	2-and-2 and capture and chinit rebound techniques	✓		✓	202
Line Drill: Defensive Rebound Addition	Basic	Defensive rebounding techniques	✓			204
Line Drill: Offensive Rebound Addition	Basic	Offensive rebounding; getting past the defender to block out, getting to a gap, making contact to move the defender closer to the basket	✓		✓	204
Rebound and Outlet Drill	Intermediate, advanced	Taking a defensive rebound off the backboard and making an outlet pass			✓	205
Rebound Number	Basic	Seeing opponent and ball when a shot is taken				206
Closeout and Blockout Drill	Intermediate, advanced	Team competition; 1-on-1, 2-on-2, 3-on-3 rebounding situations; on-the-ball and off-the-ball blockouts		✓		206
Line Drill: Full-Court Offensive Boards Without the Ball	Basic	Offensive rebounding skills				206
Advanced Figure-Eight Rebound Drill	Intermediate, advanced	Controlling the rebound				207
Garbage Drill	Basic, intermediate	Scoring on the offensive rebound		✓	✓	207
NBA (No Babies Allowed) or Survival Rebounding	Advanced	Aggressiveness		✓	✓	207
Individual Rebounding	Basic	Rebounding skills	✓			208
Rebound Progression: 3-on-0, 3-on-3	Intermediate, advanced	Rebounding skills	✓			209
Cutthroat Rebounding: 3-on-3, 4-on-4	Intermediate, advanced	Offensive and defensive rebounding		✓	✓	209
War Rebounding	Advanced	Aggressive defensive or offensive rebounding		✓		210
Team Offense						
Skeleton Offense Drill: 5-on-0	Basic	Basic team offensive formation	✓		✓	229
Team Offense-Defense Drill: 5-on-5	Intermediate, advanced	Team offense and defense		✓		229
Blitz Fast-Break Drill	Intermediate, advanced	Two-lane and three-lane fast-break offensive and defensive plays		✓	✓	230
Transition Fast-Break Drill	Intermediate, advanced	Transition basketball		✓		232
Team Defense						
Half-Court 3-on-3, 4-on-4 (Shell Drill)	Intermediate, advanced	Two-person and three-person offensive play		✓	✓	243
Half-Court to Full-Court Drills: 3-on-3, 4-on-4, 5-on-5	Intermediate, advanced	Half-court defense and transition to offense; half-court offense and transition to defense		✓		244
Full-Court Drills: 3-on-3, 5-on-5	Intermediate, advanced	All phases of defense		✓	✓	244

References

Bunn, J. 1955. *Scientific principles of coaching*. Englewood Cliffs, NJ: Prentice Hall.

Carter, J. 2006. *Noah's arc—Building the perfect shot*. Palo Alto, CA: Self-published.

Harle, S., and J. Vickers. 2006. *Quiet eye improves accuracy in the free throw*. Calgary, Alberta: University of Calgary.

Hays, D. 2006. *Developing your shot and offensive moves*. Oklahoma City: Self-published.

Jaimet, S. 2006. *The perfect jump shot*. Indianapolis, IN: Elemental Press.

Krause, J., C. Janz, and J. Conn. 2003. *Basketball skill progressions: NABC's handbook for teaching*. Monterey, CA: Coaches Choice.

Krause, J., and B. Brown. 2006. *NABC's youth basketball coaching handbook: Beyond the backboard*. Monterey, CA: Coaches Choice.

Krzyzewski, M. 2000. *Leading with the heart*. New York: Warner Books, Inc.

Martens, R. 1997. *Successful coaching*. 2nd ed. Champaign, IL: Human Kinetics.

Wolff, A. 2002. *Big game, small world*. New York: Warner Books, Inc.

Wooden, J.R. 1998. *Practical modern basketball*. 3rd ed. Redwood City, CA: Benjamin Cummings.

Index

About the Authors

Jerry Krause has been coaching the basics of basketball since 1959. He has experience at the elementary, high school, college, and Olympic levels, which uniquely qualifies him to help players improve their skills at all levels.

Krause is the director of men's basketball operations for Gonzaga University. During his first stint with Gonzaga, Krause was an assistant coach for eight years. In between his time at Gonzaga, Krause spent five years at the U.S. Military Academy at West Point serving as a professor of sport philosophy, director of instruction for the physical education department, and assistant women's coach. Prior to his latest endeavors, Jerry Krause was head coach of the Eastern Washington University Eagles. During Krause's tenure his Eagle teams compiled a 262-196 (.572) record.

Krause has been a leader in national associations dedicated to the continued growth of basketball. He served on the selection committee of the National Basketball Hall of Fame, the board of directors of the National Association of Basketball Coaches (NABC), and the NCAA rules committee. He is the NABC research chair and a member of the NAIA Basketball Coaches Hall of Fame and the National Association for Sport and Physical Education Hall of Fame. He holds a bachelor's degree from Wayne State University and master's and doctoral degrees from the University of Northern Colorado.

Krause was recognized for lifetime contributions to basketball as the 2007 Battle in Seattle honoree by Northwest Sports and Gonzaga University. He is the most widely published coach in basketball history, having written more than 30 books on coaching basketball. He resides in Cheney, Washington.

See his Web site at www.coachjerrykrauseonline.com for more information.

Don Meyer is the head coach at Northern State University in Aberdeen, South Dakota. His 860-plus wins put him in fifth place on the all-time list of coaches in men's collegiate basketball. Before his term at Northern State University, Meyer was the head men's basketball coach at Lipscomb University in Nashville for 24 seasons, where he reached the 700-win plateau faster than any other coach in college basketball. Named the National Coach of the Year in 1989 and 1990, Meyer was inducted into the NAIA Hall of Fame in 1993. See www.Northern.edu or www.coachmeyer.com.

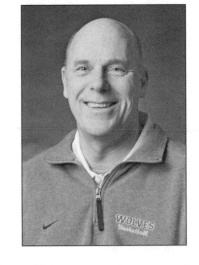

In addition to coaching, Meyer has established a coaching academy that has attracted more than 10,000 basketball coaches from all over the United States. His reputation as a coach and teacher has allowed him to attract some of the most renowned coaches, including Pat Summitt and John Wooden, to speak at his academy. He resides in Aberdeen, South Dakota.

Jerry Meyer is currently the chief analyst and scout for the Rivals.com basketball recruiting coverage. He is a nationally recognized basketball instructor whose expertise dates back to his high school playing days when he won Tennessee's Mr. Basketball award in his junior and senior seasons. As a college player for Lipscomb University and the University of Minnesota at Duluth, Meyer was a two-time All-American and became college basketball's career assist leader. Meyer has been a high school head coach, has served as an assistant at Vanderbilt University, and has been a head coach in the American Basketball Association. Jerry lives in Nashville, Tennessee.